REVOLUTIONS

D0144023

Studies in Comparative Social Science

ᔆ A series edited by Stephen K. Sanderson ᔆ

Titles Available

Revolutions: A Worldwide Introduction to Political and Social Change,
Stephen K. Sanderson (2005)

Plunging to Leviathan: Exploring the World's Political Future,
Robert Bates Graber (2005)

REVOLUTIONS

A WORLDWIDE INTRODUCTION TO POLITICAL AND SOCIAL CHANGE

Stephen K. Sanderson

Paradigm Publishers

Boulder • London

Copyright © 2005 by Paradigm Publishers

Published in the United States by Paradigm Publishers, 3360 Mitchell Lane Suite E, Boulder, Colorado 80301 USA.

Paradigm Publishers is the trade name of Birkenkamp & Company, LLC, Dean Birkenkamp, President and Publisher.

Library of Congress Cataloging-in-Publication Data

Revolutions : a worldwide introduction to political and social change/ Stephen K. Sanderson.—1st ed.
p. cm.
Includes bibliographical references and index.
ISBN 1-59451-048-2 (hardcover); ISBN 1-59451-049-0 (paperback)
1. Revolutions. I. Title.
JC491.S32 2005
303.6'4—dc22
2005004925

Printed and bound in the United States of America on acid-free paper that meets the standards of the American National Standard for Permanence of Paper for Printed Library Materials.

Designed and Typeset in New Baskerville by Straight Creek Bookmakers.

09 08 07 06 05
1 2 3 4 5

For Gunder

Contents

Chapter 6 Revolutions from Above in Eastern Europe and   **107**
the Soviet Union
State Socialism: Development and Reforms, 108 •
1989: The Revolutions Against Communism in Eastern
Europe, 113 • 1991: The Revolution Against
Communism in the Soviet Union, 123 • Explaining the
Revolutions Against Communism, 126 • The Communist
Collapse and State-Centered Theories of Revolution, 135
• Coda: The Unexpected Nature of the Communist
Collapse, 136

Chapter 7 The Outcomes of Revolutions   **139**
France, 141 • Russia, 143 • China, 145 • Cuba, 148 •
Nicaragua, 151 • Iran, 154 • The Revolutions Against
Communism, 156

Epilogue: The Future of Revolutions   **165**

Appendix: Ten Leading Students of Revolutions   **167**
John Foran, 167 • Jack A. Goldstone, 170 • Jeff Goodwin,
177 • Ted Robert Gurr, 181 • Krishan Kumar, 184 •
Barrington Moore, Jr., 188 • Theda Skocpol, 192 •
Charles Tilly, 194 • Timothy P. Wickham-Crowley, 197 •
Eric R. Wolf, 200

Suggested Readings   203

References   209

Index   223

About the Author   235

Preface and Acknowledgments

THIS BOOK BEGAN LIFE as a chapter in a proposed textbook on social change. In 1994 I signed a contract, along with two co-authors—one a sociologist and the other an anthropologist—to write a social change text that emphasized a long-term evolutionary perspective. I thought that the book needed a chapter on revolutions and state breakdowns, and my co-authors agreed. None of us specialized in that dimension of social change, but I had long wanted to read the most important literature in this area so I agreed to bite the bullet and write the chapter. This I did after spending five months reading the pertinent literature. For some reason, once I finished the chapter I had the feeling that my co-authors were not as enthusiastic about the book as I was and that they might take awhile to get their chapters written. I sent them my chapter with a note stating that when their chapters were completed I would then finish my other three. Frankly, I wasn't sure they were ever going to write anything, and it turns out that my suspicions were correct: They didn't. As a result, the chapter I'd written languished in my computer for years. It eventually became clear that our textbook was never going to see the light of day. But I had invested a lot of time and energy putting my chapter together, and I didn't want to "waste" it. I therefore hit upon the idea of investing a few more months' work and expanding the chapter into a short book.

I am very happy that I took the trouble to delve into the literature on revolutions and state breakdowns and write the chapter and the book, because I find this literature fascinating. Moreover, it represents some of the best scholarship that my own discipline, sociology, has to offer. Sociologists of revolution are among the most intellectually sophisticated of all sociologists, and one can point to their work with great pride in the knowledge that we are members of the same discipline.

The plan of the book is as follows. Chapter One discusses the nature of revolutions and addresses some important background concepts and assumptions essential to the study of large-scale social and political change. Chapter Two looks at the three most prominent historical revolutions of the past two centuries, what have been called the Great Revolutions (Skocpol, 1979): the French Revolution of 1789, the Bolshevik or Russian Revolution of 1917, and the Chinese Revolution of 1911–1949. Chapter Three follows by examining several examples of much more recent revolutions in the less-developed parts of the world, especially the Cuban Revolution of 1959 and the Nicaraguan and Iranian Revolutions of 1979.

This leads to what is really the heart of the book—a discussion of some of the most prominent explanations of revolution that social scientists have proposed. Chapters Four and Five take up this discussion. Whereas social disorder and rebellion are common and frequent, actual revolutions are relatively rare, and most attempts at revolution are abortive. The various theories attempting to explain why this is so are reviewed and critically assessed.

Chapter Six examines the state breakdowns that occurred in Eastern Europe and the Soviet Union in 1989 and 1991, respectively; it also tries to explain why they happened, and explores whether they were genuine examples of revolutions. The issue of the outcomes of revolution is a critical one as well. Do revolutions generally lead to the results desired and fought for by revolutionaries, or are their outcomes more modest? These outcomes are the subject of Chapter Seven. Given the massive forces of globalization and worldwide evolutionary change, are revolutions likely to occur in the future, or are they a thing of the past? An epilogue considers this question about the future of revolutions, while an appendix presents short biographical and autobiographical sketches of ten leading students of revolution.

I have written this book as both a contribution to scholarship and as a work suitable for the classroom. I hope instructors will find it useful not only for specialized courses in revolutions but also for courses in political sociology, comparative/historical sociology, macrosociology, social change, sociology of development, Third World studies, and the like. I have tried to make the writing highly accessible to undergraduates; if responses to my previous books are any indication, I think I have succeeded.

I am delighted that Dean Birkenkamp wanted to publish this book as part of the launching of his new company, Paradigm Publishers. I would follow Dean anywhere. He has been a successful editor wherever he has gone and has first-rate editorial judgment and great editorial integrity. Dean is also the nicest person I have ever met in the publishing industry. Dean wants to publish books because of their scholarly value. He knows, of course, that you have to make money in order to stay in business, but he strives to balance scholarly value and need with the bottom line. There is also a nice little irony in the fact that he is publishing this book. He was the very editor in charge of the ill-fated social change text that contained my revolutions chapter in 1994, having signed it for Westview Press. He left Westview shortly thereafter for Rowman and Littlefield, where, I am happy to say, he published two of my books. Now the full revolutions book has circled back to him for his own new company. What a delightful *dénouement!*

I dedicate this book to the memory of my longtime friend and epistolary colleague Andre Gunder Frank, who died on April 23, 2005. I first met Gunder at the annual meeting of the International Society for the Comparative Study of Civilizations, at Berkeley, in 1989. I presented a paper that was fairly critical of his latest work postulating the existence of a 5,000-year world economy, and he objected strenuously. (For those who know Gunder, this will not come as a surprise!) The rest of the day, over dinner, drinks, and maneuvering around Berkeley, he launched objection after objection. I countered them all, but Gunder was undaunted and irrepressible and refused to give up. At the time I thought he was pushing a set of ideas that could not possibly be correct. However, as I studied his developing work in the years to come, I gradually came to accept much of his thinking, and even cited some of it quite favorably in later works of my own. (I came to accept about half of his arguments, considerably more than the big fat zero percent I accepted at the beginning, but then well short of the 100 percent that Gunder thought was necessary!) Gunder and I eventually came to gain a great deal of mutual admiration and personal liking. I have valued his friendship and collegiality enormously. He is truly one of the most brilliant social scientists I have ever met, and, although often gruff on the exterior, inside he is a real softie! He is also incredibly bold and imaginative in his thinking, not at all afraid to challenge entrenched ideas, and also not reticent to change his mind, and to say so publicly, when he encounters new arguments or new evidence suggesting that a formerly held position is no longer valid. (For example, although one of the two major founders of radical dependency theory, in time Gunder came to acknowledge that the socialist alternative did not work and that there is probably no real-world alternative to capitalism.) It has been my privilege to know this extraordinary man and to know that he has thought highly of my abilities and of much of my work. (It came as an extremely pleasant surprise to me that Gunder even liked and accepted much of my more recent Darwinian thinking [Sanderson, 2001], quite something for a radical from the sixties!) This one's for you, Gunder—*reposes en paix.*

Stephen K. Sanderson
Indiana, Pennsylvania

Chapter One

Understanding Revolutions

The Nature of Revolutions

What is a revolution? Wilbert Moore (1963), a well-known student of social change, thinks of revolutions as a form of change that involves violence, that engages a large portion of the population, and that produces a transformation of the overall structure of government. John Dunn (1972) sees revolutions as a form of change that is massive, violent, and rapid. Samuel Huntington (1968:264), in a definition that has been favorably endorsed by many, conceives of a revolution as a "rapid, fundamental, and violent domestic change in the dominant values and myths of a society, in its political institutions, social structure, leadership, and government activity and policies."

A. S. Cohan (1975) lists six characteristics that revolutions are typically thought to have:

1. Alteration of the basic values and myths of a society.
2. Alteration of the social structure.
3. Alteration of social institutions.
4. Changes in the structure of leadership, in terms of either the personnel of the elite or its class composition.
5. Nonlegal or illegal transfer of power.
6. Presence or dominance of violence in the actions leading a regime to collapse.

1

Cohan suggests that most definitions of revolution will include several of these attributes, and it is certainly possible for a definition to include them all. Cohan himself prefers to see the attributes "violence" and "value change" as least essential. His own definition of revolution (1975:31) identifies it as "that process by which a radical alteration of a particular society occurs over a given time span. Such alteration would include (a) a change in the class composition of elites, (b) the elimination of previous political institutions and their replacement by others (or by none), or an alteration of the functions of these institutions, and (c) changes in the social structure which would be reflected in the class arrangements and/or the redistribution of resources and income." This is certainly an all-encompassing definition, but it may be too restrictive to apply to every single event that some social analyst somewhere wants to call by the name *revolution*.

Theda Skocpol, one of the foremost students of revolutions today, has formulated a widely popular definition that draws a distinction between social revolutions, political revolutions, and rebellions. *Social revolutions*, she tells us, are (1979:4) "rapid, basic transformations of a society's state and class structures; and they are accompanied and in part carried through by class-based revolts from below." *Political revolutions*, by contrast, involve the transformation of state structures without any corresponding transformation of class or social structures. *Rebellions* occur when subordinate social classes revolt but no fundamental structural change in society or politics occurs.

Jack Goldstone (1991) has used the alternative concept of *state breakdown*. For him, a state breakdown occurs when a society's government undergoes a crisis so severe that its capacity to govern is severely crippled. Only some state breakdowns become actual revolutions, which involve dramatic transformations of social and political institutions. Many state breakdowns lead to only limited social and political changes, changes that are not dramatic enough to warrant the label of revolution. Indeed, Goldstone uses the concept of state breakdown in preference to that of revolution because his interest in political crisis and change is broader than that indicated by the term *revolution*.

Another prominent scholar of the overall subject, Charles Tilly (1978, 1986, 1993), is even more general than Goldstone. He uses the term *collective action* to identify a wide range of forms of sociopolitical conflict. These include not only revolutions and rebellions but also strikes, revolts, civil wars, and the like. At the level of explanation, Tilly has formulated an overall theory, quite abstract by design, that is intended to apply to all of these conflictive phenomena.

In this book I neither formulate nor rely on any single definition of revolution conceived as superior to all others. The definitions presented above seem to do a reasonable job of addressing the most critical elements of revolutions. Moreover, avoiding any single definition at the outset helps us avoid boxing ourselves into a corner, for when we look at theories of revolution we will see that the explanations of revolutions offered by individual theorists pertain to revolutions (or state breakdowns, collective action, etc.) as they are conceived by each theorist. Although these theorists are broadly addressing the same basic issue, there are sufficient differences in the focus of each to warrant maintaining conceptual flexibility.

What, then, are some of history's more prominent and interesting examples of revolutions and other sociopolitically conflictive phenomena? At one end we have the so-called Great Revolutions. These are the French Revolution of 1789, said by many to be a "bourgeois revolution," or one that ushered in the basic economic, social, and political structure of modern capitalism; the Bolshevik Revolution of 1917 (also known as the Russian Revolution), which transformed Russia into the Soviet Union; and the Chinese Revolution that began in 1911 and culminated in 1949 with a transfer of power and major social and economic changes. These are full-scale social revolutions in Skocpol's sense of the term. To these may be added social revolutions in the Third World, such as the Cuban Revolution in 1959, the Iranian Revolution in 1979, and the Nicaraguan Revolution of the same year. Then there are the less dramatic political revolutions. In Europe and Asia these have included the English Revolution of the 1640s and the Meiji Restoration in Japan in 1868. Third World political revolutions have occurred in Mexico in 1911 and, much more recently, in the Philippines in 1986 when Ferdinand Marcos was ousted from power and replaced by a new government.

Revolutions are distinctly modern phenomena, limited at most to the last 500 years. They are a product of the modern world specifically because of the enormous changes wrought by the rise of modern capitalism and the growth of the modern state. As Tilly (1993:33) notes, with the beginnings of the modern world, states "began exerting much more extensive controls over populations, resources and activities—taxing, conscripting, commandeering, regulating, policing, erecting systems of surveillance. With the growth of massive national armed forces and the attendant growth of state budgets, almost all states erected wider, deeper, more direct systems of control. Central control extended, obviously, to property, production and political activity." As a result of these changes, "the residents of a national territory fell increasingly under the obligation to yield labour, goods, money and loyalty to the state, but also acquired rights of redress, voice and compensation. That process broadened popular politics" (1993:34).

Describing these social and political revolutions is the goal of the next two chapters. First, however, we need to consider some intellectual background.

Concepts for Understanding Revolutions

Modes of Production

A good understanding of some basic sociological and historical concepts should prove very useful in understanding revolutionary phenomena. A good starting point is the concept of *mode of production*. This is a concept that derives from the thinking of the social theorist Karl Marx (1818–1883) and is still basic to the Marxian tradition of social thinking. A mode of production is a large-scale structure of economic production characteristic of whole societies, regions within societies, or large regional or even global configurations or systems of societies. Every mode of production contains both forces of production and relations of production. *Forces of production* are primarily technological; they are the tools, techniques, and methods that people most commonly use in a given time and place in producing a living. The features of the natural environment may also be counted among the productive forces. *Relations of production*, on the other hand, refer to the modes of property ownership that characterize a mode of production. Productive relations are a matter of who owns the means of production, how they put them to use, and how they seek to use the labor of those individuals and groups excluded from productive ownership.

In his original thinking, Marx distinguished four major modes of production throughout human history, which he described as stages in the evolution of social life: primitive communism, slavery, feudalism, and capitalism. The last of these, capitalism, would eventually be replaced by a fifth—a universal socialist stage. *Primitive communism* was the oldest and earliest stage of human society. Here humans lived by hunting, gathering, simple forms of agriculture, animal herding, or some combination of these. The productive forces were little developed, which made life difficult; on the other hand, social life was not characterized by any form of private ownership of the means of production, and so people were essentially equal; no one oppressed or exploited anyone else. Because of the privations imposed by this rather primitive form of society, people were motivated to develop and expand their tools and technological methods. As they eventually accomplished this, however, communal relations of production were replaced by private ownership, and the *slave mode of production* (sometimes called the *ancient mode*) emerged. Here a small fraction of the population owned not only large tracts of land but also human subjects, which they used to produce enormous quantities of wealth. Marx thought that the slave or ancient mode extended all the way back in time to the earliest civilizations in Egypt and Mesopotamia, but he considered ancient Rome and Greece to be the quintessential examples of this stage of social life. As is widely known, Roman society was the successor to Greek civilization, and Rome evolved from a small republic into a large empire. It blossomed for hundreds of years, conquering many lands and capturing from them the many workers it needed for the large-scale slave system that was essential to the maintenance of its social and economic order.

By the end of the second century C.E., however, Rome was in a state of decline, and in the late fifth century it suffered a final collapse. This once-great civilization had disintegrated and was now overrun by barbarian invaders from various parts of Europe. They created a new mode of production, *feudalism*. Feudalism differed in several important ways from the old ancient mode. For one thing, it did not have an imperial political or military structure, being highly decentralized politically. In addition, slavery as a labor method gradually disappeared and was replaced with *serfdom*, a mode of labor organization in which unfree *peasants* become the primary labor force. Unfree peasants—more accurately, *serfs*—are not owned outright as human chattel (as are slaves); rather, they are tied to parcels of land overseen by landlords and their supervisors. Feudal society also contained free peasants, who owned their own land, and these peasants became more numerous as the feudal system advanced over time.

However, both types of peasants in feudal societies were compelled by landlords to perform labor services, to pay rent and taxes, and to accept other penalties of their status. Finally, feudal society was overwhelmingly rural, with towns and cities few and far between and life lived mostly in the countryside.

European Feudalism lasted for the better part of a thousand years. The period roughly spanning the sixth through eleventh centuries is commonly known as Early Feudalism, whereas the period from the eleventh until the sixteenth centuries is known as Later Feudalism. This latter period was marked by population growth, growth in the number and size of towns and cities, and increased commercial activity. Beginning in the sixteenth century, most observers would agree, feudalism gradually gave way to a new mode of production known as *capitalism.* The predominant economic activity under feudalism was peasant agricultural production for the benefit of landlords. Capitalism, by contrast, involved the *production of goods for profit and economic exchange through buying and selling.* Although some form of capitalism had existed in the world for thousands of years, modern capitalism's roots are to be found in the Italian city-states in the fourteenth and fifteenth centuries, especially Venice and Genoa. These societies were overwhelmingly specialized for trade, existing as they did on the Mediterranean, which enormously facilitated maritime trade. By the sixteenth century, though, the torch had passed to the Netherlands, especially the province of Holland. It became the dominant economic power in Europe in the following century. In the eighteenth century England surpassed Holland and produced the world's first *Industrial Revolution.* This was a dramatic economic and technological transformation in which machines began to replace human manual labor as the basis for getting work done. With the development of industrial machinery, the factory system emerged and capitalist society shifted from a rural to an urban foundation. Cities exploded in size and economic productivity soared. England became the world's dominant economic power in the nineteenth century, when it was known as the "workshop of the world." It had the world's most powerful economy, society, and government. But just as England had replaced Holland, so England would be replaced as well—in this case, by the United States in the twentieth century. By the end of World War II it had acceded to the position of the world's dominant economic and political power. Today we are witnessing the globalization of capitalism, with the tremendous development of societies in East Asia and massive capitalist investment throughout the less-developed regions of the world in Latin America, Asia, and Africa.

Social Classes

One cannot talk of modes of production without talking about *social classes,* for the two are inextricably intertwined. Social classes center largely around Marx's relations of production. In the ancient world of Greece and Rome, the two main classes were *masters* and *slaves*—the one owning the means of the production and the other not, the one oppressing and exploiting the other. In feudalism, as we saw, the major social classes were *landlords* and *peasants.* Like the master-slave class division, this, too, was a relationship of oppression and exploitation. The ancient and feudal modes of production were subtypes of what can be called an *agrarian mode of production,* or one in which the primary basis for human subsistence and the creation of wealth is agriculture. In classical agrarian societies there is always some sort of landowning class, often called a *nobility* or *aristocracy,* and some sort of dependent population of workers: slaves, serfs, peasants, or some other type of unfree labor. Serfs and free peasants are the most numerous source of labor in most agrarian societies, and the mode of labor organization is what Dietrich Rueschemeyer, Evelyne Huber Stephens, and John D. Stephens (1992) have called *labor-repressive agriculture.* Under this system, landowners rule the roost and compel serfs and peasants to work on pain of starvation. Serfs and peasants have few or no rights, and landowners wish to keep the system organized in that manner because they greatly benefit from it. Agrarian societies have other more minor social classes, such as merchants, artisans, and retainers. Merchants specialize in trade and commercial activity, artisans are craftsmen who produce goods to be sold and traded, and retainers are persons in the direct service of the noble classes.

As capitalism replaced the feudal agrarian economy, and as societies underwent the process of industrialization, the class structure shifted away from landowners and peasants and toward capitalists and workers. *Capitalists* are the owners of the means of production in the form of capital goods—money, land, machinery, technology, and so on—that are used as investments in order to earn profits. The aim of capitalists is to maximize their profits and to accumulate saved profit (capital) over time, a part of which can be reinvested in more capitalist production. *Workers* are the individuals who operate the machinery to produce goods that capitalists can sell for profits. They work in factories and mines and, sometimes, in agriculture. As capitalism advanced, workers became increasingly employed in factory production and lived in cities. Just as landlords sought to exploit peasants and other dependent workers, capitalists seek to exploit workers by holding their wages down to a low level. Minimizing labor costs is a common aim of both landowners and capitalists, although they employ different labor forces and use different methods of extracting wealth from them.

The Capitalist World-System

One of the most important works on the development of capitalism to appear in recent years is Immanuel Wallerstein's *The Modern World-System,* which has appeared in three volumes (1974b, 1980, 1989), with at least one or two more projected. Wallerstein views capitalism as a *world-system,* which is a very large social system consisting of many societies that interact on the basis of relations of economic production and exchange. Wallerstein argues that the world-system or *world-economy* began to develop around 1450 and has continued to evolve and expand right up to the present day. It has gone through four major phases. The first phase lasted from 1450 until about 1640, the second from 1640 until the 1760s, the third from the 1760s until the early 1900s, and the fourth (and current) phase from the early 1900s to the present. The world-system consists of economic zones or components that Wallerstein calls core, periphery, and semiperiphery. In the *core* are those societies that are the most economically developed, that use the most advanced technologies and production techniques, and that tend to compensate workers in the form of *wages* (who thus perform *wage labor*). Wage laborers are legally free to negotiate for whom to work, their rate of compensation, the conditions of the workplace, and so on. In the capitalist *periphery* we find the least developed societies that rely on the most traditional forms of technology and production methods. Historically, peripheral capitalist societies have specialized in raw materials production for export, normally using one or another method of *forced labor,* such as slavery or serfdom. They have organized large labor forces to work on plantations producing sugar, coffee, cotton, or some other mass commodity to be sold on the world market, or to engage in the mining of such ores as gold and silver. The *semiperiphery* contains societies that combine core-like and periphery-like forms of production and modes of labor organization.

In the first phase of capitalist development, the major core societies were Holland, England, and northern France. These societies engaged in capitalist forms of agriculture and many forms of industry. *Peripheral capitalism* existed in Eastern Europe—where a kind of serfdom was reinstated after having earlier been abolished—and in the Spanish and Portuguese colonies in the New World. In Eastern Europe, there was a type of capitalist agriculture in which primary agricultural products, such as grain and timber, were produced for export to Western Europe. In the periphery in the New World, the Spaniards established colonies in Mexico, Peru, and other regions devoted to large-scale agriculture and mining. Since the Spaniards encountered large, dense populations in these regions, once they conquered them they were able to use them as their primary labor force. The Portuguese established very large sugar plantations in Brazil and, not having large indigenous populations suitable for intensive labor, they imported huge amounts of slave labor from Africa to work them. Southern Europe—Spain, Portugal, southern France, and Italy—belonged to the semiperiphery, as did parts of Central Europe. Sharecropping was a major type of economic activity, and both core-like and periphery-like forms of economic production coexisted.

During its second phase, the capitalist world-system expanded but not to any dramatic extent. Prussia entered the semiperiphery, as did Sweden and the U.S. North. The U.S. South became an important part of the periphery, with its plantation agricultural system based on slave labor. The core remained much the same, although Holland's economic dominance slipped.

The third phase is what Wallerstein has called "the second era of great expansion of the capitalist world-economy." There was an enormous expansion of the system to include most of the world. *Colonialism,* begun earlier by the Spaniards and Portuguese, was expanded by such European powers as Britain and France to include much of Asia, especially India and China. The *peripheralization* of Africa began toward the end of this period (the late nineteenth century). The United States was a new society, with its northern states concentrating on mercantile and industrial capitalism and free farming, and its southern states engaged in plantation agriculture using slave labor until the mid-nineteenth century. Between about 1815 and the 1870s Britain became the number-one economic power and created a vast colonial empire around itself.

The fourth phase of capitalist development was marked by the United States' displacement of England as the number-one economic and political power. Capitalism became truly global during this period, with only the most uninhabitable regions of the world excluded from its orbit. During this period, two of the Great Revolutions occurred: the Russian in 1917 and the Chinese in 1949. This was also the period of revolutionary movements and actual revolutionary overthrows throughout the rest of the world. The conditions for revolutionary discontent were being created in this century more than at any other time in history.

Today the capitalist core, and much of the semiperiphery, is highly economically developed and industrialized. Formal colonialism has ended virtually everywhere, but much of the semiperipheral capitalist world, and all of the capitalist periphery, remains much less developed and industrialized than the core—North America, Western Europe, Australia, New Zealand, and Japan. Since the 1950s many social scientists have called the semiperiphery and periphery the *Third World*. Industrialization began in the Third World in the nineteenth and twentieth centuries, but did not become substantial until the second half of the twentieth century. Third World societies are complex mixtures of industry and agriculture, capitalists and workers, and landowners and peasants. For example, in 1900 the class structure of Mexico looked approximately as shown in Table 1.1.

How has the socioeconomic structure of Mexico changed in the past century? Although it is still a relatively poor Third World society, Mexico today is much more urbanized, much less agricultural, and more industrialized; in addition, the standard of living for the average person is much higher. For example, whereas in 1900 about 70 percent of Mexico's population consisted of peasants, today no more than 15 percent of the population earns its living through agricultural labor. Not counting the capitalist and agricultural elites, business managers, professionals, and small businessmen and civil servants, the bulk of the population now belongs to the working class, where it engages in manufacturing or the production of services. Socioeconomic structures have been transformed in similar ways throughout Latin America and much of Asia.

Table 1.1 The Class Structure in Mexico About 1900

Elite	Class comprising thirty companies and 8,000 haciendas, which owned one-third of all the surface of Mexico and a larger proportion of the useful land, less than 1 percent of the population
New upper-middle class	(Managerial and professional, private and in civil service) 200,000 individuals and their dependents, 1.5 percent of the population
Rest of the middle classes combined	1,000,000 individuals and their dependents, 8 percent of the population
Working class	2,600,000 individuals doing physical or manual work in factories, mines, etc., along with their dependents, 20 percent of the population
Agriculturalists	(Mostly peasants, most of them very poor) 9,100,000 individuals and their dependents, 70 percent of the population

Source: Chirot (1986), Table 5–4, p. 112.

Table 1.2 provides a picture of how the world looked about a hundred years ago, at the beginning of the very century during which most of the world's revolutionary movements and successful revolutions occurred.

States

The *state* is the term used by sociologists and political scientists for what most people simply call government. States are political and military organizations that exercise control over subject populations within certain geographical territories. In Europe during the era of feudalism the state was a *feudal state*. This type of state was heavily intertwined with the landlord class or nobility. The king was the most powerful landlord; he divided his land into many parcels known as *fiefs* and gave them out to powerful landlords, who became his *vassals*. Vassals were individuals who pledged fealty (loyalty) to the king and agreed to serve him militarily, when called upon, in exchange

Table 1.2 The World in 1900

A. Control of Population in Europe (26 Percent of World's Population)

Percentage of the population controlled by:

United Kingdom	10%
Germany	13%
France	9%
Minor core societies	6%
Total core	*38%*
Austria-Hungary	11%
Italy	8%
Spain	4%
Russian Empire (incl. Asian regions)	31%
Total semiperiphery	*54%*
Peripheral Europe (Portugal, Balkans)	8%
Total periphery	*8%*

B. Control of Population in the Americas (9 Percent of World's Population)

Percentage of population controlled by:

United States	52%
Total core	*52%*
The rest (incl. independent and colonial areas)	48%
Total periphery	*48%*

C. Control of Population in Asia (57 Percent of World's Population)

Percentage of population controlled by:

United Kingdom	34%
Netherlands	5%
France	2%
United States	1%
Total colonies of the core	*42%*
Japan (incl. its colonies in Korea and Taiwan)	7%
Total semiperiphery and its colonies	*7%*
China (semi-independent)	44%
Ottoman Empire (semi-independent)	2%
Remainder of Asia	5%
Total periphery	*51%*

D. Control of Population in Africa (7 Percent of World's Population)

Percentage of population controlled by:

United Kingdom	50%
France	23%
Germany	7%
Belgium	6%
Total colonies of the core	*86%*

Italy, Spain, Portugal	7%
Independent (Ethiopia and Liberia)	7%
E. Division of the World's Population	
Core societies	15%
Semiperipheral societies and their colonies	18%
Colonies of the core	28%
Other peripheral (independent and semi-independent) societies	39% (25% in China)

Source: Chirot (1977), Tables 6–10, pp. 45–47.

for the land they had received. The feudal system was characterized by *subinfeudation,* which meant that the landlords who received fiefs from the king further subdivided their own land and gave it out to their own vassals, who then pledged fealty to them. A hierarchy of lords was thus created, and a lord held political power only insofar as he controlled land and vassals. This was a highly decentralized political system in which knights fought not only against the knights of other societies or nations but, just as often, against each other.

Beginning in the late fifteenth century, these feudal states started to grow larger and become more centralized. Large, highly bureaucratized states gradually emerged and became major political actors throughout Europe. Power was concentrated heavily in the king (or queen) and his (or her) court, a form of government that was known as *absolute monarchy.* The first absolute monarchies were the regimes of the Tudors and the Stuarts in England. They were followed by such monarchs as Ferdinand and Isabella in Spain and Portugal; Louis XIV, XV, and XVI in France; the Hapsburgs in Austria; and the Hohenzollerns in Prussia. Then, of course, there were the tsars of Russia.

How Economies, Classes, and States Are Intertwined

What is the relationship between modes of production, classes, and states? In Marx's view, the state was "the executive committee of the ruling class." What he meant by this famous phrase was that the state protected the dominant economic class from its opponents both inside and outside the country, and also helped promote its economic interests. Feudal monarchies were viewed as a form of government best suited to serve the interests of landlords or nobles. The European absolute monarchies emerged at about the same time the capitalist world-economy was emerging, and some Marxists argue that the monarchies became larger and more centralized in order to protect landlords and nobles during the period when their dominant position was being challenged by the rise of the capitalist class (Anderson, 1974b). Others see the absolute monarchies as emerging to promote the interests of the rising capitalists (Wallerstein, 1974b).

There is a good deal of truth in the Marxian view of the state, but it is a considerable oversimplification as well. States are not tied to dominant classes as if by some sort of umbilical cord; states have their own interests—which are political and military—and these interests are not only different from the interests of dominant classes but often come into conflict with them. It was another famous sociologist, Max Weber (1864–1920), who stressed that the state plays a substantially independent role in society. In short, it is another type of power group that plays a major role in determining historical outcomes, especially large-scale social changes.

In time, the absolutist monarchies of Europe gave way to more democratic regimes. Parliaments, which checked the power of the king, had existed in some European countries for a long time, and they helped to provide a basis for the emergence of the type of government known as *parliamentary democracy*. This type of government is based on the existence of parliamentary bodies as independent power bases, as well as on the election of government officials by the people and the existence of constitutional rights and liberties. Parliamentary democracy began to emerge in Europe in the nineteenth century, but really took off in the twentieth. Today all Western European societies are parliamentary democracies, as are the colonial offshoots of England: the United States, Canada, Australia, and New Zealand. Democracy has spread to other parts of the world as well, such as Japan, and to some countries in Asia and Latin America.

Democracy is most often found in a highly developed form in those societies that are highly industrialized and economically developed and that have mass literacy and mass educational systems (Rueschemeyer, Stephens, and Stephens, 1992; Sanderson, 2004). The countries referred to above are such societies. Throughout much of the Third World, democracy has made some headway, but many societies are still not democratic, and those that have formal democracies often do not really contain the actual substance of democracy. There are elections and formal constitutional rights, but elections may be fraudulent and rights may not be properly respected or maintained. In many Third World countries, both recently and in centuries past, highly authoritarian and repressive regimes have been extremely common. The societies they rule over are often plagued by severe economic inequalities and high levels of poverty, both of which serve to create serious social tensions. In some of these societies, "death squads" repress the population, targeting in particular known or suspected opponents of the government and economic elites.

To understand revolutionary mobilization, and why only a handful of revolutionary movements have actually succeeded, we need a good understanding of feudal and capitalist modes of production, the ways in which they are intertwined with particular class structures, and the nature of states and how they relate to social and economic structures. With this background in place, we can now proceed to a discussion of revolutionary activity in its myriad forms.

Chapter Two

The Great Historical Revolutions

The French Revolution of 1789

French Society and Government in the Eighteenth Century

In the eighteenth century France was a largely agrarian society ruled by an absolute monarchy. In terms of its class structure, it was divided into three "orders" or "estates," groups that had a legally defined status. The two privileged estates were the nobility and the clergy. The nobility consisted of men and their families who had been "ennobled" by the king. They held a high status, commanded great respect, and were generally wealthy. Nobles enjoyed many privileges that were unavailable to other members of French society. They were exempt from many taxes, especially the more burdensome ones, and the highest positions in the government and the army were available only to men of noble status. Ministers of the king were all of noble status, as were all members of the royal court and nearly all army officers. And nobles had special rights, such as the right to put weather vanes on their houses (a sign of high status), to occupy special seats in the churches, and to keep animals, such as rabbits and doves, that did damage to crops and that those of non-noble status were forbidden to keep.

Perhaps most significantly, a very high percentage of nobles were *seigneurs*, or landlords. At the time of the revolution they owned perhaps as much as a third of all the land in France, from which they collected feudal dues from the peasants who worked the land. They also exercised rights over the land they did not own, collecting dues from it and benefiting from many other feudal obligations imposed on the peasantry. Nobles dominated the cultural and intellectual life of France, and financed most of the heavy industry. They also played a major role in high finance and banking. Overall, the nobles were not numerous, making up somewhere between 0.5 and 1.5 percent of the population (roughly 110,000 to 350,000 persons in a total population of some 26 million). The nobility was also a highly differentiated class. At the top were men of great status and wealth, but the lower ranks of the nobility consisted of men of modest means who were often barely distinguishable from some of the wealthiest peasants.

The other privileged class was the clergy, which enjoyed a special status because its members were considered mediators between God and people. The Church owned a great deal of the land of France, and it had the right to collect tithes from the peasants. Members of the clergy were exempt from most taxes. Like the nobility, the clergy was internally differentiated, and there was great variation among clergymen in status and wealth. At the top were the bishops, abbots, and abbesses of the wealthiest churches, monasteries, and convents, but below them were many men and women of modest means: priests of most of the local parish churches and nuns who served in most of the orphanages and hospitals.

The so-called Third Estate (Tiers État) was made up of everyone else, people of the status of "commoner." They composed approximately 97 percent of the population. Since they were so numerous, the Third Estate obviously consisted of many kinds of individuals who differed greatly from one another in many respects. Two social groups were the most important parts of the Third Estate. First, there was the *bourgeoisie.* Today this term is most often used by sociologists and other social scientists to refer to capitalists, but historians and other scholars have used it, and continue to use it, to refer to a broader group. Thus the bourgeoisie of the eighteenth century is usually said to include not only businessmen but also office holders, physicians, lawyers, and other professionals. In the broadest sense, the bourgeoisie were town dwellers, but economically comfortable town dwellers. Most bourgeois enjoyed a comfortable life, and many had great wealth; but one thing they did not have was a noble status, although they often sought it, and the king would from time to time confer such a status on them.

Just how numerous the bourgeois were at the time of the revolution is not precisely known, but William Doyle (1999) estimates that they constituted about 6 percent of the population. Far more numerous was that other major segment of the Third Estate, the *peasantry*, which made up around 80 percent of the population. The most hapless class in society, they bore most of its burdens and did not enjoy the exemptions of the other classes. Peasants were required to pay tithes to the Church and feudal dues of various kinds to landlords, mostly in the form of taxes and services. But peasants differed from one another just as nobles and bourgeois did. Some peasants not only owned their own land but owned a considerable amount, and as a result enjoyed a fairly comfortable living. These were large-scale farmers who constituted a kind of rural elite. Below this elite was a group known as *laboureurs*; peasants who had enough land to be self-sufficient and even to produce an agricultural surplus that could be sold. However, most peasants were neither large-scale farmers nor *laboureurs* but, rather, farmers who did not have enough land even to be self-sufficient. This means that they had to hire themselves out at other jobs just to make ends meet. In good times they could scratch out a living, but when times were bad they were at risk of being reduced to begging, vagrancy, and crime.

France in the eighteenth century was governed by kings who declared themselves to be absolute monarchs. However, they hardly ruled alone. The government of France was a complex bureaucracy with many layers and many offices. The king had a number of ministers who advised him on various matters. One of the most important of these was the minister of finance, and the individuals who filled this role in the 1770s and 1780s would play a major part in the coming of the revolution in 1789. The king of France at the time of the revolution was Louis XVI. Although Louis XVI declared himself to be an absolute monarch, and his predecessor, Louis XIV, is famed for stating, "*l'État, c'est moi*" ("I am the state"), in fact the king could not rule absolutely, or be a true despot. The government included various bodies that could overcome his will, or make it very difficult for him to achieve it. In England at this time there was a system of parliamentary government, and the king was answerable to parliament. France had no parliament before the revolution, but it did have *parlements*—provincial courts that were responsible for ratifying or registering the king's rulings before they became law.

The Fiscal Crisis and the Coming of the Revolution

The French government collected and spent an enormous amount of money—on lavish living, war, and many other things—but it did not have a well-worked-out system for collecting and spending this money. Because its financial apparatus was poorly constructed, it experienced frequent financial crises, and in the early 1770s it entered a severe one. This was to become its worst crisis ever; by 1786 the government was very nearly bankrupt. On August 20 of that year, Louis XVI's finance minister, Calonne, was forced to tell the king that the government was on the verge of complete collapse. Calonne was of the opinion that the fiscal crisis was so severe it required a massive reform of the state. In January of 1787 an Assembly of Notables, consisting of high-ranking clergy, nobles, and members of the Third Estate, was convened in order to engage in this reform. But there was extreme contentiousness concerning how the assembly should operate and also great disagreement on the nature of the reforms that were required. Calonne's proposals failed to win support and he became increasingly unpopular, causing the king to replace him with one of Calonne's major critics and enemies, Loménie de Brienne. But Brienne made no more headway than his predecessor, and the economic crisis grew worse.

The Assembly of Notables had great difficulty coming to agreement on how it should vote on proposed reforms. Nobles and most clergy wanted it to vote by order or estate, whereby each of the three segments of which it was composed would have one collective vote. If it voted this way, then the nobles and the clergy could veto any decisions made by the Third Estate. Therefore, the Third Estate wanted to vote by head—one person, one vote. The Third Estate wanted fundamental changes in government that would move it in a much more parliamentary direction, allow it a greater voice in government, and give the people more rights and liberties. Since such changes threatened the interests of the nobles and most clergy, these bodies opposed them.

While all of this was going on, there was massive public discontent, much of which took the form of demonstrations by common people over rising prices (especially that of bread) and declining real wages. The authority of the government was increasingly being challenged, and a social and political crisis was emerging alongside the growing economic crisis. Royal authority was breaking down in Paris and in various provinces, for the people blamed the government for the worsening problems they were facing. On November 19, 1787, a reform plan that had been worked out by the king's ministers was to be considered by the *parlement* of Paris, but the king demanded that the judges register the plan without actually voting on it. To such a demand the judges expressed outrage, as did much of the public. Attempts to reach a compromise with the *parlement* did not succeed despite months of efforts, and on May 8, 1788, Brienne and other ministers took the extreme measure of declaring the *parlements* abolished. But this boomeranged and increased the already-growing fear of despotism among much of the public. Resistance to the government intensified, and it ultimately had to resort to convening the Estates-General, a special body that had not met since 1614. On July 5, 1788, the announcement that the Estates-General would be convened as soon as possible was made by Brienne, who also suspended the censorship laws in order to promote open discussion among the public of political matters. The authority of the government grew even weaker, and in the months that followed violence in the streets continued.

Throughout France, people were called upon to choose the members of the Estates-General and to draw up lists of grievances, or *cahiers*, that they wanted the Estates-General to consider. The *cahiers* drawn up

> provided a complex and ambiguous picture of the population's concerns on the eve of the Revolution. All three orders' *cahiers* indicated a consensus in favor of major constitutional reforms, above all the creation of a system of representative government that would modify the king's absolute powers. The nobility and clergy were ready to accept some major modifications of their privileges, such as equality of taxation. There was strong sentiment for reform of the legal system, and most nobles favored abolition of censorship. The nobility's *cahiers* hardly foresaw the complete abolition of their order, however, and the clergy were far from favoring the creation of an essentially secular society. (Popkin, 2002:27)

As Jeremy Popkin (2002) notes, the *cahiers* amounted to a very strong protest against the whole system of noble privileges.

There was considerable delay in convening the Estates-General, but on May 3, 1789, its 1,200 elected deputies finally assembled. A critical question was how the Estates-General would vote. As in the case of the earlier Assembly of Notables, it was a question of whether to vote by order or by head. The members of the Estates-General who came from the Third Estate refused to do anything until the members of the other two orders agreed to meet and deliberate as a single body, but nobles and clergy continued to resist. Eventually, on June 17, the Third Estate voted to rename itself the National Assembly and declared that it was speaking for the nation as a whole. But the National Assembly was locked out of its meeting hall by royal officials. They ended up meeting in the king's indoor tennis court, where they took an oath not to leave or be removed until France had a new constitution. On June 23, the king offered some modest reforms but continued to insist that the three orders of society maintain their separate existence and privileges. The National Assembly was ordered out of the tennis court, but they defied the order. The king ultimately had to back down, and on June 27 he ordered the nobility and the clergy to join with the National Assembly. Nevertheless, the government had its troops at the ready.

Meanwhile, popular unrest intensified. Public opinion was highly sympathetic to the National Assembly and opposed to the aims and actions of nobles and clergy. What happened next was momentous:

> On 14 July 1789, a large crowd composed primarily of skilled artisans and shopkeepers, aided by soldiers from one of the regiments stationed in the city, surrounded the Bastille, an imposing medieval fortress-prison that had become a symbol of despotic authority. Defended by only a few hundred troops and housing at that moment only seven prisoners, the Bastille had little real significance, but when the Parisians, infuriated by the commander's refusal to give up the weapons it contained, stormed and captured it, their victory became an immediate symbol of the newly born popular revolutionary movement. The "victors of the Bastille" had defeated the forces of the old government and of the privileged groups that had depended on it. Their support enabled the reform-minded deputies to stand up to the king. But the National Assembly also recognized that it would have to reckon with these popular allies' demands. (Popkin, 2002:32)

In the words of Doyle (1999), the French Revolution was thereby officially "launched." Many important things were to happen in the weeks, months, and years ahead, however. Following the storming of the Bastille, France underwent a great wave of peasant uprisings. Peasants all over France turned against nobles, killing some and burning down many castles. The peasants demanded an end to the system of feudal obligations to which they were subject. Through these actions, known as the "Great Fear," royal authority collapsed and power passed to the National Assembly and those loyal to it. There was open proclamation of a "revolution."

The Course of the Revolution

The period between the fall of the Bastille and August 1792 has been called the "liberal revolution." During this period, a new society based on parliamentary government and a constitution was created. The seigneurial system of noble privileges as well as the absolutist system of government were destroyed. On August 26, 1789, the "Declaration of the Rights of Man and the Citizen," the new French constitution, was set forth. This established the legal equality of all citizens and their basic rights and liberties.

Count Mirabeau, a leader of the National Assembly, tried to persuade the king to accept the results of the revolution, but he remained intransigent and refused to accept the new rules of the game that the revolutionaries were introducing. His queen, Marie Antoinette, was thought to be urging foreign governments to intervene against the revolutionaries. The monarchy's unpopularity increased. On June 10, 1791, the king and the royal family attempted to flee the country, the king having left behind a manifesto denouncing the revolution. However, their flight was unsuccessful, as they were easily spotted, arrested, and returned to Paris.

There was also resistance to the revolution—that is to say, the "liberal revolution"—from those who felt that it either failed to carry through its promises or did not go far enough. In October of 1789, some members of the National Assembly formed a club that came to be known as the Jacobins, and by the middle of 1791 there were over 400 Jacobin clubs throughout the country. In the beginning the Jacobins tended to be distrustful of radicalism, but as the years went on they became increasingly radical. The early Jacobins were mostly middle class, but over time more and more poorer citizens became members. The Jacobins were one of the groups instrumental in pushing the revolution in a more radical direction. Another important group was the *sans-culottes*; commoners who were called such because they wore long trousers rather than the *culottes,* or knee-breeches, worn by the better educated. The *sans-culottes* had been largely excluded from politics. When the liberal revolutionaries deliberated on the question of who should vote in the new society, they limited voting rights to those with a certain property qualification, and the opportunity to hold office in the new legislature was given an even stricter property qualification. In July of 1792, *sans-culottes* leaders, along with Jacobins and other radicals, developed a plan to convene a National Convention, create a new constitution, and remove the king. On August 10, 1792, the radicals and a huge number of supporters engaged in combat against Swiss guards who were defending the Royal Palace and the king, massacring them in what was the bloodiest revolutionary insurrection so far. The legislative assembly that had been created in 1789 overturned the existing constitution and removed the king from his duties. Thus began the radical phase of the French Revolution, what has sometimes been called the "second revolution."

The radical revolutionaries were fiercely opposed to the king and to any vestiges of his rule. A debate ensued concerning what should be done with him: Should he be tried, or simply executed at once? A majority of the deputies of the National Convention voted to give him a trial. He was found guilty, and a narrow majority of convention deputies voted in favor of immediate execution. In January of 1793 he was sent to the guillotine.

The victory of the radical revolutionaries over their liberal counterparts would lead in due time to the establishment of a dictatorship, one that actually has been compared to modern totalitarian regimes. But we shall leave this part of the story for Chapter 7, where we consider the critical question of the outcomes of revolutions.

Was the French Revolution a Bourgeois Revolution?

The question as to why the French Revolution occurred will be taken up in Chapter 4, where we begin the discussion of the causes of revolutions. But there is an issue of critical importance that requires discussion here. This concerns the so-called classic interpretation of the French Revolution, which held sway for a long time and is still influential today.

The classic interpretation, put forth best by the eminent French historian Georges Lefebvre (1939, English translation 1947), is that the French Revolution was a *bourgeois revolution:* It represented the triumph of the bourgeoisie over the nobility and of capitalism over feudalism. In his celebrated book *Quatre-Vingt-Neuf* ("Eighty-Nine," meaning of course 1789), Lefebvre pointed out that the bourgeoisie was the class that dominated the National Assembly, which was to play a major role in the revolution. What the bourgeoisie wanted was to destroy the special status and privileges of the clergy and nobility and to establish a new form of society and government based on civil equality.

It was in the 1950s and 1960s that this interpretation was first challenged. For example, the English historian Alfred Cobban (1964) brought forth data to show that only a small minority of the National Assembly were men of commerce and that most were lawyers, office holders, or government servants. Cobban claimed that it was the peasants rather than the bourgeoisie that overthrew the *ancien régime,* and that the revolution did not promote capitalism but actually hindered it. More recently, the sociologists Theda Skocpol (1979) and Immanuel Wallerstein (1989) have criticized the classic interpretation. Skocpol argues, in the manner of Cobban, that the revolution was just as much an obstacle to capitalist development as it was a stimulus. As for the alleged political aims of the bourgeoisie, Skocpol notes that the revolution increased the executive and administrative arrangements of government more than the parliamentary and representative arrangements. She concludes that "the French Revolution was 'bourgeois' only in the specific sense that it consolidated and simplified the complex variety of pre-Revolutionary property rights into the single individualistic and exclusive form of modern private property. And it was 'capitalist' only in the specific sense that it cleared away all manner of corporate and provincial barriers to the expansion of a competitive, national market economy in France" (1979:179). And she continues:

> But we should not forget that these transformations were only a part of the story. They were in a sense simply complements to the more striking and far-reaching transformations in the French state and national polity. These political changes, in turn, were not simply or primarily "liberal" in nature, nor were they straightforwardly determined by bourgeois activity or class interest. Rather, they were the result of complex crisscrossings of popular revolts and the efforts at administrative-military consolidation of a succession of political leaderships. By virtue of both its outcomes and its processes, the French Revolution ... was as much or more a bureaucratic, mass-incorporating and state-strengthening revolution as it was (in any sense) a bourgeois revolution. (1979:179)

Wallerstein (1989) agrees that the French Revolution did not produce any significant economic transformation in a capitalist direction. Indeed, he argues that France was already substantially capitalist in nature despite the political dominance of the nobility, for the nobility had long before turned to capitalist forms of economic activity. Skocpol and others have seen the peasants as the truly insurrectionary class, and Wallerstein is sympathetic to this view. "What is clear," he says, " is that, after July 14, the peasants began to implement their demands, ceasing to pay tithes and dues, resuming collective rights they had lost" (1989:104). Moreover,

> [t]he so-called abolition of feudalism on August 4, 1789, was not the program of the revolutionary bourgeois. It was pressed upon them by the insurgent peasantry. The [bourgeois-dominated] National Assembly spent is own energy *attempting to limit the reality of this institutional transformation.* (1989:104, emphasis added)

We must consign the classic interpretation, then, to the intellectual dustbin, as in fact the vast majority of historians have done (cf. Doyle, 1999:10–34). What is to replace it will be discussed in Chapter 4.

The Russian Revolution of 1917

Russia in the Early Twentieth Century

Russia at the turn of the twentieth century was a large-scale agrarian society that was much more economically backward than the societies of Western Europe. Politically it had formed itself into an empire that extended into other parts of Europe and Asia. Most Russians, about 80–85 percent, were peasants. In 1649 Russia legally established serfdom, and by the mid-eighteenth century over half of the peasants were serfs. Serfdom was officially abolished in 1861, but this brought about no real improvement in the economic status of former serfs and in some cases made things even worse. Their lives continued much as before. The peasants held much of their land communally, and there was a village council, the *mir*, that made decisions about how the land was to be farmed and a variety of other aspects of peasant life. The majority of peasants lived in an extremely backward state and had little contact with the larger society. Many peasants still used wooden plows and relied on other highly antiquated farming techniques. They lived in little more than huts, slept on their stoves, and shared their houses with their animals. The peasant economy was at a mere subsistence level, if that. Many peasants had to hire themselves out as seasonal workers in such activities as agriculture, mining, and construction in order to make ends meet. The level of peasant discontent was very high and was one of the key elements of the revolutionary turmoil that was to come.

Russia was a late industrializer, industrialization having begun only around 1890. On the eve of the Revolution of 1917, Russia was still an overwhelmingly agrarian society with a very small working class. The industrial working class emerged from the peasantry, and most Russians classified as workers worked only seasonally, farming the rest of the year. In fact, the majority of Russia's factories were placed in the countryside in order to make access to workers easier. A full-time industrial working class living in cities developed only in mining and in such technology-intensive industries as metallurgy and machine building. In 1900 the full-time working class constituted less than 1 percent of the population. The rest of the nonpeasant population consisted of clergy, government officials, and the bourgeoisie in the broadest sense (i.e., not only businessmen but also professionals and civil servants of various types).

Politically, Russia had an extremely autocratic state headed by the tsar who, until 1905, claimed unlimited power. By this time many of the absolutist states of Western Europe had given way to parliamentary and democratic institutions, but Russia was nowhere near these political achievements. The tsar not only refused to allow any representatives from the population to have a political voice but made it a criminal offense even to question his authority. Another contrast with Western Europe was that Western European monarchs respected private property, especially that of private landlords. But in Russia, the tsar owned everything. In the words of Richard Pipes (1995:11), the tsar "claimed all the land and natural resources, he monopolized wholesale and foreign trade, and, as if this were not enough, laid claim to the lifelong services of his subjects. The upper class served him directly, in the army or bureaucracy, while commoners tilled either his land or that of his servitors. This kind of 'patrimonial' regime represented the most extreme type of autocracy."

The tsar established a large bureaucracy to protect his rule. An integral part of this bureaucracy was the police department, which played the dual role of maintaining law and order among the general population and protecting the state from popular unrest and potential rebellion. That branch of the department concerned with protecting the state against the people had extraordinary powers to enforce political conformity:

> It could engage in open or secret surveillance, search and arrest, imprisonment, and, by administrative fiat—that is, without trial—exile for periods of up to five years. Through a network of agents it penetrated every facet of the country's life; its foreign branches even tracked émigrés. Such measures were considered necessary to counteract an unprecedented wave of political terrorism by radical extremists, which in the decade preceding World War I claimed the lives of thousands of government officials. They made late tsarist Russia in many respects the prototype of a modern police state. (Pipes, 1995:16)

Russia also maintained a standing army of some 1.4 million men, the largest in the world. For hundreds of years Russia was one of the most militaristic societies in Europe and the world, engaging in numerous wars. However, the army was also employed for political repression, frequently being used for putting down internal disturbances.

Political Parties and Revolutionary Thought

Political parties were illegal, but they began to emerge nevertheless toward the end of the nineteenth century. In 1883, a group known as the Liberation of Labor was founded by several Russian exiles living in Switzerland. A prominent member of this group was Georgi Plekhanov, a major Marxist intellectual who translated Marx's works into Russian. Some years later this organization was transformed into the Russian Social Democratic Party, a party that favored the transition to a socialist economy. At a meeting held in 1903, the party split over who was to lead it. A major leader of the Social Democrats, Vladimir Ilich Lenin, argued that only the most vigorous party activists should be involved in governing it. Lenin argued against full democratic participation by the party's rank and file because he thought such participation would make it easy for the tsar's secret police to repress its activities. When the party voted on this issue, Lenin lost, but the candidates Lenin was supporting for the party's central committees won. After this point Lenin and his supporters came to be known as the Bolsheviks, and their opponents, led by Plekhanov and Leon Trotsky, the Mensheviks. This split widened over time.

The Bolsheviks and Mensheviks were divided on more than just how the Social Democratic Party should be run. They both supported a transition to socialism, but they disagreed on how that should be achieved. The Mensheviks stayed closer to the thinking of Marx, who argued that socialism could develop only after capitalism had reached a highly advanced form. Advanced capitalism was a prerequisite for socialism, Marx had argued, because only capitalism was capable of leading a society to a high enough level of industrialization to produce a large amount of wealth. In Marx's view, a society could not go directly from a feudal or agrarian stage to socialism without first passing through industrialized capitalism. The Mensheviks therefore favored a political strategy that was gradualist and that concentrated on developing capitalism in Russia before attempting a socialist revolution. The Bolsheviks took a much harder line and were impatient. They thought it was possible to create a peasant-worker alliance that would be capable of overthrowing the Tsarist state and leading Russia into a highly industrialized form of socialism. The Bolsheviks wanted to establish a "dictatorship of the proletariat," or a one-party political system that would be led by a revolutionary vanguard—a small number of the most committed socialist intellectuals. They borrowed this phrase from Marx, who had used it to describe the political system of socialism in its transitional phase. This dictatorship was needed to raise the consciousness of workers and make them truly revolutionary. Left to themselves, workers would develop only a "trade union consciousness," which would favor reform over revolution and, hence, the acceptance of capitalism rather than its overthrow.

The Political Revolution of 1905

On a Sunday—later to be known as "Bloody Sunday"—in January of 1905 a group of several thousand workers tried to present Tsar Nicholas II with a list of grievances, hoping he would take action to correct them. But the tsar had his soldiers fire on the workers, killing thousands. This led to strikes and peasant protests throughout Russia and caused the tsar to be concerned that a successful revolution might occur. To stave off such an outcome, the tsar agreed to certain reforms. Among these were the creation of a national parliament, or

Duma, which would be elected by the people, including even those who did not own property, and the granting of liberties in the areas of speech, conscience, and assembly. Nicholas also agreed to make labor unions legal, to provide health and accident insurance for some workers, to provide free primary education, and to engage in agrarian reform.

However, the tsar sent the army into areas where rebellion was still occurring and had thousands of people shot; thousands of others were deported from the country. Later on, the tsar reneged on honoring some of his proposed reforms. Elections were allowed, but they were organized in such a way that only a small minority of the adult population was able to vote. When a Duma was elected, the tsar sought to gain complete control over it; when he could not, he ignored its decisions or, from time to time, actually disbanded it. Nicholas made it clear to all that Russia was still an absolute monarchy and he its monarch. Moreover, the powers of the Department of Police remained intact. Trade unions had been legalized, but the police could and did close down particular unions. Political parties had also been legalized, but the members of revolutionary parties were still subject to arrest or exile. Even as a political revolution, the events of 1905 were for the most part a failure. Little had changed in any substantial way.

The February Revolution of 1917 and the Provisional Government

Between 1905 and 1917, Russia remained a deeply divided and extremely contentious society. Unrest continued, as did revolutionary activism. Indeed, both intensified. In February of 1917 there were large-scale strikes by industrial workers in many cities. Troops were dispatched to Petrograd (formerly St. Petersburg) to disperse the large crowd that had assembled there, but the majority of soldiers refused to fire on the protesters, and, indeed, many joined forces with them. Lacking the military support it needed, the tsar's regime, already severely weakened through its involvement in World War I, lost its capacity to rule. Nicholas was forced to abdicate on March 16 and was put under house arrest. A new Provisional Government was created. However, many problems remained and the new regime could not rule effectively. The Provisional Government was constituted mostly by aristocrats, wealthy capitalists, and professionals, and thus mainly represented the interests of the higher social classes. It was therefore regarded with considerable suspicion by the mass of the population. To make matters worse from the standpoint of stable political rule, the previously established Petrograd Soviet—a council of workers—claimed that it and not the Provisional Government had the right to rule under the new circumstances. The Provisional Government consisted mostly of liberals, whereas the Petrograd Soviet was made up of socialists. A major leader of the Provisional Government was Aleksandr Kerensky, who started out as minister of justice but later became the government's head. Since he had played a role in establishing both political bodies, he acted as a kind of liaison between them. Russia was in essence being governed by a coalition of liberals and socialists.

The Provisional Government never enjoyed any real legitimacy, and hostility to it grew throughout the spring and summer. Many demonstrations were made against it, with the demonstrators carrying banners that read "All Power to the Soviets!" (The soviets were workers' councils that had been created both before and in the wake of the February Revolution.) One major political group that did not play a direct role in the February Revolution was the Bolsheviks, many of whom had emigrated or been arrested and exiled to remote parts of the empire with the outbreak of World War I. But after the February Revolution they were eager to return to Russia. Lenin returned in April from Switzerland by sealed train via Germany, and Trotsky, a former Menshevik now turned Bolshevik, returned in May. Lenin opposed the Provisional Government and agreed with the slogan "All Power to the Soviets!" He saw the Provisional Government as representing the interests of the bourgeoisie and argued that another revolution was needed, a true Marxian proletarian revolution. In the months to follow, he was successful at pushing his fellow Bolsheviks into an increasingly hard-line position. Moreover, the Bolsheviks were attracting followers at an extraordinary rate. From at best 24,000 Bolsheviks at the time of the February Revolution, their numbers increased to over 100,000 by the end of April and to approximately 350,000 by October.

Both peasants and workers were becoming angrier and more militant. There was increasing turmoil in the countryside; "manor houses were being sacked and burned," "the peasants were seizing private and state land for their own use," and "many landowners abandoned their estates and fled from the countryside" (Fitzpatrick, 1994:55). Peasants presented petitions to the government asking that land be redistributed in an egalitarian manner. July was an especially tumultuous month. Mass demonstrations and popular disorder erupted in Petrograd and lasted for three days. The demonstrators, who may have numbered half a million, consisted of sailors, soldiers, and workers. The Provisional Government blamed the Bolsheviks—the demonstrators did include Bolsheviks among their leaders—and responded by arresting a number of Bolshevik leaders, including Trotsky. An order was made for the arrest of Lenin, but he escaped to Finland.

The October Revolution of 1917

By the end of September, the Bolsheviks had become a majority in the soviets of both Petrograd and Moscow, helping Lenin reach the conclusion that it was time for the Bolsheviks to overthrow the Provisional Government and seize power themselves. On the evening of October 24, a group of soldiers, sailors, and workers followed the order of Trotsky—who had recently been released from prison and become the leader of the Bolsheviks in the absence of Lenin—to take control of several transportation and communication centers, as well as the Winter Palace of the tsar. The insurrectionaries occupied the telegraph offices and railway stations, and set up roadblocks on bridges. There was little resistance by military personnel, few of whom continued to recognize the legitimate authority of the Provisional Government, and thus little bloodshed. The Provisional Government was toppled by the next day, and its head, Kerensky, fled.

Shortly afterward, elections for a Constituent Assembly were held. The Bolsheviks won a majority of the votes in Petrograd and Moscow, but of the total votes cast throughout the country they won only 24 percent. The most votes, 41 percent, went to the Socialist Revolutionaries, with a scattering of votes for other parties (e.g., the Constitutional Democrats, a moderate party, won 5 percent of the votes, and the Mensheviks won 3 percent). Nevertheless, the Bolsheviks gradually took control of the government and refused to give it up. In November the possibility of forming a coalition government with other parties was discussed by the Bolshevik Central Committee, but Lenin was vehemently opposed to the idea. When the Constituent Assembly met and proved hostile to the Bolshevik claim to all power, the Bolsheviks simply sent the assembly packing. The Bolsheviks certainly did not have a mandate from the people to rule, but they circumvented this problem by claiming to represent only the working class, rather than the population as a whole. They apparently thought they had received more working-class votes than any of the other parties.

The Bolsheviks renamed themselves the Communist Party in March of 1918. A social revolution had occurred in that a new social and economic structure, as well as a new government, was formed. But the new government and economy had yet to be consolidated, for there was strong opposition to Bolshevik rule from the Mensheviks and many others. It took a civil war lasting some three years before the Bolsheviks could consolidate their rule. We will continue this part of the story in the chapter on revolutionary outcomes.

Revolution in China, 1911–1949

China in the Twentieth Century

China was one of the great agrarian civilizations of the world, having gone through various dynasties and phases of political centralization and decentralization. During the famous Song Dynasty (C.E. 964–1279) it underwent a startling amount of economic development and could have been poised for an industrial revolution had certain other things gone right. In C.E. 1500 it was at least on a par with the West technologically, and many of the great technological inventions of Western Europe were originally borrowed from China. Nevertheless, at the turn of the twentieth century it was far behind Europe in economic development and moving toward a state of economic crisis. From 1644 until 1911, it was governed by the Qing Dynasty (previously spelled Ch'ing), which was Manchu rather than Chinese. This dynasty encountered increasingly severe economic and political difficulties as the nineteenth century wore on. Population pressure was reducing the standard of living, taxes increased, and peasant discontent grew. In addition, government incompetence and corruption intensified, and foreign intervention in China's economic and political affairs increased dramatically. Rebellions, some of them of major scale, became commonplace. Discontent grew even among the privileged upper classes.

The structure of China in the first half of the twentieth century was typical of an agrarian society. The vast majority of the population were peasants—some 90 percent. Lucien Bianco (1971) estimates that about 7 percent of the peasants fell into the category of rich peasants, and that they owned about 27 percent of all land. Rich peasants were those who had enough land under cultivation to meet their basic needs. Usually they were able to hire laborers to help work the land, and they were often able to produce an economic surplus from it. Some rich peasants could even rent out some of their land. About 22 percent of peasants were middle peasants, and they owned about 25 percent of the land. Middle peasants were normally able to make ends meet without having to hire themselves out as workers on someone else's land. Most peasants, however, fell into the category of poor peasants, who constituted 68 percent of the peasantry while owning only some 22 percent of the land. Poor peasants were able to make ends meet only if one or more family members went to work for someone else during at least part of the year. The economic situation of the poor peasants grew increasingly desperate throughout the nineteenth century and the early decades of the twentieth.

As is the case in virtually all agrarian societies, China had a small landowning class (in this case usually referred to as the *gentry*) that owned a very large amount of the cultivable land and from which they earned their living. The gentry exercised enormous control over the land and the peasants who lived on it. It imposed rent and taxes on the peasants, and often these were severe. In the 1930s, Chinese peasants may have given up on average as much as 45 percent of their harvests to the gentry. Peasants also had to pay taxes, which Bianco (1971:100) calls "the second great torment of rural life." Tax rates were not fixed and were subject to manipulation by those who collected them. They could be doubled, or increased even as much as tenfold. In order to pay their taxes, peasants frequently had to resort to loans, which they could take in grain or in cash. Interest rates were normally 20 to 30 percent for cash loans, but sometimes went as high as 100 percent. Bianco (1971:103) tells us more:

> In hard times, interest rates rose to incredible heights. Combined with the concurrent rise in grain prices in such times, a food loan stripped many a family of its land. Borrowing was the classic road to dispossession, to the point where many peasants were resigned to selling their children rather than mortgage their land. Nonetheless, investigations in 1929, 1934, and 1935 revealed that almost half of all peasant families (44 percent)—poor, middle, and "rich"—were in debt.

The remaining 10 percent or so of the population consisted of government administrators, merchants, craftsmen, urban workers, soldiers, and servants. The level of industrialization in China in the early twentieth century was extremely low, so urban workers constituted only a tiny fraction of the population.

The Chinese political system was an imperial one. At the top was the emperor, who claimed absolute authority and the "mandate of heaven." The emperor was surrounded by an elaborate bureaucratic administration. Government administrators were selected for their positions, and had been for some 1,500 years, by an extremely rigorous set of examinations that tested their knowledge of the Confucian classics and their administrative skills. Since the examinations were extremely competitive, few passed, and it took many years of intensive study to succeed at them. At the turn of the twentieth century, the central government included approximately 40,000 officials known as *mandarins*. They constituted a kind of class unto themselves, and most mandarins came from wealthy families. Usually it was only these families that had enough money to pay for the tutors and the many years of study required to pass the exams. Since the mandarins were part of the central government, at the local or village level they delegated authority to the gentry.

As mentioned previously, between 1644 and 1911 China was ruled by the Qing Dynasty, which consisted of foreigners who had come from beyond the Great Wall in Manchuria. Roughly the first half of the Qing period was marked by competent emperors and stable political rule; but in the nineteenth century all this was to change, with China increasingly beset by social, economic, and political difficulties. These difficulties provided the context for revolution.

The Overthrow of the Qing

Nineteenth-century China was filled with contentiousness. Discontent on the part of both the peasantry and the elite grew, and there were numerous rebellions. By the end of the century discontent was widespread and the Qing Dynasty entered a crisis. Qingyi, or "critical elite opinion," groups emerged from within segments of the elite. Many sons of the elite were having increasing difficulties in achieving elite positions and, thus, in maintaining their status. Degrees that were necessary for elite positions were increasingly being sold to the wealthiest segments of the elite, leaving those without enough wealth out of the picture. The ancient examination system was being degraded and reduced to a mere marketplace of degree buying and selling. Even those who obtained degrees often had great difficulty finding appropriate positions afterward. There was also considerable discontent of a nationalistic nature. Much of the Chinese elite resented the increasing role of Westerners and Western ideas and wanted reforms that would reestablish China's independence and prominence as a great world civilization.

In 1898 radicalism intensified. The Reform Movement of 1898, led by Kang Youwei, played an important role in consolidating elite discontent. In 1899 a famous revolt known as the Boxer Rebellion broke out. The Boxers were highly nationalistic; in 1900 they attacked missionaries, other foreigners, and Chinese converts to Christianity. In league with the government, they declared war on Japanese and Western powers and tried to expel them from the country. However, their efforts were quickly put down. Foreign troops occupied Beijing and killed thousands of people, and China was forced to accept a humiliating peace settlement that intensified its economic problems and actually increased foreign influence.

Although the Boxer Rebellion ended badly, it may have had positive long-run benefits because it helped to spur even greater discontent, as dissatisfaction grew throughout the coming decade. Discontent existed throughout the population, with elite and popular dissatisfaction fusing. Poverty had grown among the peasants, elite economic difficulties continued and grew worse, and anti-imperialism abounded. This decade witnessed the emergence of a major revolutionary leader, Sun Yat-sen, who had begun his revolutionary activities earlier, in the 1890s. In 1894 he organized a revolutionary organization that tried to take control of Canton the following year. Being unsuccessful, Sun fled the country and remained in exile for fifteen years. In Tokyo in 1905 he founded an organization known as Tongmeng Hui ("United League"). This organization sought to bring together students, popular groups, and the army into a unified revolutionary force. Sun had three basic revolutionary principles, which involved nationalism, democracy, and equality. He wanted China to fight against imperialism, and he opposed the Manchu character of the Qing Dynasty. He favored making the Chinese government into a republic, which would limit the power of the ruler and create a much more open form of political life. And he favored economic equality, advocating a single tax on land.

The United League engaged in numerous revolts and attempted to assassinate government officials, including members of the imperial family. Revolutionaries increasingly infiltrated the army. Things had reached the crisis stage. The government responded to these actions and to earlier demands for reforms by undertaking a number of changes. It moved, however weakly, toward creating a constitutional monarchy; made fiscal, judicial, and administrative changes; established a modern army; and abolished the ancient examination system. It also tried to deal with concern over foreign influence. But the reforms were too little too late. Little was done to improve China's economic position vis-à-vis Japan and the West, and poverty and a strong feeling of social injustice were still widespread. China was ripe for revolution, and there was essentially no turning back after 1908. Both the empress and the emperor died that year, and the new emperor was a child of only three. The following year brought open displays of disloyalty among some segments of the government, and there were mutinies by the army. The new educational system was increasingly graduating revolutionaries. "Revolution," remarks Lucien Bianco (1971:12), "was the next item on the agenda."

The revolution began in October of 1911, and was pulled off with surprising ease. In the words of John Schrecker:

> With amazing speed, province after province, led by the local assemblies and the army, declared its independence of Beijing. In December Sun Yat-sen returned from abroad and, in a meeting of his followers, was elected president of China. On January 1, 1912, he officially proclaimed the establishment of the Republic of China, and on February 12 the Qing Dynasty and the Xuantong emperor bowed to the "Mandate of Heaven" ... and abdicated in favor of the new government. (2004:172–173)

Chiang Kai-shek, Mao Zedong, and the Revolutionary Interregnum

This was a revolution, but it was a political rather than a social revolution because the new regime was not accompanied by sweeping social and economic changes. China was yet to have its great social revolution. What kind of government replaced the Qing Dynasty?

Sun Yat-sen was the first president of the new Republic of China, and in 1912 he created the Kuomintang, or Nationalist, Party out of the old United League. Later that year, however, he resigned and was replaced by Yuan Shikai, a leading general in the revolutionary forces. But Yuan's outlook turned out to be not all that different from the old emperors. He had the Kuomintang's parliamentary leader assassinated, which caused Sun to flee. Yuan outlawed the Kuomintang and, in 1914, dismissed the newly formed parliament. In 1915 he made it known that he planned to create a new dynasty and become its emperor. This was met with incredulity and rebellion. After his death the following year, China fell into a state of chaos and disorder that Schrecker (2004:177) has called "probably the worst disorder that China had known since the tenth century." Central authority collapsed, and rule fell into the hands of warlords who usually controlled only a province or two and who fought vigorously among themselves.

After Yuan's death, Sun returned to China and resumed his role as a Kuomintang leader. After the Russian Revolution, he sent a young military officer by the name of Chiang Kai-shek to Moscow to bring back information on Soviet military and political organization. Chiang was impressed by the organizational abilities of the Bolsheviks even though he did not support their revolutionary goals. Sun used what he learned from Chiang about Bolshevik organizational structure as a pattern for Kuomintang organization. The other major political party established in post-Qing China was the Communist Party, which was founded in 1921. Although the Kuomintang and the Communists had a number of fundamental differences, and despite the objections of Chiang and other conservative Kuomintang officials, Sun sought to bring the two parties together, and for a time they were allied. The Communists were under the direct control of the Comintern (Communist International) leadership of the Soviet Union, and Sun made use of Comintern advisers to give the Kuomintang a Leninist style of highly disciplined organization. But in 1925 Sun died, and the ensuing struggle for leadership of the Kuomintang was won by Chiang. As suggested earlier, Chiang's attitude toward the Communists was very different from Sun's. He dismantled the Kuomintang-Communist alliance and had Communists removed from important political positions. Then he went even further. The Communists had proved useful to a major military offensive launched by Chiang, the Northern Expedition of 1926–1928, but when this usefulness was finished Chiang had thousands of Communists, along with many of their supporters, executed. The two political parties became violently opposed from this time on.

Chiang ran the Kuomintang in a highly authoritarian way and seemed mostly concerned with his own power; the condition of the mass of the Chinese people did not seem to interest him. The Kuomintang became increasingly associated with, and supportive of, privileged socioeconomic groups, who had a stake in maintaining the status quo. As Schrecker (2004:201–202) comments,

> Chiang's regime did not relieve the mass poverty of China or the misery of the average person, the nation's most pressing problems. The economic modernization that did occur did not filter down. The countryside remained a disaster area, and life in the cities, except for those on top, was not much better. ... Chiang expressed comparatively little concern with the issue of economic injustice and was certainly unable to transmit what feelings he did have to the country at large. The reasons for his problems were, naturally, intertwined with all the shortcomings of the republic but were tied, most importantly, to the increasing reliance it placed on those who were exploiting the nation's distress.

Lucien Bianco (1971:110) makes a very similar point: "Almost nothing was done by [Chiang and the Kuomintang] to satisfy the peasants' most basic needs: no steps were taken to protect them against exactions and violence on the part of the military, to eliminate usury by reforming and expanding the system of agricultural credit, or to reduce the misery caused by land tax and land rent." The Kuomintang wanted to maintain the economic and political position of the wealthiest landlords, and they favored as well the commercial bourgeoisie. And the Kuomintang themselves "built vast personal fortunes from government monopolies and the management of public funds" (Bianco, 1971:115).

Under these circumstances, support for the Communist Party grew, both among intellectuals and among the masses, especially the peasants. The Communists built the Red Army, which did battle with Kuomintang forces. In 1931, under the leadership of Mao Zedong, the Red Army gained control of part of southeast China (Jiangxi province and adjacent areas), founding the Chinese Soviet Republic and making Mao its first president. But there was to be a reversal. Chiang had launched "extermination campaigns" against the Communists, and the fifth of these was successful. The Red Army was routed and had to flee. Thus began one of the most famous events in modern Chinese history—the Long March. This started in late 1934 and lasted until the end of 1935. Mao and about 100,000 men retreated from pursuing Kuomintang forces, traveling from the southeast to the southwest and then up to the northwest, a journey of some 6,000 miles. At most only a fifth of the men who started out were left when the Long March was finished. It was during this year of retreat that Mao became the unrivaled leader of the Communists.

But Mao and the Communists were able to reconstitute themselves militarily, and they continued to attract support from the peasantry, for whom they were strong advocates. Between 1937 and 1945 they expanded their influence enormously. In the former year the Red Army contained 80,000 men, but by the latter it had the better part of 1 million and a militia of more than 2 million. Moreover, in 1937 it ruled over only 1.5 million peasants in a single northern province, whereas by 1945 it governed 90 million peasants across much of northern China. The CCP (Chinese Communist Party) had grown to include over a million members by the end of World War II. Japanese aggression against China during the war proved to be a big help to the Communists; it caused the Communists to organize a rebellion that relied heavily on the peasants, which intensified their ideological zeal, organizational strength, and nationalistic commitment. But the Japanese invasion had the opposite effect on the Kuomintang and its allies, with many Kuomintang officials, landlords, and warlords fleeing from northern China.

The Communist Revolution of 1949

At the end of World War II, Chiang and Mao engaged in a number of conversations in an effort to establish a coalition government. In the last month of 1945, U.S. General George C. Marshall was dispatched to China to assist in the negotiations, but he was unable to accomplish his mission: A settlement could not be reached. The two parties had intense mutual distrust, and their ideological positions were fundamentally different. Civil war loomed.

In July of 1946 the Communists created the People's Liberation Army, and the civil war was soon under way. Many observers expected the Kuomintang to win easily, since their forces greatly outnumbered the Liberation Army, and they had superior military power as well.

But the effectiveness of the Liberation Army surprised everyone except the Communists and the army itself. What turned out to be the most important battles occurred in 1948. In April, Yanan was captured by the army, and shortly thereafter the two largest cities in the provinces of Honan, Loyang, and Kaifeng fell to Communist forces. By September the Communists had taken all of Manchuria. The most decisive battle was the Hwai-hai campaign, which was fought for two months from November of 1948 until January of 1949. This proved to be Chiang's Waterloo, for the Kuomintang forces were decimated and the Liberation Army had achieved a numerical superiority. Recognizing defeat, Chiang made known his desire to negotiate an end to the conflict. The Communists made it clear that Chiang himself had to go, and on January 21 he resigned as president. He and many of his allies fled to Taiwan, a former Japanese colony that had been reclaimed by China with the Japanese defeat in World War II. The People's Republic of China was officially founded on October 1, 1949.

Why did the Communists win even though they were heavily outnumbered? One reason is that they fought using a new tactic, guerrilla warfare, which the Kuomintang was not militarily prepared to deal with. Another reason, no less important, is that the Communists had the strong support of the peasants because they treated them much better than the Kuomintang had:

> Insofar as possible under wartime conditions, the Communists worked to improve the economic life of the average person and to equalize wealth. The Communists put their major effort into making sure that what goods were available were fairly distributed and that people had some hope of surviving. They carried out a program of rent reduction and, even more importantly, did much to free farmers from usurious credit arrangements that had kept them in thrall for generations. The party also undertook a moderate program of land redistribution. (Schrecker, 2004:207)

Lucien Bianco tells much the same story:

> As late as the spring of 1946, there were many areas in which the peasants' only concern was to avoid involvement in the warfare; when the Eighth Route Army left, the villagers stayed behind and welcomed the Nationalists [Kuomintang]. Soon, however, it became clear that the return of the Kuomintang meant the undoing of social and political

advances the peasants had thought they could take for granted, the repeal of reforms relating to interest rates, land tax, and land rent that they had presumed to be part of any postwar government program, and worst of all, a return to the traditional social and political order.

The term Liberated Areas, by contrast, ... became synonymous with the redistribution of land, the indictment of landlords, and the dictatorship of the Poor Peasants Association. ... As the true direction of the revolution became clear, the struggle grew pitiless. When the villagers realized that their hour had come, that they had gone too far to turn back, years of accumulated hatred were unleashed. Landlords guilty of exploiting their tenants were paraded from village to village and slowly chopped to bits along the way by mobs armed with pitchforks, shears, pickaxes, and clubs, which then fought over the flesh of men alleged to have gorged themselves on the flesh of the people, and mutilated their remains. (1971:187–188)

A Note on Sources

Since the main thrust of this book is explaining revolutions and taking note of their outcomes, I have kept the descriptive material in this and the following chapter to a minimum—just enough to give the reader a feel for (1) the nature of the society in question, (2) the main sources of discontent, and (3) the really big events that led up to the revolutions in question. Thus I have not felt it necessary to delve into classic works on the revolutions, relying instead on what I feel are reliable summaries presented by other authors. Since I am not a specialist in any of these revolutions, virtually all of the information I have presented has been drawn from others. If all of the sources were cited within the text, it would be cluttered with references at the end of every paragraph, not to mention the end of many sentences. This seems to me stylistically inappropriate and an imposition on the reader. Therefore I simply indicate, here and in the note at the end of Chapter 3, the main sources on which I have drawn. On the French Revolution, I have relied primarily on Popkin (2002) and Doyle (1999), but also consulted Hibbert (1980). On Russia, my main sources have been Fitzpatrick (1994) and Pipes (1995), with occasional reference to DeFronzo (1996). On China, I have consulted mainly the classic treatment of Bianco (1971) and the excellent, but much more recent, analysis by Schrecker (2004); a small amount of material has also been drawn from Skocpol (1979) and DeFronzo (1996). Readers seeking a more detailed understanding of the dynamics of the Great Revolutions are advised to consult these sources, as well as the bibliographies used by them.

Chapter Three

Revolutions in the Third World

In the last chapter we looked at the three most dramatic and consequential revolutions of all time. True social revolutions are rare in world history, but they have become somewhat more common in the twentieth century. And certainly there has been a significant increase in revolutionary *activity*. With the exception of the revolutions against Communism, which are a special case, all of the revolutions of the twentieth century have occurred in less-developed, highly agrarian societies. In this chapter we look at three social revolutions that occurred in the Third World in the second half of the last century: the Cuban Revolution of 1959, the Nicaraguan Revolution of 1979, and the Iranian Revolution of the same year. We also discuss a major revolutionary situation that ended in political rather than social revolution: the overthrow of the Marcos regime in the Philippines in 1986.

Castro and the Cuban Revolution

Cuba was one of the major slave plantation societies of the Caribbean during the eighteenth and nineteenth centuries. Whereas most Caribbean plantation societies were under the control of the British and the French, Cuba was under Spanish control. Slaves were imported from West Africa, and sugar was the main crop. Slavery was formally abolished in Cuba in 1886, although the Spanish continued their involvement after that date. The United States got involved in Cuba in the late nineteenth century, with Spain ceding the island to the United States in 1898 as a trust. Spanish rule formally ceased at the beginning of 1899, and the United States ruled Cuba militarily from then until May of 1902, when it became sovereign. From this point, the United States started to become a major player in the Cuban economy, with large-scale capitalist investment in sugar production. Throughout the twentieth century Cuba continued to be overwhelmingly dependent on sugar production. More than 80 percent of Cuban exports involved sugar, and the majority of this was exported to the United States. The main beneficiaries of this sugar monoculture were the big Cuban sugar landlords and U.S. investors in sugar production. Sugar monoculture and economic dependence on the United States made it very difficult for Cuba to develop a highly diversified economy that would experience sustained growth. What industry there was—utilities, manufacturing, oil refining, and mining—was also heavily under U.S. control.

Cuban society was dominated by landlords, and land was very unequally divided, with three-fourths of the farmland controlled by a very small minority (less than 10 percent) of farm owners. Approximately a third of sugar farms and cattle ranches was under the control of a mere one-half of 1 percent of the sugar and cattle farm owners. Farmworkers constituted the largest subordinate class, although Cuba did have an industrial working class and a surprising number of industrial workers. There were also a number of service workers who catered both to wealthy Cubans and to the large number of tourists that flocked to Cuba's shores. Perhaps a third of Cuban workers in the 1950s fell into the category of underemployed or part-time workers. Unemployment in Cuba was very high, sometimes reaching 30 percent during the dead season.

Cuba was ruled by a series of unstable dictatorships throughout most of the twentieth century. Gerardo Machado became president in 1924 with the assistance of U.S. business interests and the Cuban army. He was merely one of a long series of brutal dictators who met popular unrest with severe repression. Machado's successor was overthrown by an army sergeant by the name of Fulgencio Batista, who created a government that was led by Ramón Grau San Martín. Batista was the real power behind the scenes, however. In 1940 Batista defeated Grau for the presidency in an allegedly free election. Batista was followed by Grau and Carlos Prio between 1944 and 1952, and their regimes, like that of Batista's, were pervaded by graft and corruption of all sorts. In the words of Marifeli Pérez-Stable (1999:43), "Public officials continued to view the national treasury as their private domain." Although elections were still supposed to be held, in 1952 Batista and the army seized control of the government and ruled in a highly dictatorial and corrupt way until 1959. Proposed reforms were blocked and government repression actually intensified.

Cuban society was characterized by massive discontent affecting not just the subordinate classes but the middle classes and elites as well. University students from elite and other well-educated backgrounds often joined revolutionary groups that sprung up in the universities. One of these students was Fidel Castro, a young lawyer. There was a Cuban Communist Party, but Castro did not believe it had enough popular support to be able to generate a revolution. He joined instead the Orthodoxo Party, another oppositional party. After Batista seized power in 1952, Castro presented a legal brief in court asking that Batista be imprisoned. When the court rejected his request, Castro spurned negotiations with Batista as a means of putting an end to his dictatorial regime. At this point, Castro, his brother Raúl, and other militants decided in favor of armed insurrection and organized many opponents of the regime to this end. When one of their major military attacks ended in disaster, Castro was brought to trial and given a long prison sentence, although he served less than two years of it. After being freed from prison, Castro went to Mexico, where in 1955 he organized the famous M-26–7 movement. One of the radicals he recruited to this movement was Ernesto ("Ché") Guevara, who became a legendary revolutionary.

The rebel forces put together by the Castro brothers and Guevara gradually grew in strength and made many forays against Batista's army. They achieved more and greater victories, and the army was disinclined to venture into the mountains where the rebels hid. In 1957 and 1958 the rebels engaged in assaults in the cities that produced strong counterattacks by the army, with many revolutionaries being killed. Because the government's security forces engaged in torture as well as killing, its actions led to enormous popular outrage. Many of the victims were from the middle class, which intensified this group's opposition to Batista. Batista's actions were also of concern to the U.S. government, which stopped shipping arms to the Cuban government in 1958. This seemed to imply a more permissive attitude of the United States toward the revolutionaries and led to a severe crisis for the Cuban regime. Popular opposition to the regime continued to grow, the army's morale fell, and even some of Batista's soldiers became sympathetic to the revolutionaries. The revolution essentially came when the revolutionaries surrounded Santiago and negotiated a surrender on December 31, 1958. Castro took command of the army, and Batista fled the country on January 1, 1959.

After the revolution it was not clear for some time just what kind of government and economy Castro intended to establish. Although from the very beginning he seemed to want to turn Cuba into a Marxist-Leninist state, Castro concealed any such plans until long after the revolution. In May of 1960 Castro announced to the people that his government would not hold free elections. By the end of that year the means of production were in the hands of the state and the upper classes had been disappropriated. Cuba's economy was no longer capitalist. In April of 1961, Cuba officially became a Marxist-Leninist state.

The Sandinistas and the Nicaraguan Revolution

Nicaragua was part of the Spanish Empire until it gained its political independence in the 1820s. After independence, it became a society based largely on peasant subsistence farming and cattle ranching. Then, in the 1870s and 1880s, the economy shifted to large-scale coffee production for export, and coffee provided the basis for the economy from then until the 1950s, after which it became somewhat more diversified.

Nicaragua was formally a democracy, but it was a democracy with no real substance. In 1936 Anastazio Somoza García gained control of the government, and his family controlled Nicaragua until the revolution of 1979. Somoza was the son of a coffee plantation owner and had been educated in the United States. When he was assassinated in 1956, he was succeeded by his oldest son, Luis Somoza Debayle. When this son died of natural causes in 1967, his youngest brother, Anastazio Somoza Debayle, who had been educated at West Point, assumed office. The Somozas held elections, but these were a sham. Because elections were rigged, the two major political parties that did exist, Liberals and Conservatives, had little meaning and were largely nineteenth-century relics. The large mass of the population had virtually no input into politics. They had the legal right to strike, but in practice it was severely restricted and most strikes were declared illegal.

The Somoza family's control of the government was based on their control of the National Guard, Nicaragua's military apparatus, which was essentially the family's own personal army. The Somoza regimes enjoyed the support of the United States because they were hospitable to American capitalists and were strongly anti-Communist. The last Somoza was an extremely corrupt, repressive, and brutal dictator whose greed was seemingly boundless. He treated the state as his own personal possession and used his position to amass enormous wealth.

In 1970, half of the economically active population worked in agriculture, and the working class was small, constituting only about 10 percent of the labor force. Another 20 percent of the labor force worked in such jobs as domestic labor, construction, and transportation, and about 15 to 20 percent was engaged in middle-class jobs: small-business owners, government functionaries, and managers, sales personnel, and clerical workers. Inequality was extreme, with the top 5 percent of the income bracket earning twenty times as much as the bottom half. Land was also extremely unevenly distributed, with less than 1 percent of farm owners holding nearly a third of the farmland, and the bottom three-fifths of farm owners holding barely more than 3 percent of the land. Literacy was very low, especially in the rural areas, where only about 25 percent of the population was literate. The United Nations has estimated that in the 1970s about two-fifths of the urban and four-fifths of the rural population could be classified as poor, and over half of these were extremely poor.

Because of high levels of poverty and inequality, as well as the extreme corruption, greed, and brutality of the Somoza regime, Nicaraguan society was permeated with massive discontent. This led to the creation in 1961 of a powerful revolutionary organization, the Sandinista Front for National Liberation (Spanish acronym = FSLN). The leader of the FSLN, Carlos Fonseca, was essentially a Marxist revolutionary and thought that most of the Nicaraguan population was being victimized by capitalist exploitation on the part of both domestic and U.S. capitalists. Fonseca and other major Sandinista leaders, the most important of whom were Daniel Ortega and Lidia Saavedra de Ortega, were open opponents of the Somoza regime; they and many others were imprisoned and often tortured for this opposition. The FSLN had strong support throughout Nicaraguan society and by the end of the 1970s had grown into a mass movement.

In the late 1960s and early 1970s opposition to the Somoza regime, already strong, increased dramatically. Much of the clergy espoused the doctrine of Liberation Theology that was starting to sweep through Latin America. They told poor workers and peasants that they had a right to decent wages, a good education, and adequate medical care, and they tried to convince the poor that they could achieve these objectives. In 1972 the capital city of Managua was devastated by a massive earthquake. Millions of dollars in international aid poured into the country but, incredibly, it was largely siphoned off by Somoza and his friends. After the earthquake, there was a substantial decline in real wages, and by 1979 unemployment had climbed to nearly a third of the workforce. Even some wealthy Nicaraguans felt that Somoza's greed was simply beyond control, since Somoza siphoned off as much of their wealth as he could. This led many businesspeople to join with the poor in calling for Somoza's ouster and even to give financial support to the FSLN. After 1973, an increasing number of young people from well-off backgrounds joined forces with the Sandinistas.

In the mid-1970s the Sandinistas intensified their attacks on the Somoza regime, but these attacks were met with even more severe repression. Martial law was declared and many FSLN members, along with anyone thought to be sympathetic to their aims, were tortured and murdered. Of course, this only increased hostility toward Somoza dramatically. In 1977 Jimmy Carter assumed the presidency of the United States and was concerned about human rights violations in Nicaragua. Carter insisted that Nicaragua improve this dreadful situation in order to continue to receive U.S. military assistance, thereby forcing Somoza to discontinue martial law. The end to martial law gave the FSLN more freedom of maneuver, and the Somoza regime became partially delegitimized in the eyes of the United States.

In January of 1978 Pedro Joaquín Chamorro, a journalist who was a strong and longtime opponent of the Somoza regime, was assassinated, provoking a massive and immediate reaction from the Nicaraguan people. Angry crowds attacked businesses owned by Somoza, burning some of them, and a business work stoppage or "general strike" lasting two weeks was conducted by the business community.

When street barricades appeared all over Nicaragua, Somoza engaged in brutal repression of the protesters. As repression intensified, the Church's official nonviolent position was qualified by Archbishop Miguel Abanda y Brava, who said that armed resistance could be legitimate in some circumstances.

In April of the same year the longest and most massive strike in Nicaraguan history occurred. More than 60,000 students were involved in this strike, and "the student leadership now became the vanguard of the urban struggle" (Chavarría, 1986:154). In July another nationwide strike occurred, this time led by hospital workers. In August a unit of the FSLN took over the National Palace and held many government officials hostage. In response, martial law was reestablished and the National Guard killed over 5,000 people. Another 10,000 were injured and 25,000 became homeless. Mass uprisings began and it appeared that overthrowing Somoza was becoming increasingly likely. The FSLN had clearly captured the popular imagination. This led a number of Latin American countries to provide major aid to the Sandinistas, including major arms shipments by Cuba in 1979. Moreover, members of the Human Rights Commission of the Latin American OAS (Organization of American States) went to Nicaragua to investigate, and they condemned the regime.

The FSLN's full-time guerrilla force increased greatly between 1977 and 1979. In late May of 1979 the Sandinistas made a final military push. FSLN soldiers took several towns and cities and began to fight in Managua on June 9. A few days later, an ABC news reporter was murdered by the National Guard, and this murder was videotaped and seen on television in the United States. At this point, President Carter told Somoza to step down, and the OAS voted overwhelmingly to demand that Somoza resign. No longer able to deal effectively with the FSLN offensive, and with his regime in international disrepute and U.S. support withdrawn, Somoza did indeed flee the country. The Sandinista radio station announced the establishment of a provisional government on June 16. The first territory to be liberated in Nicaragua was Jinotepe on July 5. Two days later the revolutionaries captured León, and soon they had gained control of twenty-three towns and cities throughout the country. On July 18 the National Guard fell apart; the next day, Managua was taken over by the Sandinista soldiers and a revolutionary *junta* proclaimed. The revolution had occurred.

The Iranian Revolution

Iran is the successor state to Persia, with the modern name officially adopted in 1934. Iran's first monarch was Reza Khan, who chose the name Pahlavi for his dynasty and crowned himself shah (king) in 1926. The shah was interested in the modernization of the country and saw the Shi'ite Islamic *ulama* (clergy) as an obstacle to his plans. He therefore enacted measures to reduce their influence and importance, such as restricting the number of seminaries, enacting state control of theological centers, and requiring state approval of religious expenditures. These measures, of course, were extremely unpopular with the *ulama,* as was the shah's order that all state institutions had to accept women. During World War II the shah feared that Soviet and British invaders would depose him and put an end to his dynasty, and thus he abdicated his position. His son, Muhammad Reza Pahlavi, succeeded him in 1941, at the age of twenty. The new shah was a Western-educated playboy who would engage in extremely authoritarian rule and preside over a highly divided society marked by frequent turmoil.

At the top of the socioeconomic structure was the Pahlavi family and about sixty other families. They and several hundred additional families formed an upper class, which constituted a tiny 0.01 percent of the population. Below them was a traditional middle class of merchants and craftsmen, who made up about 13 percent of the population. Roughly half of this class consisted of *bazaaris,* who were involved in the bazaar guild system of trade and crafts. There was also a modern middle class of professionals, bureaucrats, technicians, teachers, managers, and intellectuals, which constituted about 5 percent of the population. An industrial working class, some 30 percent of the population, consisted of persons who labored in manufacturing, construction, mining, and oil operations. The rest of the population—about half of it—consisted mostly of peasant farmers.

By the time the elder shah abdicated in favor of his son, Iran had become a highly polarized society. The upper class and the modern middle class were highly Westernized and were not strongly influenced by Islam or Islamic culture. Standing opposite them were the traditional middle and working classes and the peasants. They strongly identified with Islam and traditional Islamic culture. The Islamic *ulama* was a very powerful force in Iran, but it was divided against itself. Most of the *ulama* supported the shah and had little interest in any direct involvement in politics. A minority segment of the clergy, however, which was much more fundamentalist in religious outlook, felt that the *ulama* should play a direct and major role in government. It was not only opposed to any separation of church and state but also rejected the notion of separation as an alien Western notion that was highly threatening to Islam and Islamic society. The shah feared this group and predicted that it would eventually attack his regime. And he was right—the fundamentalist *ulama* would play a major role in the revolution that was to come.

In the early 1950s the Iranian parliament voted to install a group known as the National Front as part of the government and demanded that the shah appoint its leader, Muhammad Mossadeq, to the position of premier. The National Front consisted of secularized, well-educated, middle-class Iranians who were committed to softening many of the autocratic aspects of the shah's rule and shifting control of the military to elected leaders. It wanted, in other words, to make Iran a more democratic state. Mossadeq had control over the parliament and was unpopular with many pro-shah government officials and the shah himself. In August of 1953 the shah dismissed Mossadeq from his position, angering the National Front. Soldiers sympathetic to the National Front then arrested pro-shah officials in what appeared to be an attempt at taking over the government. The shah left the country for Rome, only to return shortly after his troops prevailed over the opposition soldiers. With the shah's return, many of his opponents were jailed, executed, or driven out of the country. The shah had the support of the American Central Intelligence Agency in stopping the takeover attempt, and the CIA also played a role in helping the shah create a secret police force, the infamous SAVAK, which was established in 1957. SAVAK engaged in surveillance of the population, watching out for any opposition to the shah's rule, and murdered and tortured many thousands of Iranians.

In 1961 the shah abolished parliament and ruled in the manner of an absolute monarch. At the same time he embarked on an explicit program of social and economic modernization. He hoped to gain support from various disadvantaged groups, especially women and peasants; he also responded to pressure from the United States (under the Kennedy administration) to carry out economic reforms. Unfortunately, some of his reforms actually worsened the economic situation of many peasants, necessitating their migration to the cities.

Hundreds of thousands of peasants migrated to the capital, Tehran, where they ended up living in squalid and primitive conditions.

Ayatollah Khomeini, who was later to become the major leader of the revolution, was a staunch opponent of the shah's modernization policies and reforms. He attacked the shah for disbanding parliament and ruling as a despot, as well as for ignoring Islamic leaders and the role of Islam in the government. Khomeini's public denouncements of the shah led to his arrest in June of 1963, causing demonstrations and riots against the shah to break out in a number of cities. The shah responded by jailing over two dozen high-ranking members of the *ulama* and declaring martial law. By the time Khomeini was released from jail a short while later, his popularity had soared. He had become Iran's single most popular religious leader. When he continued to criticize the shah, he was arrested again and later exiled, eventually taking up residence in one of the holy cities of neighboring Iraq.

In the 1970s, dissatisfaction with the regime started to become more open. Government stability was made possible only through severe repressive measures, especially the actions of the hated SAVAK. People knew their actions were being monitored and that others were being tortured and killed, and this inhibited most protest and outspokenness against the government. The fact that the shah was strongly supported by the United States was undoubtedly another factor that inhibited protest.

But opposition was strong nonetheless, and it came from many places. Secular nationalists from the modern middle class wanted free elections and a much more democratic regime. Iran also had a Communist Party that was vehemently opposed to the shah. The fundamentalist religious leaders were a major source of opposition, especially after the emergence of Khomeini. They constituted a social network that had substantial influence on most social groups, both rural and urban. The large mass of the population shared the same basic values as the *ulama*. The *bazaaris* also strongly supported the religious opponents of the regime. They tended to be highly religious and had suffered economically under the shah.

After the protests of 1963 were repressed by the regime, many guerrilla movements formed. The two most important of these were the *Fedayeen-e Khalq*, which was Marxist oriented, and the *Mujahideen-e Khalq*, an Islamic leftist organization. Both groups engaged in military attacks against the regime. The *Fedayeen* was composed mainly of university students and university-educated Iranians, whereas the *Mujahideen* were drawn heavily from the traditional middle class and were very religious. One of their major intellectual inspirations was Ali Shariati, a prominent sociologist and activist. The *Mujahideen* began their military actions in 1971, and many of their members were killed in battles with the shah's troops or executed. By 1978, just prior to the revolution, the *Fedayeen* and *Mujahideen* had each split into two guerrilla groups, and so there were four instead of just two.

In 1975 the shah consolidated the two existing political parties into one, the Resurgence Party, and established a one-party government. This was designed to strengthen his regime against the growing opposition. The Resurgence Party was created to stretch its tentacles into every nook and cranny of Iranian society, and especially to control the *ulama*. The pro-Western shah thought that many members of the *ulama* were religious reactionaries and attempted to restrict their influence. His government insisted on control over the publication of theological works, and also sought to limit, if not eliminate, the more conservative clerics' control over matters concerning the family. Such actions radicalized even the more moderate *ulama*, who now began to oppose the shah quite openly.

By the end of 1977, discontent was widespread and extreme, as the shah's actions had ended up alienating almost every segment of Iranian society. Discontent was based on many considerations: worsening economic conditions, soaring inflation, massive corruption, widespread repression and regime terror, and constant attacks on Islamic tradition and the *ulama*. The shah no longer had any real supporters. The regime had lost all legitimacy, and the conditions had been created for the formation of a large revolutionary coalition intent upon bringing it down.

Ayatollah Khomeini emerged as the leader of the revolutionary coalition. Khomeini told the *ulama* to establish committees in the mosques to organize faithful Muslims and lead them in the battle against the shah. As Khomeini grew stronger and more influential, the increasingly concerned shah tried to discredit and isolate him. But this turned out to be political suicide. It boomeranged and intensified the support of the masses for Khomeini. Disorder became massive. On September 7, 1978, half a million people marched to the parliament building in Tehran chanting "Death to the Shah." The shah responded by imposing martial law. On September 8 the shah's troops massacred several thousand demonstrators, which only made matters worse. The shah then put pressure on Iraq to throw Khomeini out of the country so that he would be unable to communicate with Iranian pilgrims in Iraq. In October, Khomeini took up residence in France, but he continued to call on the Iranian people to oppose the shah. He appealed on moral grounds to the shah's troops, urging them to abandon their support for the shah on Islamic grounds; he also asked oil workers to strike in order to cause massive disruption of the economy. In November the shah imposed military rule on the entire country. Many of his government officials fled Iran with huge amounts of money, further angering the population. When President Carter assumed office in 1977, he continued U.S. support for the shah only on the condition that he liberalize his regime. By the end of 1978, however, the shah's intensifying repressive tactics caused the Carter administration to withdraw support. It became obvious to the Iranian people that the United States would not intervene militarily to save the regime.

The shah made a last desperate effort to save himself by appointing a temporary successor, Shahpour Bakhtiyar, on December 29. The shah convinced Bakhtiyar to let him take a leave of absence and later be allowed to return and act as a constitutional monarch. This was yet another action taken by the shah that had a boomerang effect, serving only to alienate the masses even more. The shah was finished, and on January 16, 1979, he fled the country. His successor was forced to allow Khomeini to return to Iran, and when he reentered the country on February 1, he was welcomed by millions of Iranians lining the streets of Tehran. A provisional government was established, and within a short time most of the air force, navy, and army pledged this government their support. On February 10 and 11, revolutionaries gained control of Tehran's police stations, prisons, and television station, and Bakhtiyar was forced to flee Iran. The social revolution that had taken place would change Iran in a fundamental way.

The Overthrow of the Marcos Regime in the Philippines

The Philippines was a colony of Spain from early in the sixteenth century until the very end of the nineteenth century, a period of nearly four centuries. Sugar was one of several important crops throughout this period, but in the early nineteenth century it moved into the top position, and the Philippine economy became heavily dominated by sugar production. As John Larkin (1993:24) notes, "in 1836 sugar surpassed rice, abaca, and indigo as chief Philippine exports and became one of the mainstays of the economy, a condition that has persisted until recent times." Between 1836 and 1916 Philippine sugar exports increased from 15,097 to 337,490 metric tons, a whopping 2,135 percent increase. Three major factors—industrialization, commercialization, and the increasing demand for sugar in the world-economy—were responsible for stimulating this huge boom.

The Philippine socioeconomic structure at the end of the nineteenth century reflected this heavy involvement in sugarcane production. Large plantations dominated the economy, and plantation owners constituted a powerful landed elite. The landowners had close ties to American economic interests and were given special access to American markets. There was a huge economic and political gap between the landowners and the plantation workers, and this inequality has persisted into modern times. In the words of James Boyce (1993:194), "The stark inequalities of wealth and power on the sugar plantations ... are the legacy of this agrarian history. The planters, or *hacenderos,* are today mostly absentee landlords living in Manila or in Bacolod, the provincial capital of Negros Occidental. The lifestyle of the *hacendero* elite was more than comfortable, at least until the economic collapse of the 1980s; mansions, servants, luxury cars, and round-the-world trips were commonplace."

In 1898, during the Spanish-American War, U.S. troops and Philippine rebels combined forces to bring a conclusion to Spanish rule. Much to the surprise and dismay of Filipinos, their country became subject, at this point, to a new type of colonial rule by the United States. In 1902 the United States created a legislature in the Philippines while at the same time indicating that it eventually planned to give the Filipinos their full independence, which came in 1946. The Philippine political system was constructed much in the image of the U.S. system. It had a president, a senate, and a house of representatives. There were two political parties. The first, the Nacionalista Party, was established in 1907, and the other, the Liberal Party, formed in 1945 as a splinter group from the Nacionalistas. However, the differences between the political parties were not dramatic. There were a series of presidents; the most famous of these was Ferdinand Marcos, who was elected in 1965 and, despite widespread dissatisfaction, reelected in 1969. Although a democracy, the Philippine government was democratic in name only, for the political process was dominated by the economic elite and was corrupt. Marcos's reelection was considered fraudulent by many. In fact, in 1972 political turmoil led Marcos to declare martial law, which lasted until 1981. During this time Marcos persecuted and often arrested his political opponents. Most of the Filipino population experienced no participation in the political process at all.

Even though the United States granted the Philippines its formal independence right after World War II, American involvement continued to be very strong. Considerable economic and military assistance was provided to the Philippines, and the United States continued to maintain several hundred military bases. Close ties existed between the Philippine government and a series of American presidents, especially Ronald Reagan, who was deemed "an old friend from way back." U.S. aid and loans for economic development increased dramatically from the mid-1960s on.

Throughout most of Marcos's rule his country experienced constant dissatisfaction and even turmoil. As suggested above, even before he was elected to a second term there was considerable opposition from various segments of Filipino society. Not only was he forced to declare martial law in 1972, but he went so far as to confiscate the holdings of some members of the economic elite and disband the private armies that these individuals had established. Throughout the 1970s his corrupt and highly authoritarian rule continued to alienate large segments of the population, although not always for the same reason. Peasants and workers wanted economic reforms that would improve their living conditions, whereas the economic elites were interested only in a change of administration. As Richard Kessler (1991:207) comments,

> although the poor and well-to-do formed an alliance against Marcos, their principal grievances and agendas were radically dissimilar. The poor wanted land reform, improved prices for their produce, basic improvements in living conditions, and personal security from an undisciplined military and a corrupt judicial system. The elites were more interested in wresting political control from Marcos so they could regain their economic power. They opposed anything but the most superficial land reform schemes and preferred low agricultural prices in order to maintain lower living costs. These differences did not weaken

the alliance, but they did suggest that once Marcos was exiled, political cooperation between the poor and the rich would cease.

In 1983 the popular Senator Benigno Aquino was murdered, and many thought it likely that Marcos had had him killed because he was a dangerous political opponent. This belief intensified antagonism and popular mobilization against Marcos. The person who emerged as the opposition's main leader was Corazon Aquino, the widow of Benigno Aquino. As Marcos's hold on power continued to weaken, he announced that a new election would be held on February 7, 1986, in which he and Corazon Aquino would be the two major candidates. However, although Marcos was the official winner of the election, it was certain that he tried to rig it, so it was not clear who the real winner was. When both sides claimed victory, U.S. President Reagan, a strong supporter of Marcos, advised Aquino to concede even though some members of the U.S. government thought she should be declared the winner. Because the Filipino reaction to Reagan's position was extremely negative, the White House changed its position. This meant that Marcos's hold on power was now extremely fragile. The last straw came on February 22, when a key segment of the military elite, which had had long-standing grievances against Marcos because of the way in which he appointed officers, rebelled against him. They urged the rest of the military to join them, and a major leader of the Catholic Church urged the people to flood into the streets. They did. Marcos was in very poor health, was isolated, and was confused and indecisive about whether to resort to violence. He finally ordered his remaining troops to attack, but it was too late because little support for him remained anywhere. He was forced to flee the country and to turn over the government to Corazon Aquino. Along with his family and a number of aides, he was taken by U.S. helicopters to Hawaii, where he remained in exile until he died from kidney failure a short time later.

Unlike the revolutions in Cuba, Nicaragua, and Iran, however, the revolution in the Philippines was a political rather than a social revolution. A corrupt and highly undemocratic regime was forced out of power, and a new regime, that of Corazon Aquino, acceded to office, but no fundamental social or economic transformations accompanied the political changes. In the words of Richard Kessler (1991:212), the regime change proved "to be less a revolution than a restoration of the ancien regime."

A Note on Sources

In addition to the following, see the note on sources at the end of Chapter 2. For the present chapter, my sketch of the Cuban revolution has drawn on DeFronzo (1996) and Pérez-Stable (1999); of the Nicaraguan revolution, on Chavarría (1986), DeFronzo (1996), Grynspan (1991), and Walker (1986); of the Iranian revolution, on Abrahamian (1989), DeFronzo (1996), Keddie (1981), Milani (1988), Moshiri (1991), and Parsa (2000); and of the Philippine political revolution, on Boyce (1993), de Dios and Hutchcroft (2003), Kessler (1991), Larkin (1993), and Parsa (2000). Again, readers wishing many more details should consult some of these sources. DeFronzo is particularly good and is written with unusual clarity.

Chapter Four

The Causes of Revolutions: I

For the most part, it is only in recent decades that scholars have undertaken to formulate general theories of revolution and other forms of major sociopolitical conflict. Earlier, historians and social scientists paid attention to revolutions, but they were more interested in detailed descriptions of their course than in why they occurred. Jack Goldstone (1982) has referred to this approach as the "natural history of revolutions." This chapter will explore the natural history approach and look at the three major theoretical approaches to revolutions that have been developed: social-psychological theories, Marxian theories, and so-called state-centered theories. The following chapter will continue the analysis of state-centered theories and explore several other related theoretical issues.

The Natural History of Revolutions

Goldstone (1982:189–192) has codified the general conclusions of the natural history approach to revolutions as follows:

1. Prior to a great revolution, the bulk of the intellectuals cease to support the regime, instead condemning it and demanding major reforms.
2. Just prior to the fall of the old regime, the state attempts to meet its sharpest criticism by undertaking major reforms.

3. The collapse of a regime begins with a severe political crisis created by the government's inability to deal with some economic, military, or political problem, rather than by the action of a revolutionary opposition.
4. Even where the revolutionary opposition to the old regime was once united, the collapse of the regime eventually reveals the conflicts within the revolutionary opposition.
5. Moderate reformers are normally the first oppositional group to seize the reins of state.
6. While the moderates seek to reconstruct rule on the basis of moderate reform, alternative and more radical centers of mass mobilization spring up.
7. The great changes in the organization and ruling ideology of a society that follow successful revolutions occur not when the old regime first falls but, rather, when the radical, alternative, mass-mobilizing organizations succeed in supplanting the moderates.
8. The disorder created by the revolution and the implementation of the radicals' control generally results in the forced imposition of order by coercive rule.
9. The struggles between radicals and moderates, and between supporters of the revolution and external enemies, frequently allow military leaders to move from obscurity to commanding leadership.
10. The radical phase of the revolution eventually gives way to a phase of pragmatism and moderate pursuit of progress within the new status quo.

As Goldstone points out, most of these ideas may constitute a useful guide to understanding the process of revolutionary change, and certain theoretical notions about the causes of revolutions might, with sufficient work, be extracted from them. Nonetheless, the ideas themselves stop well short of an actual explanation of revolutions. Let us look, then, at some major explanatory theories of revolution.

Social-Psychological Theories

Until recently some of the most popular theories of revolution were basically social psychological in nature. These theories locate the sources of revolutionary change in the feelings and attitudes of subordinated and oppressed social groups. More than four decades ago James Davies (1962) formulated a theory often called the *theory of rising expectations*. Davies argued that people do not revolt when they are at their lowest stage of misery and oppression, but only when their lives have improved sufficiently so as to give them hope that further change is around the corner. When people's expectations have risen, but those expectations are newly frustrated—that is the point at which revolution is most likely. For example, if downtrodden people have been experiencing a period of growing economic prosperity, but then this growing prosperity comes to an end and is possibly even reversed, severe frustrations set in that cause people to become hostile and aggressive. Shortly after Davies proposed his rising-expectations theory, Ted Robert Gurr (1970) wrote a famous book that developed a similar argument. In response to popular notions that misery and oppression were the root causes of revolution and rebellion, Gurr proposed that it was not the absolute level of misery that counted. Instead, it was the level of dissatisfaction that people felt *relative to what they expected out of life* that really mattered. Gurr thus rooted revolution in what sociologists have long called *relative deprivation*.

Despite their popularity, these theories leave a lot to be desired. As Rod Aya (1979) has pointed out, Davies does not give us any way of determining whether or when the gap between people's expectations and their gratifications has reached an intolerable point, or one at which it would produce a revolutionary state of mind. Moreover, Davies fails to explain how such a state of mind gets translated into actions capable of overthrowing an incumbent regime, seemingly assuming that it just occurs automatically. As for Gurr, Aya (1979:58) comments that, as strange as it may seem, he "declines to analyze the role of governments in fomenting episodes of political violence, and thereby omits from consideration the very 'collectivity' historically responsible for initiating most incidents recorded as 'civil strife,' as well as for committing the vast bulk of murder and mayhem. Nor, on principle, does Gurr's scheme ... come to grips with violent clashes that set contenders for power in the state against one another." What is missing in these theories, in other words, is a systematic analysis of the larger social framework—especially the economic and political framework—within which revolutions and revolts occur. Misery and dissatisfaction, whether absolute or relative, are extremely common characteristics of human societies—in fact, far more common than revolutions and other forms of collective sociopolitical violence. They therefore fail to take us very far in understanding the actual occurrence of such conflict (Aya, 1979; Goldstone, 1982).

It might be thought that such theories are not necessarily wrong in any fundamental sense, just highly incomplete. But they may even be wrong. In one of the few attempts to test this type of argument, David Snyder and Charles Tilly (1972) looked at collective violence in France between 1830 and 1960. They constructed an index of hardship and well-being that included an index of food prices, an index of the prices of manufactured goods, and an index of the level of industrial production. Rising prices and declining levels of production were taken as indicators of hardship. They found no relationship at all between the level of hardship or well-being and the incidence of collective violence.

Marxian Theories

In turning to consider theories that focus not on individual psychological states but, rather, on larger socioeconomic and sociopolitical conditions, we find that easily the most famous of these is the Marxian approach to revolutions. Marx himself worked out a famous conception of revolution that emphasized the socioeconomic order and the struggle between classes. As everyone knows, Marx predicted and hoped for the ultimate collapse of capitalism and its replacement by socialism, and he thought that this great transformation would most likely take place by revolutionary means. It all had to do with the logic of capitalism and the capitalist class struggle. In capitalist society there were numerous social classes, but the two that occupied center stage were, of course, the bourgeoisie or capitalist class and the proletariat or working class, the former of which exploited the latter and became rich at its expense. As capitalism advanced, the working class expanded in size not only by the sheer growth of numbers but also because other social classes gradually descended into it. But the capitalist class, through the gradual concentration and centralization of capital, actually grew smaller, and ultimately a huge working class would confront a tiny bourgeoisie. And not only this, but there also occurred an economic polarization between the two classes, which intensified the conflict between them. Moreover, with the advance of capitalism the working class came to be better organized and potentially more politically powerful. At some point the working class would rise up, overthrow the capitalist class by violence, and establish a worker's state in which private property would be abolished. Marx thought that the first revolution against capitalism would most likely occur in England, because this country was, in Marx's day, the world's most industrially advanced society. However, this revolution also had a chance of occurring in other advanced capitalist societies, such as Germany, the Netherlands, or the United States.

Unfortunately for Marxists, this theory has been largely falsified by the history of the last century. No advanced capitalist society has ever even remotely experienced a socialist revolution of any sort; on the contrary, such revolutions have occurred in overwhelmingly agrarian societies, first in Russia in 1917, and then later in China and other parts of the Third World. The peasantry, far more than the working class, has been the social class most central to revolutionary change (Skocpol and Trimberger, 1978).

Nevertheless, a number of recent theories have been set forth that, while abandoning Marx's own specific theory of revolution, at the same time draw on the general Marxian notion that economic exploitation and class struggle are the keys to revolution. In his *Peasant Wars of the Twentieth Century* (1969), the anthropologist Eric Wolf attempted to analyze revolutionary change in six agrarian societies: Mexico, Russia, China, Vietnam, Algeria, and Cuba. He saw revolutions in these societies as rooted largely in the disruption of peasant life by the gradual spread of capitalist market relations. We can let Wolf (1969:280–281) speak for himself:

> Everywhere the dance of commodities brought on an ecological crisis. … Thus in Russia land reform and commercialization together threatened the peasant's continued access to pasture, forest, and plowland. In Mexico, Algeria, and Viet Nam commercialization menaced peasant access to communal land; in Mexico and Cuba it barred the peasant from claiming unclaimed public land. In Algeria and China, it liquidated the institution of public granaries. In Algeria, it ruptured the balance between pastoral and settled populations. In Mexico, Viet Nam, Algeria, and Cuba, finally, outright seizures of land by foreign colonists and enterprises drove the peasants back upon a land area no longer sufficient for their needs.

Thus, as peasants experienced severe disturbances of their economic equilibrium, they frequently turned to revolt and revolution as a means of establishing a new equilibrium.

Another recent Marxian-inspired theory of revolution, this one focusing exclusively on the Third World, has been developed by Jeffery Paige in his book *Agrarian Revolution* (1975). Paige focuses overwhelmingly on how forms of economic organization and class structure promote or prevent peasant revolution in Third World countries where the majority of people earn their living primarily through agricultural work of one type or another. Paige delineates four types of socioeconomic situations in Third World countries. The first is the *commercial hacienda*. Here landlords and peasants both earn their living through the land. In this situation, peasants tend to be highly aversive to risk and thus to be relatively conservative in their political behavior. The commercial hacienda is therefore not conducive to revolutionary movements. It tends to produce quiescence, or, at most, *agrarian revolts,* which Paige identifies as movements aimed only at the redistribution of land and not at any larger political ends.

Another socioeconomic situation in Third World societies is the *small holding*. This is similar to the commercial hacienda in that the peasantry is dependent on land for its living. However, what is different is that the landlord or noncultivating class lives not merely from products produced on the land but through the sale of products on the market. In short, the small holding system is a type of capitalist farm. According to Paige, since members of the peasant or cultivating class are dependent on land for their living, they tend to be politically conservative, but such political agitation as they might engage in tends to be in the form of *commodity reform movements,* which are concerned with control of the market for agricultural commodities. There is no demand for the redistribution of land, let alone any attempt to seize the state, but merely a limited type of economic protest.

A third type of socioeconomic situation is the *plantation*. Here we find the agrarian upper class receiving its income in the form of capital rather than land, and the agrarian lower class receiving its income in the form of wages for work performed on the land. When the lower class receives its income in the form of wages, it is likely to be less politically conservative, and its members are likely to establish greater solidarity with one another. Nonetheless, lower-class political behavior does not tend to take a revolutionary form. Rather, the outcome is most likely the *reform labor movement,* a movement devoted to achieving higher wages and better working conditions. As Paige notes, the most common tactic of this type of movement is the strike. This means that an agrarian lower class dependent on wages behaves much like an industrial working class, which is also dependent on wages.

Finally, there is the socioeconomic situation in which the agrarian upper class receives its income from the land and the agrarian lower class receives its income in the form of wages. This is the socioeconomic form, Paige argues, that is most conducive to agrarian revolution, by which is meant an attempt to seize state power and massively redistribute land, normally through guerrilla warfare. Paige identifies two subtypes of this socioeconomic situation, sharecropping systems and migratory labor systems. The *sharecropping system* is one in which the "traditional agrarian upper class responds to new urban and export markets by intensifying pressures on the peasantry for higher rates of production or forcing the peasants to adopt new crops valuable in the export markets. The landlord then claims the export crop and pays his tenant with a share of what he himself has produced" (Paige, 1975:59). This system is usually one in which the sharecroppers have no legal rights and can be dismissed from work at any time. They have normally been politically disenfranchised, and the landlord class retains enormous control over land. Since the only real way in which they can reduce their economic deprivation is by limiting the extractions of landlords, there are strong incentives for mass political action.

Paige argues that the sharecropping system has normally been conducive to socialist or communist revolutionary movements, such as prevailed in Vietnam in the 1950s and 1960s. In the other subtype, the *migratory labor system*, revolutionary movements are more likely to be nationalist rather than socialist in nature. In this type of system, agrarian workers are paid wages for the work they perform, but this work is performed only part of the time; the rest of the time, workers depend on subsistence cultivation for their livelihood. Because migratory workers retain substantial ties to the land, they are less likely to be oriented to radical political action than sharecroppers. How, then, do we explain revolutionary movements in this type of system? The key, Paige says, is the agrarian elite. Their political interests may become similar to those of workers when "the landed estates are developed by settlers who threaten the continued political survival of the traditional agrarian leadership by the expansion of their estates" (Paige, 1975:69). Under such a circumstance, the agrarian elite is ripe for a revolutionary nationalist movement. Paige sees Algeria,

Kenya, and Angola as societies in which this type of movement has been prominent.

Paige has carried out a detailed statistical test of his argument by drawing on data on 135 agricultural export sectors in 70 Third World countries. By and large, these analyses support his argument. There are, indeed, correlations between the type of socioeconomic situation and the type of political behavior. However, none of these correlations is terribly strong, and some are quite modest, which means that there is much more going on than Paige's overall argument allows for. Paige's argument is so strongly focused on socioeconomic patterns that he allows no room for the role of governmental structures, which theorists like Theda Skocpol (1979, 1994) would insist are crucial. Moreover, Paige's arguments concern only revolutionary *movements* or *situations;* his statistical analyses include failed as well as successful movements. Basically, Paige is just trying to answer the question, "What makes peasants revolutionary?" This is an important question, but Skocpol and other theorists would insist that we cannot stop there; we must go on to consider the conditions under which some revolutionary movements fail whereas others succeed.

The biggest problem with Marxian-inspired theories is that they systematically omit one major type of social factor—the political realm—in their overwhelming focus on the economy and class relations. As Skocpol (1979) has pointed out, a consideration of socioeconomic and class relations is crucial to an adequate theory of revolution, but by itself it is insufficient. Serious attention must also be given to the organization of political life, especially to such things as the political resources peasants may be able to draw upon to press their cause, as well as the degree to which states may or may not be able to quell peasant revolutionary activity. As Skocpol (1994:115–116) puts it:

> In accounting for the causes of revolutions the theoretical emphasis [in Marxist theories] is always placed upon economic developments and class contradictions, while the capacities of state rulers, given the state organizations at hand, to cope with international pressures and, internally, with upper-class political dissidence and lower-class rebellions, are matters often treated descriptively, but never examined theoretically with an eye to identifying the social-structural conditions that might systematically affect such political capacities. Marxist scholars have failed to notice that causal variables referring to the strength and structure of states and the relations of state organizations to class structures may discriminate

between cases of successful revolution and cases of failure or nonoccurrence far better than do variables referring to class structures and patterns of economic development alone.

Charles Tilly's Resource Mobilization Theory

Since the late 1970s there has thus been not only increasing recognition of the importance of a range of political factors in revolutionary change but the explicit formulation of theories that make such factors central. Charles Tilly (1978) was among the first to formulate an explicitly political theory, one that has come to be called *resource mobilization theory.* Tilly sees his theory as relevant not only to revolutions but to all major forms of collective action or violence, and this gives the theory a remarkable generalizability and flexibility. According to this theory, collective action is the result of a combination of four factors. First, there is the extent to which the members of a group or population share common *interests.* Are they, for example, in the same economic circumstances, and do they have the same kinds of needs and concerns as a result of these shared circumstances? The second factor is *organization.* Do the members of a population share a sense of common identity, and have they built up a network of ties with one another that gives them some degree of unification? Third, there is *mobilization,* which involves the extent to which the members of a population control important resources that give them the capability of pursuing joint aims. Finally, Tilly's theory admits of *opportunity,* which involves the relationship between a population's interests and its environment. Opportunity encompasses three subcategories: *Power* involves the extent to which the outcomes of a population's interaction with other populations is favorable to its interests (when this involves interactions with governments, then *political* power is involved); *repression/facilitation* concerns the costs of collective action to a contending population (when the contending population's costs of collective action are high, then we usually get *repression,* and when these costs are low we usually end up with *facilitation*); and *opportunity/threat* has to do with the possibilities open to a contending population to press its claims.

Tilly's theory of collective action is presented diagrammatically in Figure 4.1. Basically, what this model says is that collective action is likely when populations share interests, are well organized, control important resources, have sufficient power, are not repressed by governments or other groups, and have the opportunity to act. This model is by design very general, so we need to see how it can be translated into a more specific conception of revolutionary change. Tilly argues that revolutionary situations (efforts at revolutionary change that may or may not be successful) result from three proximate conditions:

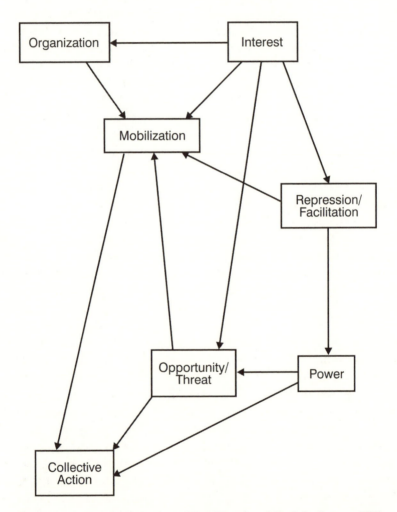

Figure 4.1 Tilly's Resource Mobilization Model. *Source:* **Tilly (1978), p. 56, Figure 3–2.**

1. the appearance of contending populations making exclusive alternative claims to control the polity,
2. the development of significant commitments to those claims, and
3. the inability of the government to repress contending populations.

The second and third of these deserve further discussion. Tilly points out that there are two types of governmental actions that tend to enhance the commitment of a population to revolutionary claims. The first involves the sudden failure on the part of the government to meet obligations that a population regards as well established and essential to its own well-being. Such failures would especially involve the provision of employment, welfare services, protection, or access to justice. The second type of action occurs when a government rapidly or unexpectedly increases its extraction of resources from the population, such as by raising taxes, commandeering land or crops, or conscripting labor for public works projects. Tilly's argument here converges considerably with the theories of Davies and Gurr, but with an important difference. Tilly (1978:207) explains:

> Assuming that sharp contractions following long expansions *do* produce revolutionary situations with exceptional frequency, however, the line of argument pursued here leads to an interesting alternative explanation of the J-curve phenomenon [i.e., rising expectations followed by a contraction]. It is that during a long run of expanding resources, the government tends to take on commitments to redistribute resources to new contenders and the polity tends to admit challengers more easily because the relative cost to existing members is lower when resources are expanding. In the event of quick contraction, the government has greater commitments, new matters of right, to members of the polity, and has acquitted partial commitments to new contenders, perhaps not members of the polity, but very likely forming coalitions with members. The government faces a choice between (1) greatly increasing the coercion applied to the more vulnerable segments of the population in order to bring up the yield of resources for reallocation or (2) breaking commitments where that will incite the least dangerous opposition. Either step is likely to lead to a defensive mobilization, and thence to a threat of revolution. Such a situation does, to be sure, promote the disappointment of rising expectations. But the principal link between the J-curve and the revolutionary situation, in this hypothesis,

lies in the changing relations between contenders and government likely to occur in a period of expanding resources.

In other words, what Tilly has done is add a political dimension that is notably lacking in previous theories of revolution.

But also critical to the formation of revolutionary situations is an inability or an unwillingness of a government to engage in the repression of the actions of contending groups. A government may simply lack the necessary coercive power to overcome contenders, and for a number of reasons: The government may have suffered a depletion of its military resources as the result of, say, war; the contending group may over time have acquired powerful military resources by, say, stockpiling private arms; or the contending group may implant itself in a rough and unknown terrain or adopt military tactics that are unfamiliar and thus difficult to combat. In addition, governments may have sufficient coercive means to put down contenders but may be unwilling for one reason or another to use them. For example, the use of coercive resources against contenders may be extremely unpopular among other segments of the population and may therefore run the risk of alienating these other segments.

So far we have been discussing only revolutionary situations. What about actual revolutionary *outcomes*—that is, successful revolutions? Tilly once again sees three crucial conditions:

1. the presence of a revolutionary situation,
2. the formation of revolutionary coalitions between contenders and members of the polity,
3. control of substantial force by the revolutionary coalition.

It can thus be seen that the conditions required for a successful revolution are many and varied. This should come as no surprise, given the relative rarity of such success. Not only must there be present all of the conditions necessary to the development of a revolutionary situation, but revolutionaries must enlist the aid of other groups and they must control enough military force to win. Accomplishing all of these ends is very difficult.

Tilly (1978:216–217) tries to pull everything together by offering a newer version of a "natural history" of revolutions. His looks like the following:

1. gradual mobilization of contenders making exclusive claims to control the government that are unacceptable to members of the polity;
2. a rapid increase in the number of people accepting these claims and/or a rapid expansion of the coalition that includes the unacceptable or exclusive contenders;
3. unsuccessful efforts by the government to repress the contenders and/or the acceptance of its claims;
4. establishment by the contenders of effective control over some portion of the government;
5. struggles of the contenders to maintain or expand their control;
6. reconstruction of a single government through the victory of the contenders, through their defeat, or through the establishment of some sort of compromise between the contenders and the members of the old government, at which point there occurs a fragmentation of the revolutionary coalition; and
7. reimposition of routine governmental control.

Although the foregoing is another example of a natural history of revolutions, it should be noted that, in contrast to past such histories, this one is much more driven by theory and is thus of considerably more use than the earlier histories.

At the time it was developed, Tilly's work constituted an extremely important advance in social scientists' thinking about the causes of revolutions. Of greatest value was his explicit recognition that revolutions are permeated by the politics of struggle and, therefore, involve much more than just people's thoughts and feelings and their socioeconomic locations. Nonetheless, he has been criticized for not going far enough with his recognition of the importance of the political dimension. In Skocpol's (1979:110) view, despite Tilly's emphasis on the importance of the state, he does not give it the proper role it deserves: "Tilly's stress upon multiple sovereignty as the defining characteristic of revolution trivializes—inadvertently, no doubt—the role of the state. The state is not seen as determining by its own strength or weakness whether or not a revolutionary situation can emerge at all."

Skocpol and others have nonetheless built on the political perspective sketched out by Tilly, and have done so primarily by giving the kind of attention to the state that Tilly did not.

State-Centered Theories

Theda Skocpol's Theory of the Great Revolutions

In her *States and Social Revolutions* (1979), Skocpol attempts to explain the three Great Revolutions we discussed in Chapter 2. Her explanation is one of the most famous, and clearly one of the most impressive, theories of revolution ever developed. Remember that Skocpol distinguishes between *social* revolutions, in which there is not only a change in the structure of government but also a structural transformation in society, and *political* revolutions, or transformations in which there is only a change in government. Her theory is developed by way of a detailed historical and comparative analysis of these three social revolutions.

A major guideline stressed by Skocpol is the need to focus heavily on the international context in which societies and governments are situated. For the past several hundred years there has existed a capitalist world-economy (Wallerstein, 1974a, 1974b, 1980, 1989) and an international system of states, and both of these, Skocpol insists, have contributed greatly to revolutionary situations and outcomes. States and societies cannot be viewed in isolation. As we have seen, the world-capitalist system has an enormous impact on the economic functioning of individual societies, and one of the most important characteristics of states is that they are involved in both cooperative and conflictual relations with other states. Skocpol stresses in particular the latter, for, as she says, "developments within the international states system as such—especially defeats in wars or threats of invasion and struggles over colonial controls—have directly contributed to virtually all outbreaks of revolutionary crises" (1979:23). Most theories of revolution have ignored this international context, Skocpol asserts, and thus have failed to take us very far.

Another major guiding assumption in the study of revolutions, according to Skocpol, involves the relationship between the state and the larger society and economy. According to Skocpol, most theories of revolution have viewed politics as largely at the mercy of economics. A classical tenet of traditional Marxism is that the state is a representative of the dominant economic class, designed to carry out its will. Traditional Marxists have thus viewed outcomes in the political realm as basically underlain and guided by economic—especially social class—considerations. Revolutions have been seen as the political effects of socioeconomic conditions. Even non-Marxists, Skocpol claims, have often seen politics as largely the expression of economics. But this is a gross oversimplification, she argues, for states maintain a remarkable autonomy with regard to society and economy. What is the state? Skocpol (1979:29) tells us that it is "a set of administrative, policing, and military organizations headed, and more or less well coordinated by, an executive authority. Any state first and fundamentally extracts resources from society and deploys these to create and support coercive and administrative organizations." Given this character of the state, its "involvement in an international network of states is a basis for potential autonomy of action over and against groups and economic arrangements within its jurisdiction—even including the dominant class and existing relations of production. For international military pressures and opportunities can prompt state rulers to attempt policies that conflict with, and even in extreme instances contradict, the fundamental interests of a dominant class" (1979:31). What all of this means is that any good theory of revolution must take the state seriously as an actor at least on a par with the actions of other groups, especially socioeconomic ones. Since most theories have failed to do this, they have come up short.

Skocpol's theory is essentially this: The Great Revolutions resulted from a coming together of two overpowering circumstances, a massive crisis within the state machineries of France, Russia, and China, and widespread rebellion and revolt on the part of the lower classes, especially the peasantry. State crises resulted both from severe international political and military pressures and economic difficulties that produced widespread dissatisfaction for various social groups. In all three societies, governments were unable to implement needed reforms or to promote sufficiently rapid economic development to allow them to deal with the military threats they encountered. Skocpol pays particular attention to the impact of war on the functioning of states. World War I, she holds, was critical to the Bolshevik Revolution, and the earlier attempted revolution in Russia in 1905 was defeated because Russia was able to quickly conclude its war with Japan. The involvement of Russia in World War I, when combined with widespread economic dissatisfactions, produced a situation of literal economic and political chaos. As Skocpol (1979:97) puts it:

> As the magnitude of Russian defeats (beginning from the spring of 1915) became apparent, the dominant strata steadily lost confidence

in the tsar and autocracy. And as the strains imposed by the endless war persisted, the lower classes, suffering terribly, became war-weary and rebellious. Finally these social discontents—given new potency due to the breakdown under wartime conditions of the usual barriers between state organizations and social groups—crystallized in the cities of Russia to give political expression to the near-universal repudiation of the autocratic regime.

In order to solidify her argument, Skocpol contrasts the cases of France, Russia, and China with those of Japan and Prussia. The Meiji Restoration of 1868 in Japan was only a political revolution, she claims, and one of the most important reasons it did not develop further is because Japan at this time was not fully integrated into the European system of states and, thus, did not suffer from the blows of war. Regarding Prussia, Skocpol finds something similar in the Reform Movement of 1807–1814. The international pressures on Prussia at this time were not as severe as those on Russia during World War I and, besides, Prussia had a state machine that was extraordinarily disciplined and efficient. It was thus able to survive attempts at massive change.

But we have told only part of the story, for political and military crises by themselves could not have led to full-scale social revolution. In France, Russia, and China the other key ingredient was present, and this was peasant revolt. As Skocpol says, neither political crises nor peasant revolt alone could have brought about social revolution; it was the combination of the two that was necessary. Although in the Great Revolutions various socioeconomic groups were part of the total insurrectionary picture, Skocpol sees peasant revolt as absolute critical. The peasantry was the largest social class, and other classes had insufficient potential to bring about a revolutionary outcome. Skocpol (1979:112) argues her case this way:

> Massive as they were, societal political crises alone were not enough to create social-revolutionary situations in France, Russia, and China. Administrative and military breakdowns of the autocracies inaugurated social-revolutionary transformations—rather than, say, interregnums of intraelite squabbling leading to the break-up of the existing polity or the reconstitution of a similar regime on a more or less liberal basis. This result was due to the fact that widespread peasant revolts coincided with, indeed took advantage of, the hiatus of governmental supervision and sanctions. ... Their revolts destroyed the old agrarian class relations and undermined the political and military supports for

liberalism or counterrevolution. They opened the way for marginal political elites, perhaps supported by urban popular movements, to consolidate the Revolutions on the basis of centralized and mass-incorporating state organizations.

Skocpol makes reference to the English Revolution of the mid-seventeenth century and the German Revolution of 1848–1850 to provide additional evidence for the importance of peasant revolt to full-scale social revolution. The former, she says, was a successful political revolution, while the latter was a failed social revolution. The reason why these were not among the Great Revolutions was the relative absence of peasant revolt in each, a situation that Skocpol attributes largely to the political power of landlords.

Skocpol's theory is without doubt a tremendous theoretical advance. Indeed, at the time her book was published, the eminent sociologist Randall Collins called it the best book on revolutions ever written. Her work has inspired many other works on revolution, some of which we examine below. But what criticisms have been made of it? One major critic of her work is Jack Goldstone, a former student. Goldstone believes that Skocpol's work has helped to establish three important points:

1. Revolutions arise from a conjunction of events such as state crises, popular uprisings, and elite actions, and each of these events may have different causes.
2. States are major actors in revolutionary struggles, and their actions are crucial in precipitating revolutionary crises.
3. Revolutions occur in the context of international pressures that impinge on individual states.

While accepting these general points, Goldstone concludes that the specifics of Skocpol's theory leave a great deal to be desired. War, he argues, should not be used as a major explanatory variable. In his words:

> The incidence of war itself provides little guidance to the long-term recurrence of revolution. Much has been made of the impact of particular wars, such as the Thirty Years' War, which preceded the seventeenth-century state breakdowns in England, France, and Spain, and World War I, which led to the Russian Revolution of 1917. Yet little attention has been paid to the even larger wars that did *not* produce

state breakdown. From 1688 to 1714, Louis XIV brought Europe into almost continual armed conflict, leading some historians to label this period the "Second Thirty Years' War." France suffered extensive defeats in these wars, which were fought with larger armies and cost far more than the first Thirty Years' War. Yet despite defeat and bankruptcy, neither France nor any other of the combatants experienced revolutions. ... As these cases make clear, the incidence of war is neither a necessary nor a sufficient answer to the question of the causes of state breakdown. (1991:19–20)

Goldstone further argues that Skocpol neglects urban disorders, which he thinks were crucial to state breakdowns. In addition, he believes she unduly overlooks cultural differences between nations as important causes. He concludes that these are "crucial deficiencies" that have greatly limited the explanatory power and impact of Skocpol's work.

One of the most important alternative theories of revolution has been produced by Goldstone himself. Although it is an alternative theory, it follows in the state-centered tradition of theorizing established by Tilly and Skocpol.

Jack Goldstone and State Breakdowns

Goldstone's *Revolution and Rebellion in the Early Modern World* (1991) is a work of enormous historical and comparative scope that rivals Skocpol's work in its impressiveness. Whereas Skocpol is concerned only with social revolutions, Goldstone focuses more broadly on state breakdowns.

Goldstone argues that state breakdowns have been cyclical phenomena that have occurred over the past several hundred years in two major waves, one peaking in the mid-seventeenth century and the other peaking in the mid-nineteenth century. These waves occurred in both Europe and Asia, and between them there was approximately a century of relative political stability. Most of Goldstone's book is devoted to an analysis of four cases of state breakdown: the English Revolution of the mid-seventeenth century, the French Revolution of the last decade of the eighteenth century, the Anatolian rebellions in the Ottoman Empire (which peaked in the mid-seventeenth century), and the fall of the Ming Dynasty in China in approximately 1644. He also gives some attention to the Fronde and the revolts in the Spanish Hapsburg Empire in the mid-seventeenth century, the revolutions of 1830 in France and of 1848 in France and Germany, the Meiji Restoration in Japan, and the Taiping rebellion in Qing China.

Goldstone's model of state breakdown is what he calls a *demographic/ structural* model. It specifically considers how population growth led to widespread social and economic dissatisfaction and state crises. Goldstone notes that the large agrarian states of early modern Europe and Asia had considerable difficulty dealing with the effects of population growth. When population grew, a whole series of negative consequences ensued. For one thing, prices increased because of increased demand. This had a negative impact on the tax system, because tax systems in these centuries were based on fixed rates of taxation. As a result, with price inflation tax revenues lagged behind prices, and this gave states no option but to increase taxes. Since it was difficult to increase taxes to the extent of being able to maintain a stable fiscal situation, state fiscal crisis normally ensued, and it was intensified if military demands on the state purse increased, as they frequently did. In addition, the growth of population had a negative impact on social and economic elites; because it increased the number of competitors for elite positions, an increasing number of aspirants for these positions saw their aims frustrated. Finally, the growth of population drove down wages. With higher prices and lower wages, both rural and urban misery increased, precipitating food riots and wage protests. The result of this concatenation of unfortunate circumstances was a widespread state crisis and, ultimately, a state breakdown.

Goldstone argues that the cyclical nature of state breakdowns in early modern Europe and Asia corresponded closely to the swings of population, and that these swings were largely determined by changes in mortality. Population grew when mortality fell, and stabilized or declined when mortality increased. What, then, caused the changes in mortality? The answer, according to Goldstone, has to do with changes in the incidence of virulent disease. Goldstone describes the fluctuation of population in early modern Europe and its relationship to state crises in the following terms:

> The growth of population that occurred throughout the temperate regions of Eurasia from about 1500 is well known.... [F]rom 1500 onward the recurrent visitations of plague, which reappeared in Europe roughly every thirty years since the fourteenth century, ceased.... [I]t is generally well established that a combination of favorable climate

and receding disease led to a doubling of the population in most regions between 1500 and the early 1600s.

These conditions did not last. The climate turned distinctly cooler and more variable after 1600; plague returned, accompanied by smallpox, typhoid, and other infectious diseases. By 1650, outside of a few exceptional pockets of growth, population increase had halted worldwide. There followed a century of high mortality, in which population in most regions stagnated or declined. Yet for those who lived, conditions, paradoxically, improved. With population nearly constant, agricultural improvement immediately raised per capita food supplies; food prices thus widely stabilized or fell. With the labor force not growing but trade and output increasing, real wages began to climb upward. Elite composition stabilized, and elite incomes and royal revenues were no longer eroded by inflation. ...

Sometime in the late seventeenth century, the peak of poor climate and epidemics was passed; by the early eighteenth century, the population had recovered its early-seventeenth-century levels and then began to surpass them. By the second half of the eighteenth century, pressure on the land, and accompanying inflation, were evident throughout Europe and China. Renewed expansion of the cities and of the pool of aspirants to elite positions, combined with falling real wages, led to concentrations of the ambitious and the impoverished in European capitals. In nations with weak financial structures and high expenses, such as France and China, administrative structures were crumbling by the end of the eighteenth century. In nations that had used the favorable interlude of 1660–1760 to streamline expenses and expand their incomes, such as England and Prussia, administrative structures held, although they faced recurrent elite and popular protests throughout the first half of the nineteenth century, culminating on the continent in the revolutions of 1848. (1991:25–26)

Goldstone has attempted to quantify his approach to state breakdown by constructing an index he calls the Political Stress Indicator, or *psi*. Figure 4.2 shows the *psi* for France between 1680 and 1789. Notice that the index increases dramatically beginning in the 1760s and peaks right at the time of the French Revolution of 1789. *Psi*'s for other cases of state breakdown generally support Goldstone's argument.

Goldstone's theory is a fascinating and impressive one—in fact, as impressive and compelling as any theory of revolution we have. But, of course, no work on this grand a scale covering such a huge historical territory could possible escape criticism. John A. Hall (1992) applauds Goldstone's emphasis on demography, noting that he wisely does not

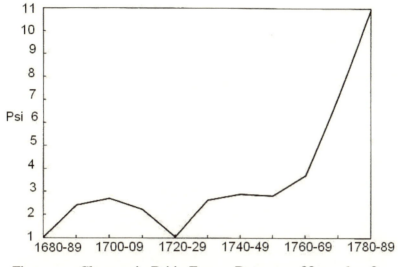

Figure 4.2 Changes in Psi in France Between 1680 and 1789.
Source: **Goldstone (1991), p. 282, Figure 8.**

make this the whole story. Population increase is a causal determinant of state breakdowns because it sets in motion various dimensions of state fiscal crisis, and it is this crisis that actually leads to a state breakdown. On the other hand, Hall argues that Goldstone has overstated the role of population growth. It has sometimes been important in state break-downs, but in other instances it seems to have played little or no role. Said Arjomand (1992) also thinks that the role of demography may be overstated. He seems to agree with Hall that demographic growth cannot explain certain cases. Arjomand mentions in particular the French Revolution and state breakdown in the Ottoman Empire in the seventeenth century. He notes that population growth in England was only 25 percent in the forty years prior to the English Revolution, and only 15 percent in France in the four decades before the French Revolution. Arjomand argues that these are very small rates of growth compared to many of the population growth rates of modern times, and that revolutions in the modern world have been rare occurrences. In fairness to Goldstone, however, it must be acknowledged that whether a population growth rate is significant in producing a fiscal crisis depends on the nature of the state, the level of technology, and a host of other things. The rates Arjomand refers to for seventeenth-century England and eighteenth-century France were, in fact, fairly high for that historical period.

Chapter Five

The Causes of Revolutions: II

THE ANALYSIS OF STATE-CENTERED THEORIES of revolutions in the previous chapter concentrated on the Great Revolutions and other revolutions in Europe and Asia. This chapter continues the analysis of state-centered theories by looking at revolutions in Latin America and other parts of the Third World. It seeks to provide an overall evaluation of these theories and explores two additional questions crucial to explaining revolutions: What is the role of ideology in revolutions? Are revolutions the product of human will and deliberate intent, or do they happen as the result of external circumstances over which individuals have little control?

State-Centered Theories of Third World Revolutions

Timothy Wickham-Crowley's *Guerrillas and Revolution in Latin America* (1992) is an extremely painstaking analysis of guerrilla movements in one region of the Third World, Latin America, in the second half of the twentieth century. In examining Wickham-Crowley's explanation of Latin American revolutions we need to bear in mind that explaining Third World revolutions is a somewhat different task from explaining earlier historical revolutions. The reason for this has to do with the contrast between the historical context of the second half of the twentieth century and that of Eurasia hundreds of years ago.

As Wickham-Crowley notes, the guerrillas who lead revolutionary movements tend to be urban, well educated, and middle class, and the university has been a major source of such political activists. The key problem is to understand why guerrillas win or fail to win the support of the peasantry, because this support is generally necessary for the success of revolutionary movements. Wickham-Crowley proposes a number of conditions that may predispose peasants to support guerrillas. He accepts much of what Jeffery Paige (1975) argues as to what makes peasants revolutionary, but he points to other possible conditions as well. For instance, he provides evidence showing that "squatters"—peasants under serious threat of losing their lands, crops, or even lives—are also likely to be strongly supportive of guerrillas. He also contends that there have been in Latin America certain "rebellious cultures" such that peasants in some regions of some countries have had a long history of rebellion; a certain tendency toward rebellion has seemingly been transmitted, generation after generation, as part of the culture. He concludes that "neither class structure alone, nor historical changes therein, exhaust the correlates of peasant support for guerrillas. Variations in regional political cultures, especially their sheer 'ornery'-ness in the face of exactions and exertions by central government, are also related to regions' propensity to provide haven and support for the challengers to government, including those of the radical left" (Wickham-Crowley, 1992:152).

But guerrillas need more than just peasant support to be successful. They also need military strength. Wickham-Crowley argues that this is a factor consisting of three major subfactors: the internal financing of the guerrillas' armed forces, the internal solidarity of guerrillas as fighting forces, and the extent to which a guerrilla army wins the support of various actors outside the state. Militarily strong guerrilla forces obviously have a much better chance of revolutionary success than weak forces. But even when guerrillas are strongly supported by peasants, and even when they are also militarily strong, another factor is crucial: the nature of the state, especially the extent of its vulnerability to revolutionary movements. It is with respect to this last factor that Wickham-Crowley makes his most distinctive contribution to a theory of Third World revolutions.

As Wickham-Crowley shows, in the second half of the twentieth century successful revolutions occurred in only two Latin American countries: Cuba in 1959 and Nicaragua in 1979. What is it that made these societies and their states distinctive? Let us look at Cuba first.

Wickham-Crowley identifies what he believes are six distinctive features of Cuban society and the Cuban state that made Cuba especially vulnerable to the actions of a revolutionary movement. First, the Cuban middle and upper classes were relatively weak politically, which means that they had little capacity to influence the functioning of the state. Second, Cuban political parties were weakly institutionalized and never came to be constituted along class, ethnic, or religious grounds. They were often opportunistic, corrupt, and venal. Third, the Cuban military was weak and controlled personally by Batista, Cuba's president. The army literally became Batista's personal army, ensuring his control over the state. Fourth, the revolutionary movement that overthrew Batista in 1959 was a large-scale coalition. This coalition drew heavily on the peasantry, but it also included the middle class, the working class, and even portions of the upper class. In effect, virtually all of Cuban society was opposed to the Batista regime and wanted it overthrown. Fifth, the Cuban mass media strongly favored the anti-Batista forces and sent out messages to that effect.

All of these factors were important, but the sixth is the most important of all. Cuba had a very distinctive type of state that has variously been called a *patrimonial praetorian regime*, a *neopatrimonial regime*, or, in Wickham-Crowley's words, a *mafiacracy*. This is a type of regime in which a highly corrupt ruler turns the state into his own personal property: He personally controls the military, suppresses political parties, and dispenses rewards and favors (and punishments) in a highly personalized manner. In short, the ruler dictatorially controls all of the state and society and bends them to his own personal whims. It is precisely this type of regime, Wickham-Crowley argues, that is most vulnerable to overthrow because the personal dictator eventually ends up alienating virtually all major social groups. This is what makes possible a broad revolutionary coalition—a coalition that includes groups that normally have strongly opposing interests.

What, then, of Nicaragua? It turns out that a description of Nicaraguan state and society is strikingly similar to the one for Cuba. Nicaragua also had weak upper and middle classes that had little influence on the state, weak political parties, a nonprofessional army, and a state that was dominated by a dictator (Somoza) who engaged in massive corruption, personal control of the military, and violent attacks on his political opponents. In short, Nicaragua also had a neopatrimonial state or mafiacracy, and this state, as in Cuba, was

Table 5.1 Revolutionary Situations and Outcomes in Latin America

Cases	Favorable Conditions					Outcomes
	Guerrilla attempt	Peasant (and/or worker) support	Guerrilla military strength	Patrimonial praetorian regime	Government loses US support	Social revolution?
I. Winners: Successful Revolutions						
1. Cuba 1956–59	1	1	1	1	1	1
2. Nicaragua 1971–79	1	1 (P,W)	1	1	1	1
II. Also-Rans: Other Guerrillas with Peasant Support						
3. Venezuela 1960s	1	1	1	0	0	0
4. Colombia 1960s	1	1	1	0	0	0
5. Guatemala 1960s	1	1	1	0	0	0
6. Colombia 1970–90	1	1	1	0	0	0
7. Peru 1980s	1	1	1	0	0	0
8. Guatemala 1975–90	1	1	1	0	1	0
9. El Salvador 1975–90	1	1 (P,W)	1	0	0	0
10. Argentina 1974–78	1	1	0	0	1	0
11. Brazil 1970s	1	1	0	0	0	0
12. Argentina (*Montoneros*)	1	1 (W)	1	0	1	0
13. Mexico 1970s	1	1	0	0	0	0
14. Uruguay (*Tupamaros*)	1	1	1?	0	0	0
III. Losers: Failed Guerrilla Movements						
15. Argentina 1958–63	1	0	0	0	0	0
16. Peru 1965	1	0	0	0	0?	0

17. Bolivia 1967	1	0	0	0	0
18. Nicaragua 1958–63	1	0	1?	0	0
19. Dominican Republic 1963	1	0	0	0	0
20. Ecuador 1962	1	0	0	0	0
21. Haiti 1960s	1	0	1	1	0
22. Paraguay 1958–59	1	0	1	0	0
23. Honduras 1965	1	0	0	0	0
24. Brazil 1960s (urban)	1	0	0	0	0

IV. Absent Rural Guerrilla Movements

25. Costa Rica	0	0	0	0	0
26. Panama 1959–85	0	0	0	0	0
27. Panama 1985–89	0	0	1	1	1
28. Paraguay 1960–89	0	0	1	0	0

1 = present, 0 = absent, P = peasant, W = worker.

Source: Wickham-Crowley (1992), p. 312, Table 12-3.

overthrown by a large-scale revolutionary coalition. Wickham-Crowley (1992:299) summarizes the importance of state vulnerability for revolutionary success as follows:

> Patrimonial praetorian regimes, or mafiacracies, have shown themselves to be strikingly vulnerable to revolutionary overthrows because of their peculiar lack of supports in civil society, and because of their corresponding tendency to elicit cross-class opposition to the patrimonial ruler. Collective military regimes allied to the upper class, in contrast, have shown themselves consistently able to suppress revolutionaries, even those with deep and widespread peasant support and substantial military firepower. Finally, elected democratic regimes appear to be the strongest of all in the face of insurgency, and they achieve this strength largely because the populace becomes *indifferent*, if not actively hostile, to the insurgents' cause.

Wickham-Crowley summarizes his argument in Table 5.1. It can be seen that for genuine social revolution to occur, all of the conditions we have discussed above must be present, plus possibly an additional one, that of the loss of support from the United States. Successful social revolution, in the Third World as in earlier historical periods, is obviously not easy. The table also shows that revolutionary movements in Latin American countries that lacked neopatrimonial regimes could nevertheless create a lot of worry, and sometimes come close to revolution, if they were militarily strong and had peasant support. Venezuela and Colombia in the 1960s, Guatemala in the 1960s and between 1975 and 1990, Colombia from 1970 to 1990, Peru in the 1980s, and El Salvador between 1975 and 1990 all had revolutionary guerrillas who were militarily strong, and who had peasant or worker support; but in each instance a neopatrimonial regime was absent, and thus a revolution failed to occur.

The cases of El Salvador and Guatemala are especially instructive. According to Wickham-Crowley, instead of a neopatrimonial regime, El Salvador had a *collective military regime* (cf. Goodwin, 2001). For many years, power in El Salvador involved an alliance between military officers and an upper class that consisted principally of just fourteen extremely wealthy families. The upper class was in nearly complete control of the economy, whereas the military ran the government. In the nearly two decades between the early 1960s and 1980, the main opposition to these groups came from the Christian Democratic Party (Spanish acronym = PDC) and its main leader, José

Napoleon Duarte. The PDC had the support of substantial segments of the middle class, the working class, and the peasantry. In Wickham-Crowley's view, because the ruling collective military regime governed in close association with the upper class, there could be no widespread class coalition of the type that brought about revolution in Nicaragua and Cuba. In his words:

> The Salvadoran insurgency began against a collective military regime that ruled hand in glove with the upper class, not against a patrimonial praetorian regime like Batista's Cuba or Somoza's Nicaragua. Only patrimonial regimes tend to elicit cross-class, populist uprisings that isolate the government from all organized support; an uprising against an upper-class-backed military regime will instead tend to take the form of a class war. That is precisely what happened in El Salvador. That turn to class warfare hardened any wavering upper-class reformists against the insurgency. There is no greater difference from Nicaragua: there the upper class turned against the regime from "the left" beginning in 1972; in El Salvador, the upper class instead had been united to support the old military regime, and then turned against any "reformist" governments, attacking them from the right. (Wickham-Crowley, 1992:286)

The result in El Salvador was thus a kind of stalemate between the regime and the opposition forces. El Salvador gradually drifted toward a kind of electoral democracy, but it was more a formal than a substantive democracy. The upper class and the military remained very dominant political actors.

The situation in Guatemala was strikingly similar. Wickham-Crowley points to five fundamental similarities between El Salvador and Guatemala and their revolutionary potential:

1. Collective military alliances ruled for long periods between the early 1950s and the 1980s.
2. There was a gradual move toward formal electoral democracy, but elections tended to be highly fraudulent or heavily restricted; the military retained control of the government despite elections.
3. The military governments strongly supported and even promoted the claims of the upper class to their property and their control over the labor of peasants and workers.
4. The military and the upper classes were strongly anti-Communist in both countries.

5. There were occasional political openings to the opposition, but they were either not allowed to take office or, if they did, not allowed to govern in an unrestricted way.

The outcome in Guatemala was essentially the same as that in El Salvador: class warfare and political stalemate, or, in the words of Jeff Goodwin (2001), protracted low-intensity conflict.

If guerrilla movements failed to attract peasants, and if they were not militarily strong, they got nowhere. This was the case, for example, in Argentina between 1958 and 1963, in Bolivia in 1967, in the Dominican Republic in 1963, in Haiti in the 1960s, and in Honduras in 1965. And where guerrilla movements themselves failed to develop— even if a neopatrimonial regime was present, discontent was widespread, and sporadic rebellions occurred—nothing of major political significance happened. For example, Panama in the late 1980s had a neopatrimonial regime (headed by the infamous Manuel Noriega) and even lost the support of the United States, but it had no guerrilla movements and so nothing even remotely approaching social revolution occurred. The overall message seems clear: Actual social revolution takes the full combination of five conditions to become a reality, and this is why it is a rare event even under the most oppressive of social, economic, and political conditions.

Goodwin and Skocpol (1989) are supportive of Wickham-Crowley's emphasis on state vulnerability, but generalize it. They point to several additional examples of neopatrimonial states that succumbed to social revolution. One of these, Iran, had a classically neopatrimonial regime. As we have seen, the shah was an extremely brutal dictator who only got worse over time. He used his state to enrich himself, his family, and various state officials. As Farrokh Moshiri (1991:125) notes, "By the late 1970s, the corruption within the royal family had reached unbelievable proportions, with the shah's sister Ashraf being involved in international drug trafficking." The more the shah encountered opposition, the greater the extent to which he used repressive methods. He once had the support of some segments of Iranian society but eventually ended up disgusting and alienating all groups: the traditional and modern middle classes, workers, peasants, and (especially) the entire Islamic clergy. The brutal repressiveness of his regime led to precisely the same type of widespread revolutionary coalition of disparate groups as that which formed in Cuba and Nicaragua.

Goodwin and Skocpol also suggest that there is another type of Third World state that is highly vulnerable to revolution: the *directly ruled colony*. As examples of such regimes that were overthrown by revolution they cite Vietnam, Algeria, Guinea-Bissau, Angola, and Mozambique. They claim that directly ruled colonies are similar to neopatrimonial regimes especially in the fact that they provide a common and highly identifiable focus of opposition for a wide range of social groups:

> Direct colonialism undermines actual or potential moderate and reformist leaderships since, unlike indirect colonialism, it does not attempt to preserve a traditional indigenous elite or to create a new one so that formal political power may one day be "safely" transferred to the colony without jeopardizing the colonizer's economic interests. Direct colonial rule also tends to create more indigenous elite and middle-class opposition than indirect colonial rule. Important business and professional opportunities, as well as upper-level administrative positions, are reserved by and for the colonists. That exclusion from such positions is based on an explicitly racial criterion, and not on education or ability more generally, can only heighten the alienation of indigenous upper-class and middle-class elements from the colonialists. (Goodwin and Skocpol, 1989:501)

By contrast, when a colony is ruled indirectly—when the colonizing power is more detached and less intensively involved in day-to-day administrative affairs of the colony—the colonizer tends to be more cohesive, militarily stronger, and more capable of providing the colony with a transition to an independent state that is more inclusive of various social groups, or that may even be constructed on democratic foundations. Goodwin and Skocpol (1989) point to several indirectly ruled colonial regimes that were able to suppress mass revolutionary insurgency during the 1940s and 1950s: the Philippines, Kenya, Malaya, India, Indonesia, and Burma.

Wickham-Crowley's theory of Third World revolutions is clearly the best we have ever had, but it cannot be completely correct since there is at least one case that is an exception—the Philippines. As Jeff Goodwin (1994b) points out, if Wickham-Crowley were completely right the Philippines would today be ruled by the Communist Party. As we saw in Chapter 3, the Philippines was ruled by a highly corrupt dictator, Marcos, who essentially headed a neopatrimonial regime. What happened in this country to produce a political rather than a social revolution? Goodwin's answer is that there are different subtypes of neopatrimonial regimes, some of which are less vulnerable to social revolution. In Cuba and Nicaragua the regimes dominated the military, and economic elites were especially weak. (The shah of Iran heavily controlled his military as well.) But Marcos did not dominate his military apparatus to the same extent that Batista, Somoza, and Shah Muhammad Reza Pahlavi did, and the Philippine economic elite was stronger than the elites in Cuba and Nicaragua. Therefore, instead of joining forces with subordinated classes, the Philippine elite attempted a *coup d'état* on its own, and this *coup*, though initially a failure, set the stage for removing Marcos. As Goodwin (1994b:745) expresses it, "it was an abortive coup d'etat, in fact, that led to the outpouring of 'people power' that finally convinced Marcos, with some behind-the-scenes arm-twisting by the United States, to cede power to Aquino and her elite-dominated circle. The guerrillas of the NPA [Communist New People's Army] were thereby (figuratively speaking) left out in the cold." The Philippine elite wanted a political but not a social revolution—new political leadership without any fundamental change in the social and class structure—and conditions allowed it to obtain that. Because of its strength, it was able to avoid forming a coalition with subordinated classes, whose interests it did not share.

Given Goodwin and Skocpol's general endorsement of Wickham-Crowley, it will come as no surprise that there are striking similarities between Wickham-Crowley's argument and Skocpol's interpretation of the Great Revolutions and the Iranian Revolution. Both emphasize the coming together of two major factors, peasant insurrection and state vulnerability, as crucial for revolutionary change. Table 5.2 summarizes Wickham-Crowley's analysis of key parallels among all these revolutions. Jack Goldstone's (1991) analysis of state breakdowns, though critically different in some respects from the theories of Skocpol and Wickham-Crowley, is nevertheless similar to those theories in its emphasis on state weaknesses and crises. These broad similarities in the most important recent analyses of revolutions suggest that real progress is being made in our understanding of revolutionary change. We are far ahead of where we were just two or three decades ago.

Table 5.2 Revolutionary Predispositions in France, Russia, China, Iran, Cuba, and Nicaragua

Cases	France, Russia, China	Iran	Cuba, Nicaragua
Regime type	Agrarian protobureaucracy headed by hereditary monarch	Rentier-state-cum-patrimonial absolutist rule	Mafiacracy, i.e., patrimonial praetorian dictatorship
State-dominant class relations	Landed elite lodged within the state (France, China)	Monarch excludes, even attacks, upper class	Dictatorship excludes, even attacks, upper class
Taxation of masses?	Yes	No	Little
External pressures?	Yes (massive in Russia)	Modest US pressure (at end) for regime shift	Loss of external support
Weakened armed forces: source?	Recurrent or intense war	Patrimonial meddling weakens esprit de corps	Patrimonial meddling weakens esprit de corps
Key structural weakness	Upper class blocks state, fiscal reforms	Monarch-state is focus of cross-class demands, unrest	Personal dictator is focus of cross-class unrest
Sources of lower-class insurrection (internal): lower-class solidarity?	In peasant villages (France, Russia)	In urban bazaars	Unimportant (some role in Cuba)
Sources of lower-class insurrection (external): mobilization by outsiders?	Rural China, by Red Army	Unimportant	Dispersed rural squatters and/or urban *barrios*, by guerrillas

Source: Wickham-Crowley (1992), p. 300, Table 11-3.

Strengths and Weaknesses of State-Centered Theories

The state-centered perspective is the one that has guided the best analyses of revolutions reviewed in this and the preceding chapter. It appears to be the most useful perspective we have and a significant advance over earlier ones. However, since no perspective can explain everything, Goodwin (2001) has tried to summarize the main strengths and limitations of this approach. On the positive side, Goodwin argues that the perspective has shown itself capable of providing persuasive answers to at least four fundamental questions:

1. Why are revolutions unique among all the major forms of social and political conflict in being distinctively modern? As Goodwin points out, no revolutions ever occurred prior to the seventeenth century, and they have become increasingly common as we approach the present. The reason, Goodwin suggests, is that *revolutions require states.* In fact, this is really true by definition, since a revolution involves the overthrow of a state structure and its replacement by a new one. And states themselves—or at least *national* states—did not really exist until the last few centuries. As Goodwin (2001:41) puts it, "prior to the emergence of modern national states, revolutions as we now understand them … were simply impossible and generally unthinkable. Until the modern era, that is, no institution had sufficient infrastructural power—with the possible exception of the Catholic Church—to reform extensive social arrangements in more or less fundamental ways; the national state, however, made it possible to do—and to think of doing—just that."

2. Why are revolutionary movements concerned with smashing the state and seizing state power? Why must the state collapse for a revolutionary movement to succeed? The answer is, because the state holds the key to bringing about the fundamental social changes that revolutionaries want. It was Lenin himself who said that the key to successful revolution is gaining control of the state. The old state must be brought to the point of collapse or surrender, and an entirely new state apparatus must be erected that will change the social order in a fundamental way. No other institution in society is capable of bringing about such a change.

3. Why do revolutions occur when and where they do? This question is especially important when we remind ourselves that rebellion and revolt, and civil disorder of many different types, are quite common and yet true revolutions are rare. The reason is that it usually takes a precise combination of circumstances for a revolutionary movement to succeed. Revolutionaries need to be powerful enough, and opportunistic enough, to be able to topple the state. Moreover, strong states are virtually never toppled, so there must be some inherent weakness in the state for it to collapse when severely threatened.

4. Under what circumstances are highly militant revolutionary groups able to attract broad social support? Goodwin argues that the state-centered approach points to five basic conditions that will help a revolutionary group gain support: (a) The state seeks to preserve social and economic arrangements that are widely perceived as unjust. This makes the state a target for people's grievances. (b) The state represses mobilized groups or excludes them from power. This serves to antagonize large segments of the population even more. States that limit repression of their opponents, or that even seek to include them within the state machinery, are often successful in draining away revolutionary anger. (c) The state engages in indiscriminate, but not actually overwhelming, violence against its political opponents. The more indiscriminate state violence is, the greater the resentment it provokes against itself. If this violence were overwhelming, then political opponents would usually be left without any political openings. But if the violence fails to be overwhelming, then popular movements gain a foothold and can use it to expand their level of anti-state mobilization. (d) The state has a relatively weak coercive capacity. As Goodwin (2001:49) puts it, "revolutionaries may become numerous and well organized if the state's policing capacities and infrastructural power more generally are chronically weak or geographically uneven. … And revolutionaries are doubly fortunate if they confront states that are ineffectual due to corruption or bureaucratic incoherence." (e) The state engages in highly arbitrary forms of personalistic rule. This point was strongly emphasized above, in the discussion of neopatrimonial regimes as the types of states that are most vulnerable to revolutionary coalitions (see Figures 5.1 and 5.2).

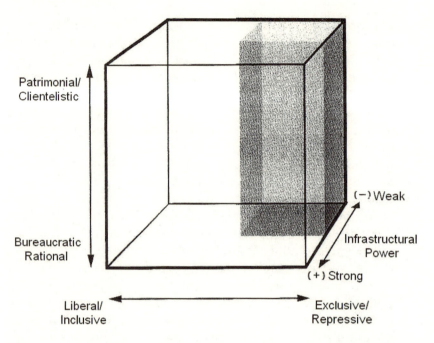

Figure 5.1 States Most Likely to Produce Revolutionary Movements (shaded area). *Source:* **Goodwin (2001), p. 29, Figure 1.3.**

Already discussed were the Batista regime in Cuba, the Somoza regime in Nicaragua, and the shah's regime in Iran, but many others could be added to the list, such as the Chiang regime in China, the Díaz regime in Mexico, and the Ceauşescu regime in Romania.

Though a strong proponent of the state-centered approach, Goodwin is fair to a fault. He identifies certain criticisms of the approach that he believes are wide of the mark, but he also acknowledges three criticisms that he concedes have some validity:

1. State-centered approaches tend to neglect or underemphasize the importance of *associational networks* outside the state that play a role in the success or failure of a revolutionary movement. These are networks based on ethnicity, kinship, neighborhood communities, religious communities, or rural villages. Goodwin

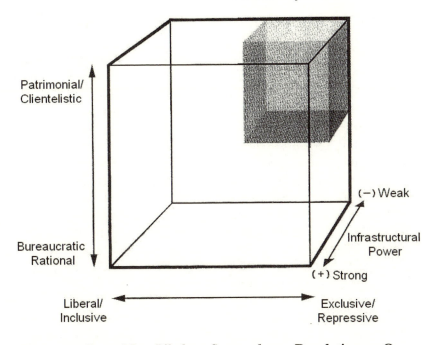

Figure 5.2 States Most Likely to Succumb to a Revolutionary Overthrow (shaded area). *Source:* **Goodwin (2001), p. 29, Figure 1.4.**

concedes that state-centered theorists could do more to examine the role of such networks and to acknowledge that their nature involves much more than just what the state is doing in any given society. As he says, "associational networks and practices have their own dynamics and emergent properties that need to be taken seriously and analyzed in their own right. Revolutionaries themselves, for example, may act in ways that expand or corrode their ties to other people. For these reasons, a state-centered perspective on the associational networks of civil society is inherently limited" (2001:56).

2. State-centered approaches underplay the role of the *availability of material resources* in empowering revolutionary movements. It was originally Charles Tilly, with his resource mobilization theory, who stressed the importance of such resources. State-centered theorists in fact readily admit that the presence or absence of such resources is important. However, they could pay more attention

to them than they have; indeed, this endeavor will probably be on the agenda for future research.

3. State-centered theorists do not give sufficient attention to the *independent role of beliefs and social identities* in shaping the actions of revolutionaries. Goodwin counters, however, that beliefs and social identities do not simply emerge from nowhere but, rather, are apt to relate to the social relations and state structures that people find within their society. Nevertheless, he does acknowledge that "like associational networks, revolutionary ideologies and strategic repertoires are also rooted in a variety of social relations and cultural systems that are not shaped wholly or much at all by state practices. Such ideologies have their own substantive properties that demand to be taken seriously and analyzed in their own right . ... For these reasons, a state-centered perspective on culture and ideology—like that on ties and resources—is inherently limited" (2001:58).

In sum, state-centered approaches cannot answer all important questions about the causes of revolutions and revolutionary movements. However, they seem vastly superior to what has come before them, and they can be appropriately modified in future research so as to generate even more explanatory power.

Ideologies and Revolutions

In recent years there has been a resurgence of interest in the role of ideologies in the generation of revolutions and revolutionary movements. To what extent do the widely shared beliefs of various revolutionary groups matter in leading individuals to form themselves into such groups and persist in their revolutionary efforts? And to what extent do these shared beliefs make a difference in producing actual social revolutions, or in shaping the future once a social revolution has occurred?

William Sewell, Jr. (1985), for example, takes Skocpol to task for ignoring the role of ideology in revolutions. Sewell accepts much of Skocpol's analysis, but argues that she has not made her model of causation multiple enough. State and class structures matter, but ideologies matter too, Sewell argues. Sewell tries to make his case by way of an analysis of the French Revolution. Critical to an understanding of that revolution, Sewell claims, was the new ideology of the Enlightenment that was so influential in France (and other parts of Europe) in the eighteenth century. The Enlightenment rejected the ideology of the Old Regime, which emphasized divine rule by a monarch and a nobility or aristocracy that deserved its privileged role in society. Enlightenment philosophers wanted to abolish the monarchy and noble privilege and reconstitute society along what they thought were much more rational lines. Once the Old Regime went into crisis, Enlightenment ideas provided revolutionary groups with the philosophical foundation for a new social and political structure.

Sewell claims that the French Revolution had an ideological dynamic consisting of four general dimensions. First, the revolutionary ideology became progressively radicalized throughout the 1790s. Robespierre became the embodiment of this revolutionary ideology, and the revolution "spoke through him." Second, although there developed different ideological variants of revolutionary ideology (Constitutional Monarchist, Girondin, Jacobin, and *sans-culottes*), these were all variations on certain common Enlightenment themes, especially popular sovereignty, the general will, representation, property, natural law, and virtue. Third, the way in which the new social institutions developed was shaped largely by Enlightenment ideology. And finally, Enlightenment ideology was itself transformed in certain unexpected ways. New ideological discourses developed, perhaps the most important of which was the concept of revolution itself. The very notion of revolution as the replacement of one government by another at the hands of the people was a product of the revolution.

John Foran (1997a) is another recent proponent of the role of shared beliefs in revolutionary action. He argues that what he calls *political cultures of resistance and opposition* are critical to the revolutionary process. His argument is "that prior to revolutions, different groups in society elaborate multiple political cultures of opposition to the regime, and that these may draw on diffuse folk beliefs and historical memories of struggle, shared 'structures of feeling' fashioned out of common experiences, and eventually, perhaps, explicitly revolutionary manifestos and formally articulated ideologies" (1997a:209). Foran sees ideology as having been highly influential in the French Revolution. Along much the same lines as Sewell, Foran argues that Enlightenment ideas were critical. Printers, fiction writers, pamphleteers, philosophers, and publishers, he claims, were among the major ideological actors who contributed significantly to the revolutionary process.

Goldstone (1991) agrees with Skocpol that ideologies probably play a limited role as causal forces in revolutions, but he insists that they play a major role in determining how states get rebuilt once a revolution or state breakdown has already occurred. It is crucial to understand, Goldstone argues, that revolutions proceed through phases. The kinds of material and social forces emphasized by Skocpol and other state-centered theorists are the critical causal factors in the first, or breakdown, phase. However, "ideology and culture develop a momentum of their own" and in later phases, those involving state reorganization and rebuilding, come to play the leading role. Goldstone stresses, though, that there is never one single ideology that seeks to dominate state reconstruction. It is normally the case that many, often highly contrasting, ideologies prevail, and conflict between groups with different ideologies is normal and often intense. Moreover, these ideologies are not static but continue to evolve in the course of political and ideological struggle. As Goldstone (1991:429) puts it, the various "twists and turns in the role of ideology are comprehensible only when we cease to consider revolutions as single events and recall that they are *processes* with multiple phases, in each of which ideology may play a different role. The guiding ideology of the French Revolution moved from an attack on privilege in general—led by representatives of all classes—to an attack on those individuals who claimed privilege—led by the representatives of the Third Estate—to an attack on anyone considered an 'enemy of the nation'—led by the Jacobins—and finally, under Napoleon, to the pursuit of national glory."

Foran (1997a) sees ideology as relevant not only to the origins of revolutions but to their outcomes as well. In the case of Cuba, he argues, once the revolutionary break occurred, the revolutionary forces were held together by the population's enthusiasm for, and commitment to, the new political culture of socialism that they had created. Socialist ideas arising from the University of Havana, he claims, helped create the revolution and played a critical role in how the revolution played out. And in Nicaragua, the Sandinistas learned from the experiences of Cuban and other revolutionaries how to avoid a postrevolutionary society that was rigidly Marxist-Leninist. They attempted to incorporate the middle classes and elites and to construct an essentially democratic political regime.

What should we make of these calls for greater emphasis on the role of ideology? In response to Sewell's critique, Skocpol (1994) acknowledges that revolutionary ideologies are often important components of revolutions. But she makes several points against Sewell. First, she quite rightly notes that the ideologies and belief systems of would-be revolutionaries are not free-floating, disembodied sets of ideas; on the contrary, the ideas that groups develop tend to be those that arise from these groups' social and political positions and that help them accomplish their objectives. Second, she says that "we should not make the mistake of assuming that the talkers and the legislators could ever straightforwardly shape outcomes according to Enlightenment principles" (1994:206). Some of the most moralistic attempts to enact various principles of the Enlightenment never became permanently established, she notes. Third, even when we are dealing with huge intellectual transformations on the order of the Enlightenment, there is little real evidence that such transformations are in and of themselves actual causes of revolutions. When we look at other revolutions, such as more recent Third World revolutions, epochal intellectual transformations are not even involved and, therefore, cannot possibly explain these revolutionary phenomena. "Modern social revolutions," Skocpol says, tend to be "fought out primarily by contending armies rather than by Leninist parties, militant clerics, or well-read legislators" (1994:207).

Although he would not claim that culture and ideology play no role at all in revolutions, Wickham-Crowley (1997) is, nonetheless, largely dismissive. He not only agrees with Skocpol's response to Sewell but thinks she could have gone further. She could have made the point, he says, that in the French Revolution the peasant uprisings that destroyed landlord privilege—uprisings that were a critical component of that revolution—were very much like previous peasant uprisings in that their goal was mainly to protect the peasants' economic situation. From the peasant point of view, their aim was narrowly economic and hardly broadly ideological. In no sense were they based on principles deriving from Enlightenment thought or a self-aware Jacobinism. Wickham-Crowley continues with respect to the two other Great Revolutions: "For China and Russia, the notion that revolutionaries consciously guided by communist ideologies brought down the old regimes is laughable: the Bolsheviks were underground and Lenin in Swiss exile when February food riots and garrison desertions brought down the old regime in 1917; Mao Zedong was but a child and the Chinese Communist Party not yet in existence when the Manchu dynasty collapsed in 1910–12" (1997:41–42).

Another difficulty faced by those who argue strongly for the role of culture and ideology is that their analyses are often limited by the examination of a single case of revolution and the unique cultural or ideological features of the society in which the revolution has occurred. Sewell, for example, limited himself to the French Revolution and to the role of the French Enlightenment. Wickham-Crowley (1997:64) tells us what is wrong with this approach:

> Thus a French cultural theorist certainly could tell us something about the "Frenchness" of the French Revolution, just as, say, an English cultural theorist might convey the "Englishness" of the English Revolution of the 1640s. But the peculiar "cultural" traits of the people or of the revolutionaries are very unlikely ever to tell us why a revolution occurred here but not there, now but not then. For there is simply too much variation within the taxonomic universe of "culture-types" to provide clear answers to crucial questions about the systematic recurrence, or not, in different cultural contexts of mass grievance, lower-class insurrections, and social-revolutionary transfers of power.

Even Goldstone (1991) himself recognizes that the importance of ideology is likely to be limited to revolutionary outcomes rather than revolutionary origins or causes. As he says, invoking "culture" is of little or no use for long-term causal explanation. This is undoubtedly why Goldstone studiously avoids invoking it in his overall theory of the actual causes of major revolutions in Europe and Asia.

Structure and Agency in the Revolutionary Process

Closely related to the issue of the role of culture and ideology in revolutionary origins and outcomes is the debate over *structure versus agency*. This is actually part of a much broader debate within sociological theory and the social sciences—one that traces its origins to the hoary philosophical debate between "determinism" and "free will." The question is essentially this: To what extent are revolutions made by revolutionaries on the basis of their conscious intentions and goals (*agency*) or the result of external social, economic, and political forces over which individuals have little control (*structure*)? Can individual action shape revolutions, or are individuals simply caught up in a swirl of forces that bring about outcomes they never intended and may not want?

Skocpol has come down firmly on the side of structure. She argues that any good theory of revolution must be a *nonvoluntarist, structural* theory. Most theories of revolution, she says, focus heavily on the intentions of revolutionaries and their allies as if revolutions are the simple result of the deliberate actions of these groups. She claims that such a notion is extremely misleading, for "the fact is that historically no successful social revolution has ever been 'made' by a mass-mobilizing, avowedly revolutionary movement" (1979:17). In this regard she quotes Wendell Phillips to the effect that "revolutions are not made; they come" (1979:17). What does it mean to say this, that revolutions simply "come"? It means that in most revolutions, and most assuredly in the Great Revolutions, many different groups are involved in complex ways that are difficult to understand, and the actual outcome— a revolutionary transformation—has little to do with, and in fact is often at odds with, the intentions and actions of many of these groups.

Skocpol insists that revolutions be viewed as the outcome of objective conditions, especially conditions in the economy and the polity. She tells us (1994:200) that "no single acting group, whether a class or an ideological vanguard, deliberately shapes the complex and multiply determined conflicts that bring about revolutionary crises and outcomes." However, Skocpol makes it quite clear that she is not ignoring the obvious fact that there are real, deliberately acting individuals and groups in revolutions, and that these individuals and groups have conscious intentions and goals. *Of course* individuals make up the revolutionary process; how could it be otherwise? What Skocpol is denying is simply that these individuals' intentions, goals, and actions are sufficient to carry the day and bring about the consequences they want. Revolutions are much more complex than that, and revolutionary crises and outcomes much more unpredictable. What happens is that "differentially situated and motivated groups become participants in a complex unfolding of multiple conflicts that ultimately give rise to outcomes not originally foreseen or intended by any of the particular groups involved" (1994:111). To understand revolutions, Skocpol asserts, one must try to rise above the perspectives of the participants and look for the common conditions that these participants are caught up in.

Skocpol does, however, admit of at least one exception to her argument that revolutions are not consciously made by individuals: the Iranian revolution against the shah (Skocpol, 1982). She admits that there was highly organized, self-conscious action on the part of major Islamic leaders, and that the actions of these leaders contributed in a very significant way to the revolution. But this represented a sharp departure, she insists, from the more general rule. Moreover, as we have already seen, the Iranian revolution conformed to the general state-centered structural perspective advocated by Skocpol. The shah's regime was a type of neopatrimonial state, and its weakness allowed the Islamic revolutionary forces to win. Without these structural conditions, no revolution would have occurred in Iran.

Usually those who emphasize culture or ideology as a causal force also come down heavily on the side of agency, or a *voluntaristic* approach. A major exception is Sewell (1985). He is unusual in advocating a strong role for culture or ideology, but in a structural way. Ideology is not a matter of the conscious intentions of individuals, Sewell contends, but is "transpersonal," "anonymous," and "collective." It is not exactly clear what this is supposed to mean, but Sewell is a follower of such French thinkers as Louis Althusser and Michel Foucault, who have advocated such an approach. Many sociologists, however, are baffled by it and admit that they do not really understand it (this is certainly true of the present author). It can readily be seen that ideologies may persist throughout the generations, so that individuals can come to absorb in a rather automatic and unconscious way the beliefs of previous generations. But, even if this is true, the ideas themselves had to originate in the conscious minds, and thus as part of the conscious intentions, of at least *some* thinkers.

More typical are Eric Selbin (1997) and John Foran (1997a), who want to stress both ideas and agency. Selbin (1997:123) proposes "that ideas and actors, not structures and some broad sweep of history, are the primary forces in revolutionary processes." Selbin wants to stress that revolutions are "human creations," and that the focus of our attention should be on "choices," not "determinism." And Foran concurs, for he clearly gives his "political cultures of resistance and opposition" a voluntaristic thrust (and see Foran's autobiographical sketch in the Appendix).

But this emphasis on agency runs up against sharp limitations fairly quickly. As Selbin (1997:133) himself candidly admits, "People's actions clearly confront certain limits that structures engender; often structures demarcate a certain range of possibilities. But structures do not unconditionally dictate what people must do." Of course Selbin is exactly right: Structures by no means strictly determine what people do. But no one has ever claimed that. Structures simply make it more or less likely that people will do this rather than that. Wickham-Crowley's (1997:64) conclusion seems warranted: "Structural theories are here to stay, and their analytical points, far from being blunted by the critics, will probably extend ever more deeply into the postrevolutionary milieu."

Explaining Revolutions: Conclusions

My grand conclusions on the theories of revolution discussed in the last two chapters can be summarized approximately as follows:

- Social-psychological theories miss the most important social conditions that contribute to revolution, and do not even seem to be supported by empirical evidence.
- Marxian theories are important in emphasizing the role of class oppression and exploitation, for subordinate classes play an important role in revolutionary crises. However, Marxian theories have been unable to predict when and where revolutions will occur because they virtually ignore the critical role of the state.
- Political conflict theories like resource mobilization theory were a major step in the right direction, but they still do not give the state a sufficient role in the revolutionary process.
- State-centered theories work best, but they represent "unfinished business" and can still be improved upon. Their advocates are working to improve them and make them more applicable to a wider range of revolutionary phenomena.
- Culture and ideology play little direct causal roles in revolutions and are themselves largely determined by the social and political positions of their carriers. Ideologies often develop and evolve as strategic devices that best suit actors' revolutionary objectives.
- Ideology plays a larger role in revolutionary outcomes—how states come to be rebuilt—than in the actual revolutions themselves, although even here structural forces constrain the choices leaders can make and the legacies of old regimes continue to live on in new state structures.

- In revolutionary action, people are, of course, acting in accordance with their interests and goals, but revolutions themselves are for the most part the result of unintended consequences. People do not really "make revolutions," and certainly not without the necessary structural forces behind them.

Chapter Six

Revolutions from Above in Eastern Europe and the Soviet Union

AFTER THE RUSSIAN REVOLUTION, the newly formed Soviet Union became the world's first socialist society. Then, after World War II, it invaded several Eastern European societies and brought them under its political and military control as parts of an expanded Soviet Empire. Yugoslavia experienced an internal revolution in 1945, and also became socialist. In all of these societies, the economy became nationalized and subject to state control. Capitalist production for profit was officially abolished, and the existing capitalist classes were eliminated from the scene. Marxism-Leninism—or, more accurately, Leninism—became the form of government and the official political ideology. The Communist Party became not just the ruling party but the *only* party.

Yet in 1989 and after, Communism collapsed as revolutions occurred in all of these societies. Table 6.1 lists the major state socialist (Leninist) societies and their current status. Today these societies are most commonly called *postsocialist* or *post-Communist* societies. They are in a state of transition from the old state socialist economies and Leninist governments to essentially capitalist societies with more open or democratic modes of government. In this chapter I describe the

Table 6.1 Leninist Regimes

Society	Year of Transition to Leninism	Current Status
Soviet Union	1917	Abandoned Leninism and fragmented into Russia and other successor states after 1991.
Albania	1944	Abandoned Leninism after 1989.
Yugoslavia	1945	Abandoned Leninism after 1989 and fragmented into Bosnia-Herzegovina, Croatia, Macedonia, Slovenia, and Yugoslavia (Serbia and Montenegro).
Bulgaria	1947	Abandoned Leninism after 1989.
Czechoslovakia	1948	Abandoned Leninism after 1989 and separated into the Czech Republic and Slovakia in 1993.
Hungary	1948	Abandoned Leninism after 1989.
Poland	1948	Abandoned Leninism after 1989.
Romania	1948	Abandoned Leninism after 1989.
East Germany	1949	Abandoned Leninism in 1989 and reunified with West Germany in 1990.

Note: Only Leninist regimes that have experienced revolutions or state breakdowns are included.

nature of these revolutions and consider what happened in these societies to produce them. First, however, we need to examine what these societies were like before the revolutions.

State Socialism: Development and Reforms

Once the Soviet Union was formed and consolidated in the 1920s, private ownership of the means of production was almost completely eliminated. Most of the industrial sector and part of the agricultural sector were nationalized. Except for small amounts of land cultivated by collective farmers and a handful of very small enterprises (e.g., people selling flowers or vegetables on the street), the entire economy was brought under centralized economic planning, and a *command economy*, as opposed to a market economy, was created. The Soviet state owned and operated all major industries: mining, heavy construction, railroads, communications, power production, urban retailing, and various others. All workers worked for the state (Kornai, 1992; Lane, 1985). The Eastern European societies that were incorporated into the Soviet Empire were based essentially on the Soviet model, although they had more capitalist or market-oriented economic activity (especially Yugoslavia and Hungary) (Abonyi, 1982). Yugoslavia attempted to create something called *market socialism,* which involved retaining a command economy while at the same time permitting substantial development of capitalist businesses.

In command economies, such crucial economic phenomena as prices and wages are set not by market principles but by government fiat, and thus are not sensitive to the laws of supply and demand. And the greater the extent of a command structure, the less the forces of supply and demand contribute to economic equilibrium. As we shall see, this absence of a market structure has had enormous consequences for the functioning of state socialist economies and their historical development.

At the time the Soviet Union was formed, the level of industrialization was very low, with most of the population still consisting of peasant farmers. Under Josef Stalin, a major effort to industrialize the Soviet Union began in the 1930s, and extraordinarily rapid industrialization was carried out. The Soviet Union was transformed in an astonishingly short time from a largely peasant agrarian society into a highly industrialized society. The major Eastern European societies were already more industrialized than Russia, but industrialization continued apace in those societies after the Soviets took control. However, although state socialism produced a great deal of industrialization, none of the state socialist societies were able to catch up with Western capitalism. They never did attain the extremely high levels of economic prosperity and the level of production of mass consumer goods characteristic of Western capitalism. Even by the late 1980s the state socialist societies had attained per capita incomes that were only about one-third to one-half of those found in Western capitalist societies.

It is striking that all state socialist societies have been characterized by highly authoritarian, and sometimes brutally dictatorial, states. Milovan Djilas (1957:37), once vice-president of Yugoslovia, remarked many years ago that "everything happened differently in the U.S.S.R. and other Communist countries from what the leaders—even such prominent ones as Lenin, Stalin, Trotsky, and Bukharin—anticipated. They expected that the state would rapidly wither away, that democracy would be strengthened. The reverse happened." Djilas referred to the bureaucratic elite that ruled state socialist societies as a "new class," and claimed that its power was the "most complete known to history."

Socialist states have often been called *Marxist* or *Marxist-Leninist* states, but, as suggested above, it seems more accurate to call them simply *Leninist* states (Chirot, 1986; Jowitt, 1978). The reason is that in a political sense these societies have departed significantly from what Marx himself envisioned. Marx used the phrase *dictatorship of the proletariat* to describe what he thought newly emergent socialist societies would be like politically in their initial stages. Revolutionaries would take power and rule in the name of the working class, which he thought would eventually come to constitute the great mass of society. This transitional government would be required to consolidate the new society and economy; it would have to be highly authoritarian to restore order and to prevent capitalists and their sympathizers from trying to bring about a restoration of capitalism. If people did not voluntarily go along with the new system, they would have to be forced to do so. However, in time—perhaps a generation or two, but Marx never really said—this authoritarian government would "wither away" and be replaced by a much more democratic system. People either would see on their own that socialism was in their economic interests or would be psychologically conditioned to accept the new system. Many people view this line of thinking as naïve, but it did seem to be what Marx actually thought. Hence it is hard to imagine that he would have approved of what actually happened in these societies—a *permanent* dictatorship *over* the proletariat.

In Leninist states, the Communist Party not only monopolizes political power but outlaws other political parties; the state legitimizes its rule by appealing to the political philosophies of Marxism and its Leninist reinterpretation; the Communist Party considers itself the only valid interpreter of truth, both scientific and political, and thus does not allow its decisions or actions to be questioned by the citizenry; and people's daily lives are closely regulated and strict limitations are placed on the political freedoms that are widely recognized in modern parliamentary democracies, such as freedoms of speech or assembly.

Did state socialism work as a feasible alternative to capitalism? The answer to this question depends not only on one's political allegiances but on the meaning of the word *work*. The Soviet Union, as already noted, was certainly successful in achieving very rapid industrialization, and for a time it appeared to some observers that the Soviet Union might even catch up with or surpass Western capitalism in economic productivity. However, although state socialism was fairly good at achieving heavy industrialization—steel, electrical machinery, and so on—it proved to be extremely poor at creating quality consumer goods on a large scale (Chirot, 1991). Moreover, by the 1970s the Soviet economy, and to some extent the economies of the Eastern European socialist societies, began to stagnate and, by the mid-1980s, to enter a period of crisis. Robert Leggett (1988) has pointed out that for several decades economic growth was declining, there were shortages of both energy and labor, and productivity was chronically low. In the period between 1981 and 1985, gross national product grew less than at any time since the end of World War II. Living standards were declining, popular discontent was growing, and, as Tatsuo Kaneda (1988) has noted, the Soviet economy was wasteful, technologically dependent on the West, losing international competitiveness, and facing increasing shortages of necessary goods. At the same time, black markets were expanding, bribery and corruption were rampant, debt was increasing, and alcoholism, drug use, illness, and mortality were becoming more common.

It was this economic crisis that led the newly elected general secretary of the Soviet Communist Party, Mikhail Gorbachev, to undertake major economic reforms beginning in 1986. Gorbachev introduced a reform strategy called *perestroika,* which, translated literally, means "restructuring." The most fundamental aspects of this plan of economic reform involved three major dimensions: (1) Although centralized economic planning was to be continued, increased responsibility was to be given to individual firms to make decisions about economic production. Firms would be required to compete with each other, being judged in terms of their degree of profitability, and insufficiently profitable firms would be eliminated. And the managers of firms would now often be elected rather than achieving their positions through the traditional political bureaucracy. (2) Greater wage differentials were to be introduced as an incentive for workers to work harder and be more conscientious. Moreover, unlike the past, when it was impossible to fire a worker for incompetence or shirking, workers could now be fired if they performed their work poorly or for being absent from work excessively. Previously impossible, unemployment would become a possibility. (3) Soviet officials would seek out new joint ventures with Western firms in order to attract Western capital and improve both the quantity and quality of the production of consumer goods (Kushnirsky, 1988; Lapidus, 1988; Leggett, 1988; Zemtsov and Farrar, 1989).

Perestroika was based on a recognition that the crisis of the Soviet economy was rooted in the limitations of centralized economic planning; it was designed to increase the role of the market in Soviet economic functioning, or, in other words, to make it more "capitalistic" (Aganbegyan, 1988, 1989; Lapidus, 1988). The Hungarian economist János Kornai (1992), one of the world's leading experts on the political economy of state socialism, has argued that the economic difficulties that motivated Gorbachev's reform efforts were inherent in the socialist system from the very beginning, even if it took Soviet leaders a long time to recognize this. According to Kornai, when market principles are absent from an economy, that economy has no way to achieve rational wages and prices. Since it is bureaucratic fiat rather than the level of consumer demand that establishes prices, the level of supply will fail to be in harmony with demand. Whatever is produced will be consumed; and, since producers are not motivated by considerations of profit to produce any given product, large quantities of that product, or a product of high quality, production is adjusted to giving the minimum effort or simply to meeting established quotas. This leads to underproduction and chronic shortages. Moreover, the socialist economy was structured so that there was little incentive to innovate technologically, which meant that it lagged technologically and therefore became technologically dependent on the West.

Perestroika as a strategy of economic reform was accompanied by a strategy of political reform known as *glasnost,* which means "openness." It was oriented toward giving more freedom to the media to report events accurately and thoroughly and to providing greater freedom of speech and artistic and intellectual expression. It also provided for the election of some public officials to office. *Glasnost* was the political counterpart of *perestroika.* Gorbachev and other Soviet leaders seemed to think that a more market-oriented economy required a much more liberal and open political system (Kumar, 2001). However, *glasnost* was only the bare beginning of political change in this part of the world.

In most Eastern European countries, as noted at the beginning of the chapter, market principles played a larger role in the economy, especially in Yugoslavia and Hungary, and most of the countries introduced reforms in the 1980s (Bulgaria had its own version of *perestroika,* and Hungary its own versions of both *perestroika* and *glasnost*). Hungary went the farthest (Holmes, 1997; Stokes, 1993). By 1980 Hungary had involved itself the most in the world market, with the largest number of private enterprises and consumer goods, and by 1983 it had established the most capitalistic joint venture regulations of any Eastern European country. By 1985, "various alternate forms of ownership had become a vital part of the Hungarian economy, producing about one-third of the national income" (Stokes, 1993:85).

1989: The Revolutions Against Communism in Eastern Europe

In mid- to late 1989, Poland, Hungary, East Germany, Czechoslovakia, Romania, and Bulgaria experienced major transformations in their authoritarian regimes. In each society, the Communist Party lost its monopoly over political power and steps were taken toward more democratic and open political regimes. (In 1990, Yugoslovia split apart into five separate states, most of which moved in a more democratic and capitalist direction, but there was really nothing that could be called a revolution.) Let us look at the specific events in each of these countries.

Poland

Poland was the first of the Eastern European socialist societies to experience overt discontent on the part of the masses during the decade that led to the breakdown of Communism. In 1980 the party known as Solidarity (*Solidarnösc*) was formed under the leadership of Lech Wałęsa, an electrician in Gdansk. The party's main concerns were a desire for economic reforms that would provide workers with greater security, the legalization of unions and strikes, and greater democracy. Protests started slowly but, as they became more widespread, Communist Party head General Jaruzelski decided that the government needed to act. Some of Solidarity's leaders were arrested, martial law was announced, and Solidarity was made illegal. However, the movement by no means disappeared; it was merely driven underground. It continued to work behind the scenes and retained widespread popular support. In fact, not even all of its activities went underground, for demonstrations and protests still occurred from time to time. Throughout the 1980s, it seemed clear to Jaruzelski that Solidarity was a force to be reckoned with, and he appeared to recognize that the government would have to share some power with the opposition. In September of 1986 he offered complete amnesty to underground Solidarity leaders, but there was disagreement among these leaders about whether to accept it. Wałęsa concluded that Solidarity should accept a partial amnesty, with some of its members emerging into full view and others remaining underground and continuing their clandestine activities. And, indeed, this is what happened (Stokes, 1993).

Later, Jaruzelski established a special council that included representatives from diverse segments of Polish society. He also followed in the new Soviet tradition of *glasnost* and liberalized censorship, allowing, for example, the publication of the works of previously forbidden authors such as George Orwell and Milan Kundera. Jaruzelski was attempting to make concessions toward a more open society in order to stabilize the country. The government even agreed to share power with Solidarity (although not on an equal basis), making it clear that the Communist Party would still be the leading political force in society (Stokes, 1993).

Throughout the 1980s economic conditions grew consistently worse, and this intensified popular discontent against the regime. The worsening economy, combined with the new political openings that were occurring, led to major strikes in 1988. At this point the government knew that it had to enter into more serious and open negotiations with Solidarity. Negotiations began, and on April 6, 1989, a series of agreements were reached. Solidarity would be relegalized. A bicameral legislature would be established, consisting of an upper house, or Senate, and a lower house, or Sejm. Seats in the Senate would be openly contested, but the seats in the Sejm would be filled somewhat differently, with 65 percent of them contested only by the Polish United Workers Party and 35 percent contested by candidates from the opposition. (Then, in four years, elections would become completely open and free.) Finally, it was agreed that the two houses of the legislature would elect a president of the country (Stokes, 1993).

The elections were held two months later, and the results were extraordinary. All 161 seats in the Sejm were won by representatives from Solidarity, as were 99 of the 100 seats available to them in the Senate. Moreover, 33 of the 35 principal Communist candidates were unable to garner the 50 percent of the vote they needed in order to be considered in a runoff election, and so the Sejm would have little representation from the Communists. The outcome was clear: Voters had overwhelmingly rejected Communist leadership (Gross, 1992; Stokes, 1993).

But the president and prime minister still had to be chosen. The Sejm elected Jaruzelski president, and wanted General Kiszczak as his prime minister. However, this choice proved to be extremely unpopular, and much political wrangling followed. The person eventually chosen was Tadeusz Mazowiecki. On August 24, 1989, he was installed "as the first non-Communist prime minister of an East European state in almost forty years. The sad-faced Mazowiecki was so overwhelmed that he fainted during the ceremonies. No wonder. The dramatic turn of events had left the entire world somewhat lightheaded" (Stokes, 1993:130).

Hungary

Opposition to the Communist regime existed in Hungary in the 1970s and early 1980s, but it was very minor and had little effect. The situation began to change in 1985, and it is probably not coincidental that this is the year that Gorbachev came to power in the Soviet Union. In the same year, elections were held that, under a new law requiring multiple candidates for office, brought 43 independent candidates into the parliament. In 1986 democratic opponents of the regime, along with other critics, met to discuss political reform, and in 1987 and 1988 the reform process picked up speed. In May of 1988, the aging general secretary of the Communist Party, János Kádár, was removed from office and replaced by Károly Grósz. By the end of the year, "dozens of new clubs and organizations had appeared, the regime was on the verge of permitting political parties, and the Hungarian Socialist Workers' Party had moved away from its claim to be the sole legitimate political force" (Stokes, 1993:93–94). Political and economic reformers had begun to gain the upper hand, and Hungarian versions of *perestroika* and *glasnost* were under way (Stokes, 1993).

In early 1989 power was passing into the hands of the most radical of the reformers. Imre Pozsgay declared the socialist path to have been completely misguided, and some weeks later the party's central committee, in a draft of a constitution it was writing, rejected the idea that Marxism-Leninism should be the leading power in society. In March a series of organized celebrations and demonstrations began.

November 7 had been a national holiday to celebrate the October Bolshevik Revolution, but the opposition requested that March 15 become a national day of celebration in its place; the government consented, and on the day in question some 30,000 people showed up to celebrate. This new holiday had great symbolic meaning for the opposition, because it represented a discrediting of Marxism-Leninism. A second demonstration involved a march of approximately 100,000 people that had been carefully organized by opposition forces. In the words of Gale Stokes:

> Organizers meticulously planned this march so that over a five-hour period it stopped at six locations in central Budapest that had significant links to both Hungarian revolutions, the one of 1848 and the one of 1956. For instance, the first stop was the statue of Sándor Petöfi, the poet of the 1848 revolution whose statue marked the spot where the demonstration of October 23, 1956, started. The last stop was Batthyany Square, the traditional end point of antigovernment demonstrations in 1956 and once again a memorial to a hero of the 1848 revolution. (1993:100–101)

But the largest and most significant demonstration was still to come. On June 16, 1989, some 250,000 people assembled in Heroes Square in Budapest in order to engage in another act of great political symbolism. The body of Imre Nagy, a Hungarian leader of the defeated revolution of 1956, was disinterred and scheduled for reburial. This combined demonstration-celebration, which lasted eight hours, was broadcast on national television and watched by millions of spellbound Hungarians. In the days leading up to this great demonstration, and for many days afterward, negotiations between Communist Party officials and the main opposition leaders were carried out. The outcome was an agreement to construct a new government, for which elections were eventually held in March and April of 1990. The Hungarian Socialist Party—essentially the old Communists—won only 8 percent of the seats in parliament. The Hungarian Democratic Forum won the largest number of votes (43 percent), followed by the Independent Smallholders (11 percent). A new government was formed that officially embraced the principles of liberal democracy and that was committed to helping steer the Hungarian economy in a much more capitalistic direction (Bruszt and Stark, 1992; Stokes, 1993).

East Germany

By the late 1980s political tensions in the German Democratic Republic—East Germany—had grown significantly. A unique feature of East German society was that its largest city, Berlin, was physically, socially, economically, and politically divided, and its two segments belonged to two different sovereign states. Since the standard of living in West Berlin was much higher than in East Berlin, it was easy for East Berliners to see how far behind they were, not to mention their lack of cultural, intellectual, and political freedom. This contributed significantly to the growth of political tensions. A certain amount of immigration to West Germany from East Germany had long been permitted, but many more East Germans wanted to leave the country than the immigration quotas allowed for.

In May of 1989 the barbed wire along the border between Hungary and Austria was torn down by Hungarians, and hundreds of East Germans tried to cross the border illegally. Many other East Germans made their way to West German embassies in Warsaw, Prague, and Budapest (Naimark, 1992). On September 11, it was announced that East Germans "waiting in Hungary and any who wished to do so in the future could cross into Austria and make for West Germany. Eleven thousand people immediately crammed themselves into buses, trains, and chugging two-stroke Trabant cars and set out for arrival centers already prepared for them in West Germany" (Stokes, 1993:136). The desire to flee had become intense.

By October mass demonstrations were occurring throughout East Germany. On October 2, a demonstration occurred in Leipzig and, following a visit by Gorbachev on October 7, mass demonstrations occurred the next day in Leipzig, Berlin, Potsdam, Dresden, and other cities. The situation became critical on October 9; rumors of a severe military crackdown on the demonstrators had spread, and in fact Erich Honecker, the East German president, apparently did order that the demonstrations should be put down by force. Nevertheless, 70,000 to 80,000 demonstrators took to the streets in Leipzig shouting "We are the people" and "Gorbi, Gorbi." The size of the demonstrations escalated, markedly and quickly. By October 16 there were 150,000 demonstrators, a week later some 200,000, and on November 6 as many as half a million. In the midst of these demonstrations (on October 18), Honecker resigned and was replaced by Egon Krenz. Since many people regarded Krenz as worse than Honecker, this may actually have contributed to the escalation of the demonstrations. But the more important factor was undoubtedly people's recognition that the government was, in the end, not willing to use force to stop them (Naimark, 1992).

The climax came on the evening of November 9. Demonstrators gathered along the Berlin Wall and, within a short time, began to tear parts of it down, an event that was broadcast live on television throughout the Western world. November 9 became "the day the frontiers were opened" (Brown, 1991). Less than a month later, on December 3, the entire East German Politburo and Central Committee resigned, and the East German state essentially collapsed. Talk of reunification with West Germany, already in the air, intensified, and reunification became a reality on January 1, 1992.

Czechoslovakia

Czechoslovakia lagged well behind the Eastern European countries already discussed in the vigor and size of its oppositional movements, but it did have them. The main oppositional group, known as Charter 77, was led by Vaclàv Havel, a Czech playwright. Because of their outspokenness, Havel and five other critics of the regime were imprisoned in 1979. Havel was released in 1983, but only because he contracted pneumonia. Charter 77 consisted primarily of intellectuals, most of whom were Czechs. Among Slovaks, there were few Charter 77 members, and opposition existed more in the form of everyday people who engaged in pilgrimages and who signed a petition opposing the government. In 1988, political opposition became somewhat more confrontational. The leader of the Czechoslovak Communist Party, Miloš Jakeš, publicly stated support for Gorbachev's reforms, but when things became tense he had demonstrators arrested and put in "preventive detention." In December of 1988, demonstrators were sprayed with hoses, and the person who supervised this spraying, Miroslav Štìpàn, indicated that the government was not interested in any kind of dialogue. On January 15, 1989, around 4,000 individuals assembled in Wenceslas Square in defiance of a government ban. The crowd was charged by the police, who beat several hundred and arrested a hundred. For five consecutive days, street crowds and the police battled each other. One of the demonstrators to be arrested was Havel, who was given a nine-month prison sentence (Stokes, 1993).

Tensions grew in the months to come, reaching the boiling point in November. On November 17 the Socialist Youth Union organized a student ceremony in Prague intended to commemorate the killing of a Czech student fifty years earlier by the Nazis. There were some 30,000 participants, and leaders spoke out against the regime, calling for economic reforms and democratization. Several thousand demonstrators made their way along Narodni Street toward Wenceslas Square, but their way was blocked by the police and some of the students were beaten. Things escalated rapidly after that. On November 18 some 400 theater people voted to go on strike and "On Strike" signs were placed in front of theaters throughout the country. That evening Havel organized a meeting of the principal oppositional groups. On November 19, in Bratislava, a number of Slovak writers, artists, and intellectuals met and formed a group known as *Verejnost' proti nasiliu,* or VPN (in English, "Public Against Violence"). On the evening of November 20, Wenceslas Square was filled with hundreds of thousands of people chanting such slogans as "Now is the time" and "This is it." For several nights to come, huge crowds continued to gather in Wenceslas Square and in other cities. On November 22, a message from Alexander Dubček, the leader of the Prague Spring of 1968, was read to the crowd in Wenceslas Square, and the next day Dubček addressed some 50,000 people in Bratislava. On November 24, Jakeš resigned as general secretary of the Czechoslovak Communist Party, and on November 25, Havel addressed hundreds of thousands in Prague. On November 27, a two-hour general strike took place in cities throughout the country. On December 9, the Czechoslovak president, Gustav Husák, resigned, and a coalition government consisting mostly of non-Communists took power. Soon thereafter, Havel was elected president. A revolution—what was later to be called a "velvet revolution" because of the absence of violence—had occurred in yet another Eastern European country in the same fateful year (Judt, 1992; Stokes, 1993).

Romania

Romania was one of the poorest of the Eastern European state socialist societies, and it remains so today. For a quarter-century it was led by Nicolae Ceauşescu, the closest thing in Eastern Europe to a Third

World neopatrimonial dictator. His regime was so focused on his and his family's self-aggrandizement that Romania has been jokingly referred to as a case of "socialism in one family." What was Ceauşescu like, and how did he govern?

The Romanian economy was extremely inefficient in its use of energy for heavy industry, and thus Ceauşescu allowed citizens to have only one 40-watt light bulb in each room of their house. Cities and towns had little light in the evenings, and in the winter apartment temperatures seldom rose above the mid-50s. Sometimes people actually froze to death in their own homes and apartments. Ceauşescu also encouraged fertility and child birth in order to increase the supply of labor. To make sure women were not having abortions (which were illegal, as were oral contraceptives), he required women to submit to random gynecological examinations at their workplaces. These examinations were intended to check on whether women were having their menstrual cycle and, if pregnant, whether they were carrying their pregnancies to full term (Stokes, 1993).

Ceauşescu also used his dictatorial powers with respect to the economy and the workplace (Stokes, 1993). For example, when production levels in the coal mines declined, he ordered work schedules of twenty-four hours a day, seven days a week; miners were given two days off for May Day celebrations, but they had to make up the missed work in overtime. When food supplies were short, he ordered all farmers with private plots to provide the state with a pig, a cow, several dozen chickens, ten rabbits, or a swarm of bees per year; if they failed to do so, they were at risk of losing their plots. Stokes (1993:159) tells us more:

> And what about the food shortages, the lines, the brownouts, and the rusted-out buses that were hauling Romania back into the nineteenth century? Nonsense. The official statistics showed that the consumption of agricultural goods was growing every year "in accordance with the needs of the population." And what if the statistics did not show this in reality? Make them up. In October 1989 Ceauşescu announced that grain production that year had reached sixty million tons. In fact, figures released after the revolution showed it had been fewer than seventeen million tons.

Ceauşescu was also inclined toward massive construction projects that would glorify the state, and, of course, himself in return (Stokes, 1993). In one case he had a beautiful eighteenth-century monastery, one of the largest in southeastern Europe, razed and built a huge complex in its place. Called the Center of the National Councils of Workers' Democracy, it consisted mostly of a large number of meeting halls, one of which would have had a capacity of 12,000 and a dome three times the size of St. Peter's in Rome. The building was never actually completed. In another case, he evicted thousands of persons from their homes and destroyed eighteen churches and dozens of historically significant structures in order to put up something called the House of the Republic. This was a gigantic palace that has been compared to Nero's palace in ancient Rome. The building was completed on the outside but never on the inside, "a grandiloquent monument to Ceauşescu's utter lack of feeling for the human dimension of life and his desperate need for contrived and unassailable grandeur" (Stokes, 1993:160). And there was more—much more.

In addition to all this, Ceauşescu maintained a secret police force, the Securitate, that allowed him to persist in his severe political repression of the overall population. The Securitate was the Romanian version of the famed Soviet KGB and Iranian SAVAK. Under all of these circumstances, it was difficult for opposition to take root and, if it did, to come out into the open. But in 1989 it did at last. Several poets and literary figures were among the first. Doina Cornea, a specialist in French literature, wrote Ceauşescu an open letter accusing him of destroying people's innermost being and of humiliating their aspirations; the poet Mircea Dinescu praised the Soviet reforms when he visited the Soviet Union in 1988 (as a result of which he lost his editorial post); three editors of Romania's second most important newspaper, *România Liberă*, tried to publish an anti-Ceauşescu edition of the paper (for which they were given death sentences); and six former senior officials of the Romanian Communist Party sent a letter to Ceauşescu in which they listed what they considered to be his huge failures. However, none of these acts of protest had any real impact on the leader, and even in late November, with Communism collapsing all around him in other Eastern European countries, Ceauşescu convened the Fourteenth Party Congress, gave his traditional six-hour speech, criticized other Eastern European countries for abandoning socialism, and accepted reelection as president of Romania (Stokes, 1993).

Ceauşescu may have felt secure, but he was nothing of the kind. On December 10, some parishioners organized a vigil outside a church in Timişoara to protest the removal of their minister, László Tökés. (Tökés was being sent to a church in a remote village because he had criticized the regime on a number of counts.) The crowd was small at first, but it grew to about a thousand by December 15. By the next evening, some 5,000 persons had assembled around party headquarters in Timişoara. On December 17, Ceauşescu ordered that the demonstrators be gunned down, and that night the army fired upon the crowd and killed some hundred persons. Demonstrations continued nonetheless. On December 19, the army, unhappy with Ceauşescu for a variety of very good reasons, began to withdraw and, within a few days, essentially switched its loyalty from Ceauşescu to the people. Stokes (1993:165–166) tells us how the revolution came to be:

> The events of the next three days were then and remain today enormously confusing. Fundamentally, what happened is that the army decided to side with the people in the streets, probably in cooperation with a group of plotters who quickly arranged to form the National Salvation Front (*Frontul Salvarii Nationale—FSN*). Serious fighting seemed to break out in the center of Bucharest on December 22, the day the self-selected leaders of the FSN appeared on television to proclaim themselves the new provisional government. This fighting ... was ostensibly between the army, now loyal to the nation, and the Securitate forces, still loyal to Ceauşescu.

By the evening of December 22 crowds were threatening the central committee building in Palace Square. Ceauşescu, still somehow believing in his powers to command the masses, tried to speak to the people, but the microphone did not work, and it became apparent that the crowds were entering the building. Along with Elena, Ceauşescu managed to flee by helicopter only a few steps ahead of the angry insurgents. The Ceauşescus had several options at this point—to fly to a prepared military location and fight back, to escape abroad, or, apparently as Nicolae himself preferred, to fly to an area like his native Oltenia, where he felt the workers supported him. Instead, the helicopter that was supposedly taking them to safety landed before reaching whatever was to be its destination. After a farcical commandeering of a passing truck the Ceauşescus fell into the hands of the new government. Three days later, on December 25, after a kangaroo trial that lasted nine hours, Nicolae and Elena Ceauşescu were found guilty of genocide and shot to death by a firing squad.

With the old government destroyed, a provisional government took over, and Ion Iliescu, leader of the National Salvation Front, was elected president of Romania on May 20, 1990, capturing 85 percent of the vote.

Bulgaria

The 1980s in Bulgaria was a period of economic crisis, which grew especially severe in the second half of the decade. Bulgaria's leader, Todor Zhivkov, claimed to have been introducing economic reforms—*pereustroistvo*, the Bulgarian *perestroika*—that would alleviate the crisis, but in fact there was much more talk than action. In 1988 Zhivkov faced opposition within his own party. In July of that year, during a party plenum, a faction of the party began to discuss not only the need to replace Zhivkov but also how they were going to accomplish it. Much of the Bulgarian intelligentsia no longer supported the regime, and their opposition continued to grow into the early months of 1989. As many as nine opposition movements may have existed by March. In July, over a hundred persons, some of them prominent oppositionists, appealed to the national assembly over the government's expulsion of Turks, claiming that it was humiliating to the country. In August they made another, even stronger, appeal. In October, Petur Mladenov, the minister of foreign affairs, sent a letter of resignation to Zhivkov, accusing him of dragging the country down to the level of Romania. On November 9—the very same day that the East Germans began dismantling the Berlin Wall—a majority of the Bulgarian politburo came out against Zhivkov. This faction of the party controlled the army, and in fact had already moved four army units into Sofia in case Zhivkov would not go willingly. But, in fact, he did, resigning the very next day. He was replaced by Mladenov, who later announced that it was necessary for Bulgaria to become a democratic and pluralist society. He expelled Zhivkov from the party, permitted freedom of speech, renounced the party's leading role, and called for free elections to be held in the spring of 1990 (Stokes, 1993; Todorova, 1992).

1991: The Revolution Against Communism in the Soviet Union

When Gorbachev inaugurated *perestroika* and *glasnost* after 1985, he intended them as reforms within state socialism itself. He did not want to replace socialism with capitalism, but only to make it more market oriented. And he did not want to replace the Communist

Party as the leading political force in the Soviet Union, but only to make the political system more open and democratic. However, Gorbachev in fact unleashed forces that he incompletely understood and was ultimately unable to control. These forces in the end spelled his own undoing, and that of the Soviet Union itself.

Shortly after the momentous events of late 1989 in Eastern Europe, momentous events began to unfold in the Soviet Union. In March of 1990 Gorbachev was elected to the new position of president of the Soviet Union, although by the Party Congress rather than by the people. In June, the Russian Supreme Soviet elected Boris Yeltsin president of the Russian Republic. Gorbachev and Yeltsin had once been allies but had turned into enemies, and Yeltsin's election intensified the power struggle between them. In July the Communist Party held its Twenty-Eighth Congress, during which Yeltsin resigned from the party, along with the mayors of Moscow and Leningrad. The legitimacy of the party was thus being increasingly called into question. Indeed, this was already becoming obvious earlier in the year. In March, Article 6 of the Soviet Constitution, which guaranteed the Communist Party the leading role within Soviet political life, was abandoned (Holmes, 1997).

By mid-1990 the three Soviet Baltic republics—Estonia, Lithuania, and Latvia—had announced their intention to become independent states. They were quickly followed by Ukraine and the Russian Republic itself. In March of 1991 a referendum was called on whether the Soviet Union should be preserved. The referendum was boycotted by six of the fifteen Soviet republics, but a majority of Soviet citizens who voted favored the retention of the Soviet Union in one form or another. Following this referendum, Gorbachev held talks with the leaders of the republics that had not boycotted it, and they signed a pact—often called the Novo-Ugarevo agreement—declaring an intention to preserve the Soviet state. The signing of the Novo-Ugarevo agreement seemed to bring Yeltsin and Gorbachev closer together, but this was illusory, or at any rate did not last (Holmes, 1997).

Nevertheless, what Gorbachev and Yeltsin did have in common was that they were both reformers who favored a more market-oriented and democratic society. Both had to contend not only with each other but with the conservatives as well. These were the Communist hardliners who strongly opposed reforms altogether. In August of 1991, a small group of hardliners attempted a *coup d'état* against Gorbachev. While Gorbachev was spending a few days at his *dacha* (country home), the *coup* plotters, led by Soviet Vice-President Gennadii Yanaev and a number of other leading officials, took him hostage and claimed control of the government. But the *coup* failed miserably, lasting a mere three days. It turned out to be a major precipitating event, however, because it created a kind of political vacuum that Yeltsin and his supporters were able to exploit in order to gain control of the major political institutions in the various republics. Back in Moscow, Gorbachev was humiliated on national television by Yeltsin, who clearly now had the upper hand. Gorbachev and the Communist Party became increasingly discredited, and Gorbachev's formal political life from this point on was essentially finished, as was the Soviet Union. The *coup* attempt created fears in the various Soviet republics that another attempt (this time successful, perhaps) was always possible. In the context of already-existing strong nationalistic sentiments, the republics formulated plans, one after the other, to secede from the Soviet Union and establish themselves as sovereign states. On Christmas Day, 1991, Gorbachev resigned his post and the Soviet Union was officially dissolved (Hahn, 2002; Holmes, 1997).

Gorbachev had been caught between the proverbial rock and a hard place. His reforms alienated the hardliners, but his failure to pursue them far enough and fast enough alienated the more radical reformers, such as Yeltsin. These vicissitudes caused Gorbachev to become politically disoriented, first turning one way and then another (and then back again), and his vacillations contributed heavily to his undoing. And the failed *coup* was the great turning point. As Gordon Hahn (2002:448–449) has remarked:

> The coup and its failure largely exhausted the possibilities of gradual change by imposed or negotiated transition and permitted the final overthrow of the party apparat from above. The intimidated hardliners lost control over their key institutional power bases.... The correlation of political forces shifted clearly in favor of the opposition, aborting the Novo Ogarevo pact under a new Union Treaty. Regime hardliners and softliners were weakened by the failed coup and the dissolution of key regime institutions. Regime softliners were discredited by their association with the regime and were no longer able to pose credibly the hardline coup threat to contain opposition moderates.
>
> The institutional arena was fundamentally transformed, as the CPSU [Communist Party of the Soviet Union] and other basic institutions of the partocratic regime were swept away in Russia's takeover of political

power and numerous Union structures. ... The party and its apparat were banned, the USSR parliament replaced, the KGB, military, and MVD discredited, and their leaders replaced. The regime's overthrow in turn facilitated almost complete collapse of the Soviet state....

By December, Russia's revolutionaries would complete their extra-legal seizure of political power with little mass participation and no violence, execution, emigration, or counter-revolution.

Explaining the Revolutions Against Communism

With a few notable exceptions, everyone was surprised by the collapse of Communism (Goldstone, 1995; Lipset and Bence, 1994). It was hard to believe that a party with the level of political and military control that the Communist Party had achieved could be removed from power except with great difficulty. But, indeed, it happened. As to why it happened, there have been a variety of explanations. Explaining the Communist collapse is a somewhat different matter for Eastern Europe than for the Soviet Union, and the revolutions in Eastern Europe occurred two years earlier than the Soviet state breakdown, so I shall discuss them separately.

Eastern Europe

Revolutions, or at least most of them, involve discontent on the part of large segments of the population. However, as we have seen, discontent usually produces only revolutionary *situations* rather than revolutionary *outcomes*. It takes more than simply discontent to produce something as substantial as a genuine social revolution. Discontent had long been present in Eastern Europe, although it was greater in some countries than others and greater at some times than others. But it was basically a constant throughout Eastern Europe since the advent of Communism there.

There were two major revolutionary situations in Eastern Europe that failed to turn into revolutions. In 1956, a revolutionary situation occurred in Hungary. Former Prime Minister Imre Nagy, a relative liberal by Communist standards who was briefly returned to power, advocated radical change. He announced Hungary's desire to withdraw from the Warsaw Pact, a coalition of state socialist nations, and he wanted the United Nations to recognize Hungary as a neutral country. The Soviet Union, however, refused to tolerate such actions and invaded Hungary with tanks. People took to the streets to resist, but some 20,000 were killed by Soviet soldiers. The uprising was crushed and the revolutionary situation neutralized (Holmes, 1997). Then, in 1968, Czechoslovakia's liberal leader, Alexander Dubček, pushed for liberalization of the Czechoslovak regime and, again, people demonstrated. But the result was similar to that in Hungary a decade earlier. Soviet tanks appeared in Prague and the uprising was quickly defeated, although there was little bloodshed this time.

What was different about 1989? Why did revolutionary situations in this year produce revolutionary outcomes when revolutionary actions were forcibly repressed in 1956 and 1968? The answer is the changed relationship between the Eastern European countries and the Soviet Union (Kumar, 2001). For several decades the Eastern European countries were satellites of the Soviet Union and were expected to conduct their affairs only with Soviet consent. They had a limited capacity to act autonomously, and this certainly did not extend to abandoning socialism and the dominance of the Communist Party. But by 1989 Gorbachev had made it clear that the so-called Brezhnev Doctrine, requiring Eastern European allegiance to the Soviet Union and its principles, was no longer in effect. Eastern Europe now had the freedom to go its own way. This meant that the Soviet Union would not intervene militarily to quell popular discontent in Eastern Europe. Thus, it was no longer dangerous, as it had once certainly been, to challenge Soviet authority and try to liberalize the Eastern European political regimes. To put it in the language used earlier in discussing the causes of both the Great Revolutions and revolutions in the Third World, the changed attitude of the Soviet state had made states in Eastern Europe *much weaker and highly vulnerable* to revolutionary discontent. It is in just such circumstances that movements to overthrow an old system in favor of a new one are most likely to succeed. With Soviet authority in Eastern Europe now gone, people were no longer afraid to take to the streets and demand that the long-hated repressive regimes be dismantled. This is what had changed—or at least it was one of the major things that had changed.

And the matter was made much easier for ordinary persons when their outlook was shared even by many members of the Eastern European Communist elites themselves. In fact, what exactly was the role of the masses in bringing about the 1989 revolutions? According to Krishan Kumar (2001), their role was largely that of destroying structures that were already in a state of advanced decay. In his view, one shared by many other scholars (e.g., Banac, 1992; Bruszt and Stark, 1992), the Eastern European revolutions were primarily *revolutions from above*. These are revolutions led by one segment of the political elite against the remainder of that elite. In true revolutions from above, mass action either does not exist or is inconsequential in determining the outcome. The Eastern European revolutions were not pristine examples of this type of revolution, since mass action was involved in every single case and played at least some role in bringing down the old regime. But the "from above" element clearly took priority over the "from below" element. Let us allow Kumar (2001:44–45) to speak for himself:

> In book 8 of *The Republic* Plato observed that "in any form of government revolution always starts from the outbreak of internal dissension in the ruling class. The constitution cannot be upset so long as that class is of one mind, however small it may be." This statement may need some qualification, but its essential truth stands up remarkably well. Was that not shown, as well as anywhere, in the revolutions of 1989? No one has doubted the widespread feeling of discontent, even despair, among the populations of East European societies for many decades. The evidence has been plain to see, not the least in the revolts or urgent attempts at reform in East Germany in 1953, in Hungary and Poland in 1956, in Czechoslovakia in 1968, and in Poland again in 1980. All were suppressed, sometimes brutally. After the suppression of Solidarity in 1981, many observers predicted a long period of resentful quiescence in the countries of the Soviet bloc.
>
> They were wrong. In the second half of the 1980s first Poland, then with gathering speed other communist societies, began to reform. Reform turned, in the space of a few breathless months in 1989, into revolution. How was that possible? Popular rebellions had repeatedly failed. Liberal attempts at reform had been crushed. The dissident intelligentsia was largely impotent. Why did change finally occur at that time—and change on a scale scarcely dreamed of by even the most hopeful reformer?
>
> The answer, in a word, is as banal as it is inevitable: Gorbachev. Gorbachev was replaying Khrushchev with a vengeance. Just as the

latter's denunciation of Stalin at the Twentieth Congress of the Communist Party of the Soviet Union in 1956 sparked the Hungarian and Polish uprisings of that year, so the former's unleashing of the forces of *glasnost* and *perestroika* sparked the revolutions of 1989.

Kumar (2001:269–273) goes so far as to suggest that Gorbachev did much more than just *permit* the 1989 revolutions; he was directly involved in them and thus actually *encouraged* them. To wit:

Item: In East Germany, Soviet military advisers were told to tell Honecker not to use force against the demonstrators in Leipzig on October 9, 1989. It may well have been the case that Soviet advisers were instructed to intervene if necessary in order to prevent a massacre of the type that had occurred in Tiananmen Square in China. Moreover, when Gorbachev visited East Germany on October 7, he told Honecker that Soviet troops would not come to East Germany's support against the demonstrators, and also encouraged Egon Krenz and other party leaders to get rid of Honecker.

Item: In Czechoslovakia, a government commission concluded that the beating of demonstrators on November 17, 1989, was actually carefully orchestrated by the head of the Czechoslovak state security police in conjunction with the KGB. "Their plan was to create the violence in which the marchers were beaten in Narodni street. To this end, *agents provocateurs* who were actually StB [state security police] officers but posing as student leaders led the demonstrators into the confined space where the beatings took place. One of the StB officers then impersonated a mathematics student, Martin Smid, and a further conspirator, Dragomira Draşska, carried the news of Smid's supposed death at the hands of the security forces to dissident sources.... The primary purpose was to cause the overthrow of the Jakeš and Husák regime as a result of popular fury and to open the way for the installation of a moderate reformist communist, Zdenek Mlynar, as president in place of Husák" (Prins, 1990:116–117; also cited in Kumar, 2001:270).

Item: In Hungary, at a special meeting of the Hungarian Socialist Workers' Party in May of 1988, Soviet officials "gave their blessing" to the removal from office of Hungarian President János Kádár. Later that year, Soviet reformer Alexander Yakovlev said on a visit to Hungary that the Soviets did not object to the Hungarian Communist

Party's abandoning its monopoly on power. In March of 1989, new Hungarian President Károly Grósz returned from a visit to Moscow to report that Gorbachev had indicated that he did not intend to intervene in Hungary's process of economic and political reform. In April, Soviet troops began to withdraw from Hungary. And at the June 16, 1989, celebration in which the body of Imre Nagy was scheduled for reburial, the leaders of all of the Warsaw Pact countries except Romania sent delegations, "thereby symbolically giving their acquiescence and approval to Hungary's bloodless revolution" (Kumar, 2001:271).

Item: In Poland, Soviet leaders appeared quite willing to accept the reforms that were occurring in which Jaruzelski's government gave up its monopoly on power and entered into a coalition government with Solidarity. In July of 1989, Romania's Ceauşescu asked Gorbachev to intervene against Solidarity, but he steadfastly refused.

Item: In Bulgaria, Soviet leaders gave their support to the plotters of the coup against Zhivkov. In November of 1989, Petur Mladenov, one of the coup's leaders, made a stop in Moscow on his return from China, during which he apparently was given a "final briefing" by Soviet officials on just how to handle the coup.

Item: Soviet leaders had long wanted to see Ceauşescu deposed, and their opposition to his policies was clearly stated at a Warsaw Pact meeting in Bucharest in 1989.

Nonetheless, in every one of the Eastern European revolutions there was at least some mass action, and it did play some role in bringing the revolutions about. It is instructive to compare these revolutions in terms of the relative contributions of "top-down" and "bottom-up" forces. Ranking the revolutions from the most to the least top-down would produce, I think, essentially the following list: East Germany, Czechoslovakia, Bulgaria, Hungary, Poland, and Romania (Bruszt and Stark, 1992; Holmes, 1997; Stokes, 1993). However, things become somewhat more complicated when we realize that the top-down forces emanated from either the national Communist elite, the Soviet Communist elite, or some combination of the two. Let us look at each of these six cases with these ideas in mind.

In East Germany, Erich Honecker's regime took a consistently hard line, and even intended to fire on protesters during some of the mass demonstrations. However, the real problem for East Germany was its recognition that it did not have the backing of the Soviet Union, which it felt it needed in order to retain its regime. Thus, the top-down forces in the revolution in East Germany were essentially Soviet forces rather than East German ones. Much of the mass action in Germany resulted from the fact that the people, and not just the government, realized that Soviet troops were unlikely to intervene to quell popular discontent.

In the Czechoslovak case, its oppositional movements were relatively weak and gained strength only toward the end of the 1980s. There was a great deal of mass action in November of 1989, but, as noted earlier, some of the demonstrators were apparently Czechoslovak security police officers who were orchestrating, in conjunction with Soviet officials, the limited violence that did take place. Thus, both the Czechoslovak elite and the Soviet elite were the major forces in bringing Communism down in Czechoslovakia, making the revolution there very much a top-down affair.

The revolution in Bulgaria was also largely a top-down affair (Holmes, 1997). Todor Zhivkov faced a great deal of opposition in his own party and lost the support of the intelligentsia. His effort to expel the Turks embarrassed many of his own party members, and Soviet officials as well. Zhivkov was brought down primarily by a *coup*, to which Moscow not only consented but may have been instrumental in planning.

Of all the Eastern European societies, Hungary engaged in the most extensive economic and political reforms in the 1980s. From an early point it had introduced more market principles than any other Eastern European society, and an incipient capitalist class had begun to form (Stokes, 1993). As of 1985, after the Thirteenth Party Congress, the party reformers ascended into the majority, and forty-three independent candidates were elected to parliament. In 1988, when János Kádár was replaced by Károly Grósz, Hungary's own version of *perestroika* began, and the Hungarian press strongly promoted it. By 1989 the radical reformers had clearly gained the upper hand. The critical moment, if there was one, was the celebration in Heroes Square in Budapest to rebury Imre Nagy, before, during, and after which negotiations took place between the government and the oppositional forces concerning the establishment of a multiparty electoral system (Bruszt and Stark, 1992; Stokes, 1993).

Poland was similar to Hungary in that it was also a case of negotiated compromise between the oppositional forces and the government.

However, in Poland the oppositional forces were stronger and the radical reformers weaker. Jaruzelski realized in 1989 that he had little choice but to relegalize Solidarity and negotiate a compromise with it. Solidarity emerged in 1980 but was declared illegal in 1981. Nevertheless, it remained powerful as an underground force and, in fact, grew more powerful throughout the 1980s. Jaruzelski devised various ways to deal with Solidarity leaders while keeping his regime intact, but his successes were only temporary. As Stokes (1993:122) has commented,

> Since 1986 at the latest, party leaders had "recognized the opposition as a lasting element on the country's political map," and in cautious ways they had been putting out feelers to that opposition ever since. That is why, when in August 1988 a second wave of strikes erupted, this time much more severe and much more widespread than in May, the government, realizing that these strikes introduced a qualitatively new element into the social equation, finally decided, after almost seven years of stonewalling, that it was time to negotiate openly with Solidarity, the enemy whom, at least, it knew.

Finally, what of Romania? On the surface, the bringing down of Ceauşescu's regime looks like a largely bottom-up affair. There was a great deal of mass action—the role of the masses in bringing down the Romanian government was greater than in any other Eastern European country (Holmes, 1997)—and demonstrators were fired upon by Ceauşescu's troops. The army switched sides and supported the people, and Ceauşescu and his wife were hunted down, tried, and promptly executed. Stokes (1993:166) comments to the effect that "it would be a mistake to concentrate on conscious actions put into effect by plotters [among the elite]. The Romanian revolution was accomplished by the spontaneous and self-activating actions of hundreds of thousands of people across Romania who acted courageously at a time when it was not at all clear that several decades of serious repression was about to end." However, appearances can be deceiving, for there was also a great deal of top-down activity in Romania. Ceauşescu was replaced by Ion Iliescu and his allies, the National Salvation Front, who were members of the Communist Party. It appears that Iliescu and his associates had been planning a *coup* against Ceauşescu for many months, and it has even been suggested that the conflict between the army and the Securitate was staged, although this has been strongly disputed (Verdery and Kligman, 1992). Katherine Verdery and Gail Kligman's (1992) suggestion seems the most sensible. They argue that the Romanian revolution was a more or less equal combination of top-down and bottom-up forces:

> It is virtually certain that without the popular uprising a coup d'etat would have had great difficulty overthrowing Ceauşescu (unless aided by foreign troops), and, at the same time, without the support of not just the army but at least a portion of the Securitate, no popular uprising could have succeeded. In our view, the revolution came from a fortuitous convergence of several elements: superpower interests, events in neighboring countries that permeated Romania's borders via the air waves, some sort of conspiracy at the top, and a long-incubated "movement of rage," culminating in a genuine popular uprising. None of these elements alone would have been sufficient. (1992:121–122)

To conclude, I think we end up with something like the following (but cf. Goodwin, 2001):

- *Largely Revolutions from Above:* East Germany, Czechoslovakia, Bulgaria.
- *Primarily Revolutions from Above, but with a Negotiated Transition:* Hungary, Poland.
- *Revolution from both Above and Below:* Romania.

The Soviet Union

If Gorbachev's renunciation of the Brezhnev Doctrine was so critical to the revolutions in Eastern Europe, what of the Soviet Union itself? The revolution there was essentially a pure case of revolution from above (Hahn, 2002). Mass action was negligible or nonexistent, and the regime was brought down by infighting within the political elite, which was severely divided on the direction the country should take. There were at least three major factions. First, there were the softliners, represented by Gorbachev himself, who endorsed economic and political reforms within the framework of maintaining the leading role of the Communist Party and the integrity of a socialist economy. To their right were the hardliners, who wanted little or no change in the old Communist system, from which they continued to benefit. It was the hardliners, of course, who led the failed August 1991 *coup.* Then to the softliners' left were the more radical reformers, led by Yeltsin, who felt that the softliners were too soft and that more radical and more rapid changes in the Soviet system were needed. Among these contending factions, we know who won.

Nevertheless, although the causes of the Soviet collapse were fundamentally political, these political causes were themselves rooted in the severe problems of Soviet economic functioning. As we have seen, Gorbachev's economic reforms were designed to deal with the problems of the Soviet economy that became especially serious after the mid-1970s. Randall Collins and David Waller (1992; Collins, 1986) have suggested that the Soviet state's overextension of its empire— the incorporation of previously sovereign states into the Soviet Union after 1917, and then again after World War II, and its political and military domination of Eastern Europe—resulted in huge economic costs, especially in military buildup, that became increasingly intolerable. It is extremely expensive to try to maintain an empire as large as that of the Soviet Union. Such an empire requires a large military apparatus and a host of additional political officials: Weapons have to be produced and soldiers have to be recruited, trained, and paid, as do the necessary political functionaries. Moreover, and even more significantly, quite apart from the huge costs of empire, a command economy suffers from enormous limitations (Chirot, 1995; Kornai, 1992). Soviet socialism worked relatively well for a time in achieving a fair amount of industrialization, but it was structurally incapable of making the transition to the production of the large number and variety of consumer goods characteristic of Western capitalism. The Soviet Union also suffered from severe international competition and the pressures of the surrounding capitalist world-economy (Chase-Dunn, 1982, 1989; Halliday, 1995). After several decades of steady and respectable economic growth, severe economic stagnation set in and major reforms were undertaken to cope with it. However, although Gorbachev was intent on retaining the basic political structure of the Soviet Union, his reforms set in motion political forces that after a certain point he could no longer control, especially in the form of severe infighting within the Soviet political elite. It was these political forces that were the proximate (or immediate) causes of the Soviet collapse (Hahn, 2002), even though the political forces were themselves rooted in economic difficulties that were the ultimate (or long-term) causes of the collapse.

The Communist Collapse and State-Centered
Theories of Revolution

Were these transformations social revolutions in the sense that we have been discussing them? Most people, scholars and laypersons alike, seem to think so. Indeed, Goodwin (1994a, 2001) has argued that there are a number of close parallels between the oppositional movements of the Communist world and those of the Third World. He lists five: They were multiclass movements, they involved widespread anger against state authorities, they were united by nationalism or patriotism, they were led by radical leaders, and these leaders had imitative and reactive ideologies. Goodwin goes even further in his search for parallels in suggesting that the Communist revolutions were made against the types of states that have been shown to be especially vulnerable to revolution in the Third World—neopatrimonial dictatorships and directly ruled colonial regimes. He says that both Communist and Third World revolutions overthrew states that were highly independent of weakly organized middle and upper classes, interest groups, and associations; were economically or militarily dependent on foreign powers, or perhaps directly installed by them; were intensely repressive of oppositional movements; and were highly involved in the ownership or control of important sectors of the economy.

It can be granted that, broadly speaking, the parallels suggested by Goodwin are real enough. But Goodwin also points to three major differences between Communist and Third World revolutions: the highly spontaneous and peaceful character of the Eastern European revolutions, the fundamentally urban nature of popular mobilizations in Eastern Europe, and the relative absence of counterrevolutionary violence in Eastern Europe. Charles Tilly (1993:234) notes that the Communist revolutions also "lacked multiple features of the past's great revolutions: the vindictive violence, the class base, the charismatic vision, the faith in politics as an instrument of constructive change, and the resistance of old powerholders to removal." To this should be added the critical point that the Communist revolutions were primarily revolutions from above, which distinguishes them sharply from all of the other revolutions discussed in this book. The events of 1989 and 1991 were, then, different in several important respects from other social revolutions.

Nonetheless, I think it is still valid to call these events social revolutions in the sense that we have defined them: There were both major transfers of state power and major transformations of the social and economic structure. Or at least that is true in most of the cases (cf. Tilly, 1993). It has been claimed by some that Romania's revolution was not so much a revolution as a neo-Communist restoration (Bruszt and Stark, 1992). And the collapse of the Soviet Union, though most certainly a state breakdown, was in some respects more of a political than a social revolution (a point to be discussed more fully in the next chapter when we consider revolutionary outcomes). But in most cases a major transformation of the economic structure has occurred; remnants of the old state socialism remain, but capitalism has largely replaced it.

Coda: The Unexpected Nature of the Communist Collapse

The collapse of Communism, especially the suddenness of it, took almost everyone by surprise, the present author included. And yet there were a number of scholars who predicted it. Jack Goldstone (1986) anticipated uprisings in Hungary and Czechoslovakia some three years before they occurred, although he did not predict the actual events themselves in those two countries, nor did he anticipate revolutions elsewhere in Eastern Europe or in the Soviet Union. Later he argued that social scientists should have seen those revolutions coming (Goldstone, 1995)

Others came surprisingly close to the mark, as Lipset and Bence (1994) have noted. Zbigniew Brzezinski (1969), a political scientist who was national security adviser in the Carter administration, published essays by a number of scholars on the Soviet Union, and six of the authors—Robert Conquest, Merle Fainsod, Eugene Lyons, Giorgio Galli, Isaac Don Levine, and Brzezinski himself—stressed the very real possibility of collapse in the medium-term future. About the same time, Andrei Amalrik (1970) noted that the Soviet Union was becoming increasingly decrepit and predicted that it was more likely to collapse than to be regenerated. Amalrik even got the timing right, anticipating collapse in the 1980s. The eminent sociologist Randall Collins (1986), in an essay originally written in 1980, predicted nationalistic movements for independence in Eastern Europe and the ultimate collapse of the Soviet Union as the result of the severe economic costs of imperial overextension. Historian Richard Pipes (1984), a specialist on the Russian Revolution, suggested a year before Gorbachev took office that a revolutionary situation was a real possibility in the Soviet Union. Twenty years after his initial prediction of a Soviet collapse, Brzezinski (1989) renewed his prediction, and in fact said that it would not take much longer. Daniel Patrick Moynihan, a sociologist who later became a U.S. senator, predicted in 1979 that the Soviet Union would eventually "blow up," and that this might well be the defining event of the 1980s. Moynihan based his prediction on the deterioration of Soviet social and economic life, and said that the best U.S. strategy for dealing with its longtime enemy would simply be to "wait them out."

But perhaps the most stunningly accurate prediction of all was made by Bernard Levin (1993). He not only anticipated a revolution from above in the Soviet Union but got the timing almost unimaginably close (as far as major predictions go). Here is what he said:

> [The revolutionary leaders] are there ... at this very moment, obeying orders, doing their duty, taking the official line against dissidents. ... They are in every respect model Soviet functionaries. Or rather, in every respect but one: they have admitted the truth about their country to themselves, and have vowed, also to themselves, to do something about it.
>
> There will be no gunfire in the streets, no barricades, no general strikes, no hanging of oppressors from lamp-posts, no sacking and burning of government offices, no seizure of radio stations or mass defections among the military. But one day soon, some new faces will appear in the Politburo—I am sure they have already appeared in municipal and even regional administrative authorities—and gradually, very gradually, other, similarly new, faces will join them. Until one day they will look at each other and realize that there is no longer any need for concealment of the truth in their hearts. And the match will be lit.
>
> There is nothing romantic or fantastic about this prognosis; it is the most sober extrapolation from known facts and tested evidence. That, or something like it, *will* happen. *When* it will happen is neither possible nor useful to guess; but I am sure it will be within the lifetime of people much older than I ... let us suppose, for neatness' sake, on July 14, 1989. (Levin, 1993:64–65; orig. 1977; quoted in Lipset and Bence, 1994:200–201)

This can only go down as one of the best predictions ever made by a social scientist.

Like Goldstone, Lipset and Bence argue that social scientists should have seen the collapse of Communism coming, and they point out that several classical sociologists—especially Max Weber, Robert Michels, and Vilfredo Pareto—developed theories that could easily have been used to predict the collapse. Weber (1968; orig. 1923), who lived to see the Russian Revolution, predicted that state socialism would be an extremely inefficient, bureaucratically top-heavy, and oppressive system that was unlikely to succeed.

Chapter Seven

The Outcomes of Revolutions

WHAT DO REVOLUTIONS ACCOMPLISH? Do they produce the results that various revolutionaries want? Do they reduce oppression and exploitation and lead to a better, more humane society? Revolutions and revolutionaries are often viewed in somewhat romanticized terms, and thus many people assume that they accomplish their goals, or at least some of their most important goals. But extreme caution is in order. The accomplishments of revolutions are limited at best, and they often simply trade one kind of oppressive situation for another. Both Goldstone (1991) and Skocpol (1979) stress that a major outcome of social revolutions has been the creation of stronger and more bureaucratic states that are just as oppressive as, if not more oppressive than, their predecessors. Goldstone notes that the English Revolution of 1640 was followed shortly by the military rule of Cromwell; that the French Revolution of 1789 was soon followed by the dictatorial Napoleonic Empire, and that the smaller-scale revolution in France in 1830 was again followed by an imperial despotism; that in Germany the revolution of 1848 gave way to the bureaucratic and military empire of the kaiser; and that in Russia the revolution of 1917 was soon followed by decades of Stalinist despotism. Goldstone concludes that "history shows an almost uniform tendency of episodes of state breakdown to culminate in populist, usually military dictatorship" (1991:479). Revolutions, he says, are not so much part of the solution to tyranny as they are part of the *problem* of that tyranny.

Theda Skocpol agrees and marshals just as much evidence as Gold-stone to support her point. And Foran and Goodwin (1993), focus-ing in particular on the outcomes of the Iranian and Nicaraguan revolutions, reach similar conclusions. Why do revolutions turn out this way? A large part of the answer involves the objective conditions of state building that revolutionaries must deal with once they win. Successful revolutionary coalitions are generally made up of groups whose interests are otherwise opposing, often strongly so. Once a coalition wins state power, it must then work out a plan for rebuild-ing the state, and at this point extensive bickering normally begins and a struggle ensues over which part of the coalition will be able to determine the future. Just as significantly, the objective conditions that center on rebuilding the state make that task daunting. Just re-gaining control and restoring order are difficult enough, but then the new state must try to restructure society in a feasible way. The many difficulties and contradictions of statecraft emerge as para-mount, and the ideologies of revolutionaries are normally strained beyond the breaking point. Skocpol (1979:170–171) explains:

> Jacobin ideologues shared in the rule of revolutionary France for only about one year, and the "Reign of Virtue" failed completely to take hold. The Jacobins accomplished instead more mundane tasks—of state build-ing and revolutionary defense—indispensable to the success of the Revo-lution that devoured them. In Russia, the Bolsheviks were pummeled by the exigencies of the attempt to take and hold state power in the name of Marxist socialism in an agrarian country shattered by defeat in total war. They found themselves forced to undertake tasks and measures that di-rectly contradicted their ideology. In the end, triumphant Stalinism twisted and upended virtually every Marxist ideal....
>
> In short, ideologically oriented leaderships in revolutionary crises have been greatly limited by existing structural conditions and severely buffeted by the rapidly changing currents of revolutions. Thus they have typically ended up accomplishing very different tasks and further-ing the consolidation of quite different kinds of new regimes from those they originally (and perhaps even) ideologically intended.... [R]evolutionary crises have particular forms, and create specific con-catenations of possibilities and impossibilities, according to how these crises are originally generated in given old regimes under given cir-cumstances.... [M]any conditions—especially socioeconomic condi-tions—always "carry over" from the old regime. These, too, create spe-cific possibilities and impossibilities within which revolutionaries must operate as they try to consolidate the new regime.

But perhaps there is a psychological factor at work as well. The leaders of revolutions are intensely committed individuals who are "true believers." They believe so intensely in their cause that they find it extremely difficult to entertain alternative positions. This is especially true of successful revolutionaries—that is, revolutionaries who have actually brought about a social revolution—because it takes extraordinary zeal and unswerving commitment to make a social revolution happen. In a sense, there is a kind of Darwinian natural selection process at work in which those individuals with the most dogmatic and fanatical personalities are most likely to attain the heights of revolutionary leadership. Once the revolutions they led have occurred, they usually feel a strong need to suppress those with opposing views, even if they were an important part of a revolutionary coalition. One sees clear evidence of this in all of the Great Revolutions and Third World revolutions discussed in previous chapters. The French Revolution, as we shall see below, produced a steady parade of intolerant true believers who executed their opponents but who, in turn, were themselves executed. Regarding the Russian Revolution, it is often said that Stalin was the person responsible for corrupting it, but clearly Lenin was a major part of the problem. He was an extremely intolerant and autocratic individual who had nothing but contempt for his political and class enemies, thinking nothing of executing them. And in the case of Iran, Khomeini preached an extremely intolerant version of Islam that was, in fact, his primary motive for overthrowing the shah. Many other examples could be added to the list.

These things having been said, let us look at the specific outcomes of the revolutions we have examined in this book.

France

In late 1792 a National Convention was convened and control of the Jacobins was gained by the Montagnards, the more radical wing of the Jacobins led by the famous Maximilien Robespierre. The Montagnards were responsible for the creation of a revolutionary dictatorship. Militant *sans-culottes* went into the countryside and forced farmers to turn over grain. The government sought to silence any political opposition by such means as censoring the newspapers and establishing surveillance committees around the country whose

members would identify anyone who might be even suspected of disloyalty. The revolutionary government also tried and executed a number of prominent political figures. Robespierre argued that "a temporary dictatorship was the only way to achieve the constitutional
freedoms that had been the original object of the Revolution"
(Popkin, 2002:84), and thus that the government should have unlimited power until it had defeated all of the "enemies of the people"
(Popkin, 2002).

The provisional government of Robespierre was so concerned with
rooting out all of its real or suspected political enemies that it engaged in large-scale Terror (with a capital *T*) (Popkin, 2002:90–91):

> The Montagnard leaders engaged in a constantly intensifying hunt for
> hidden conspirators whose activities they blamed for the Revolution's
> continuing difficulties. In the provinces, some of the deputies on mis-
> sion interpreted their mandate to "make terror the order of the day"
> in extreme terms. At Nantes, Jean-Baptiste Carrier ... rid himself of the
> several thousand suspected rebels crowding the prisons by mass execu-
> tions in which victims were thrown into the Loire River. To end rural
> resistance ... republican troops scoured the countryside, burning vil-
> lages and fields, and killing civilians indiscriminately....
>
> Another spectacular feature of the Terror was its use against an in-
> creasing number of the Revolution's most dedicated supporters....
> Those executed in October and November 1793 had included promi-
> nent leaders of the revolutionary movement of 1789 as well as dedi-
> cated republicans from 1792. In the winter of 1794, the Terror swept
> up the major enragé spokesmen and a number of Convention depu-
> ties accused of corruption or involvement in a murky "foreign plot"
> against the Revolution.... The journalist Jacques Hébert, author of *Père
> Duchêne*, the pamphlet-journal that had become the symbol of radical
> patriotism, and several of his supporters were tried and executed on
> trumped-up charges....
>
> Having brought the sans-culottes under control with the execution
> of Hébert, the Committee then turned against a group of Convention
> deputies who had raised their voices against the extension of the Ter-
> ror and who seemed to have support among the middle classes....
>
> Rather than reassuring the Committee, the executions of the
> Hébertists and Dantonists merely accelerated the pace of the Terror....
>
> How a revolutionary movement begun in the name of individual
> liberty could have culminated in so much bloodshed, and how
> Robespierre, an eloquent advocate of human rights, could have be-

come the Terror's main proponent, are questions that continue to be debated after more than two hundred years.

There was poetic justice in the fact that Robespierre's own supporters would eventually turn on him. On 9 thermidor (a new revolutionary calendar had been installed and thermidor was the new name for November), some of Robespierre's opponents accused him of having become a dictator. Along with several of his supporters, he was arrested and taken to the guillotine. At this point the machinery of revolution began to be dismantled (Popkin, 2002).

The period between 1794 and 1799 is known as the Thermidorian Reaction because it involved a basic return to order. But not only did the Thermidorians put an end to the Terror; they also dismantled a good deal of what the revolution had accomplished. The constitution of 1793 was abandoned and replaced by a new one that essentially removed the common people from politics by restricting to the wealthy the right to vote and hold office. At the end of this period, a coup occurred on 18 brumaire VIII (November 9, 1799) that brought Napoleon Bonaparte to power under the title of first consul. The counterrevolution that had been occurring during the Thermidorian period continued and intensified, with Napoleon becoming an extremely powerful dictator. In 1804 Napoleon crowned himself emperor. With Napoleon's defeat in war and his political downfall, the Bourbon dynasty was restored and Louis XVI's brother became king (Louis XVIII). But the new king did not govern in the same way as his brother. He followed a written constitution, and did not seek to reinstate the old privileges of the nobility. He himself was overthrown by a political revolution in 1830; there followed another political revolution in 1848, and a second Napoleonic empire was established in 1852 and lasted until 1870 (Popkin, 2002).

Russia

The period between 1918 and 1921, often known as War Communism, constituted the first period in the building of Communism by the Bolshevik Party. Although they claimed to represent the proletariat—indeed, to be a "Dictatorship of the Proletariat"—in fact the Bolsheviks took little time in building a police state that was a dictatorship *over* the proletariat. Workers quickly came to be deprived of even the limited rights they had under Tsarism, such as the right to elect union officials and to strike. The peasants, who of course were far more numerous, fared much worse. A massive campaign against the peasantry was initiated, with Bolshevik representatives entering the countryside to claim from the peasants whatever they considered to be surplus production. When the peasants were defiant and the collection of grain was meager, Lenin was furious, especially at the kulaks, or richer peasants. "Merciless war against these kulaks," he said. "Death to them" (Pipes, 1995:209). The Bolsheviks also sought to quickly destroy market forces and to nationalize industry. By the autumn of 1919 some 80 percent of large-scale industries had been nationalized, and in late 1920 small-scale industries began to be nationalized (Fitzpatrick, 1994; Pipes, 1995).

The Bolsheviks also wasted little time in creating a security police force, the Cheka, that was responsible for watching over any individuals and groups suspected of counterrevolutionary or anti-regime activities. The Cheka soon engaged in mass terror in the form of arrests and executions without trial. No opposition to the Bolshevik Party was tolerated, from either the inside or the outside. In 1921, Lenin established the New Economic Policy, or NEP, which involved a relaxation of controls over social, cultural, and economic life. However, there was to be no relaxation of controls in the sphere of politics, with the Bolsheviks, now renamed the Communists, exercising control even more ruthlessly than ever. All political parties other than the Communist Party were declared illegal, as was factionalism within the party. Lenin began the first of what were to be many party purges, with some 25 percent of Communist Party members being judged unworthy and expelled from the party (Fitzpatrick, 1994; Pipes, 1995).

In 1923 Lenin became ill, and he died in 1924. A struggle over who would eventually succeed him began, with Zinoviev, Kamenev, and Stalin on one side and Trotsky on the other. Trotsky lost out to the other three. But, politics being what they are, Stalin then broke with his two allies in 1925, who later joined with Trotsky. Stalin defeated the three of them without difficulty. In 1927 Stalin's opponents were finally expelled from the party or assigned to jobs in distant locations. With Stalin now in control, the powers of the police state were intensified. In order to carry out a massive state-led industrialization of the country, Stalin liquidated much of the peasantry (Fitzpatrick, 1994).

A recent book by the French historian Stéphane Courtois and his colleagues, *The Black Book of Communism* (Courtois et al., 1999), estimates that some 20 million people died in the Soviet Union as the result of Communist rule, through either mass starvation or execution when they protested or rebelled. This figure does not take into account the enormous suffering of millions of others in labor camps who did not die. In the first five years after the revolution, tens of thousands of prisoners were executed without ever having been tried, and hundreds of thousands of rebellious workers and peasants were murdered. In 1922 a major famine wiped out 5 million. Between 1918 and 1930, tens of thousands were murdered in concentration camps. Criminal convictions escalated enormously in the first dozen years after the revolution; 578,000 were convicted in 1926, 709,000 in 1927, 909,000 in 1928, and 1,778,000 in 1929. After forced collectivization of agriculture began under Stalin, things got much worse. Two million peasants were deported in the early 1930s, many of them dying as a result. In the great famine of 1932–1933, 6 million peasants died. There was a continual struggle between peasants and the state, with Soviet leaders regarding the peasants with extreme disdain. Naturally enough, the peasants wished to keep as much of their harvest as they could in order to provide for their own needs, but the state constantly demanded that they give up more. If the peasants refused, which they often did, their harvests were taken from them by force, or they were even starved out. Under the Stalinist regime, absolute conformity to the party line was demanded, and anyone suspected of political deviation was executed; in 1937–1938 alone there were some 700,000 political executions. The system of concentration and forced labor camps was also greatly expanded during the horrendous decade of the 1930s, nearly doubling in size between 1935 and 1941.

China

In China after 1949, a dictatorial regime very similar to that in the Soviet Union was established. Extreme measures were taken to identify those who could be expected to be a threat to the new system. Many members of the old gentry were tried and executed, as were those thought to be local tyrants or collaborators with the Japanese during the war. Mao himself admitted to a million executions, but some estimates have been as high as 5 million. In the early years of the People's Republic of China, Mao stayed close to the version of Leninism espoused by the Soviet Union, taking many instructions from Soviet officials. Later, however, China broke with the Soviet Union and began to follow its own path; that of Maoism. However, Maoism, like Leninism, assumed that the people were politically unsophisticated and needed proper guidance from above. They should put themselves in Mao's hands and submit unswervingly to his authority (Schrecker, 2004).

In 1956 Mao launched his famous Hundred Flowers Campaign, which implied an opening up of the political process since its motto was "Let a Hundred Flowers Bloom, Let a Hundred Schools of Thought Contend." Intellectuals and economic specialists were prodded to share their views on how the economy should be run. But if ever a movement or campaign was misnamed, this was it. In fact, within a short time those persons who actually suggested new lines of thought or were critical of existing policies lost their jobs or were even arrested and sent to labor camps. Later Mao claimed that he was not really serious about the Hundred Flowers Campaign; he introduced it, he said, as a means of discovering secret opponents of socialism in general or of his regime in particular (Schrecker, 2004).

There next followed the two periods that are most closely associated with Maoism, the Great Leap Forward (1958–1961) and the Cultural Revolution (1966–1976). Both were unmitigated disasters. In the Great Leap Forward, government repression was intensified, and new economic policies were put into effect. These policies involved a turn toward the extreme collectivization of agriculture and the formation of People's Communes. These were larger communes that combined existing agricultural collectives and their associated villages into administrative units of, on average, about 25,000 people. In the smaller collectives, farmers were paid based on how much work they did, but in the new People's Communes they received no pay at all; they were simply supplied with whatever they needed. All remaining private plots of land were abolished, as indeed were all items of personal property. Everything became the property of the state, and families were required to eat in huge dining halls. Although the Great Leap was intended to increase agricultural efficiency, the exact opposite occurred: Agricultural yields actually declined. Why did yields fall? One reason was that the relentless demands to increase agricultural production led teams of supervisors to ignore long-established and time-tested agricultural traditions and wisdom. Even more significantly, the pressure placed on farmers was intolerable. They were already working virtually as hard as they could, and to be asked to work beyond the limits of human endurance, and for no personal or family incentive, produced an unbearable situation. The end result was massive famine. Millions of people died, with estimates running as high as 40 million. The disaster for farmers also led to terrible consequences for other aspects of Chinese society. Factories were affected, many having to close down. Progress in medical care, education, and public welfare in general, which had been advancing, came to a halt (Schrecker, 2004).

The Cultural Revolution was another attempt at radical reorganization. Mao organized youth into Red Guard units, which were told to identify and root out all remaining Western or "capitalist" elements in Chinese society. John Schrecker (2004:229–230) tells us more:

> Because the ideology behind the Cultural Revolution saw no strengths in Chinese tradition and precious few in the practice of Marxism-Leninism, its only basis could be the thought of Mao Zedong himself. Mao therefore encouraged an unprecedented cult of personality centered on himself and his infallible wisdom. The most famous symbol of the cult became the *Selected Quotations from Mao Zedong*, the so-called "Little Red Book," which was printed and distributed in over a billion copies and became a talisman for overcoming all obstacles.
>
> Once goaded on by such authority, the youth proved zealous. In addition to the propaganda urging them forward, they were also stimulated by the fact that the educational advances of the previous decade had left a larger group of talented and trained young people than China's still relatively backward economy could accommodate. At the same time, schools were closed down partly because they were under party control and also said to be unfairly biased toward the elite. However, the basic reason they were closed, aside from freeing the young for political activism, was to promote the idea that nothing was worth teaching, either in China's long-term past or in its recent Communist heritage.
>
> In this nihilistic atmosphere, the youth and the older people who decided to go along with them, either out of fear or self-interest, began attacks on everything from music to the organization of factories. Cultural treasures, buildings, and artworks were defaced and sometimes destroyed. Industrial production declined. Most seriously, however, the followers of the Cultural Revolution began widespread abuse of party members, intellectuals, and social leaders of all sorts.

It was a time of humiliation, beatings, killings, and suicides, and those who perished probably numbered upward of half a million. Even more people were sent to prisons and work camps....

By the late 1960s, with the cities in chaos and rural China beginning to suffer, it was obvious the Cultural Revolution was a fiasco....

There was still terror among thinking people and attacks on all deviations from the revolutionary line.... More tragically, millions of young people, former Red Guards, joined their victims in jail and on prison farms.

In 1976, Mao died, and the Cultural Revolution was brought to an end. From this point on, China embarked on a capitalist path of economic development, although the Communist Party has retained power. However, it is probably only a matter of time before this party is itself overthrown, or a more democratic system evolves gradually through the buildup of the preconditions for democracy.

Courtois and his colleagues (1999) have shown that the human consequences of Communism were worse in China than in any other Communist society. As many as 65 million people may have died from the time Mao came to power in 1949 to his death in 1976. Total government incompetence in agriculture contributed, between 1959 and 1961, to what is undoubtedly the worst famine in the history of humankind, when somewhere between 20 million and 43 million are estimated to have died. The concentration camp system was huge, with at least 1,000 camps through which as many as 50 million people may have passed; nearly half of these died in the camps.

Cuba

As noted in Chapter 3, although the Cuban Revolution took place at the beginning of 1959, it was not until 1961 that Fidel Castro made clear his intent to turn Cuba into a Communist society. Castro set up a one-party dictatorship with himself as its head and his brother, Raúl, and Che Guevara as close associates. Cuba thus followed in the tradition of other revolutions that had replaced one type of dictatorship with another. It has been politically repressive: Basic political freedoms to criticize the government have been nonexistent, dissidents have often been arrested and given long prison terms, and in some cases there have been political executions. These executions, how-ever, have occurred on a very small scale compared to the Soviet Union, China, and the other brutally authoritarian Leninist regimes discussed earlier. In fact, for the most part, the Communist regime in Cuba appears to have been the most benign of all such regimes.

Most Leninist regimes have been marked by the dominance of a major leader: Stalin in the Soviet Union, Mao in China, and so on. But Castro has played a personal role in Cuban leadership on an unmatched scale. Early on, Castro wanted to avoid closely following the Soviet example and to map out a distinctive Cuban form of so-cialism. Part of this involved keeping bureaucracy, which he regarded as a scourge and a great evil, to a minimum (Selbin, 1999). Castro emphasized his own personal rule, or *personalismo*, as the key to the Cuban system. In the words of Eric Selbin (1999:46), "Forty years after political victory, the Cuban revolution remains overwhelmingly dominated and transfixed by the figure of Fidel Castro." Susan Eckstein (1994:20) adds the following:

> In many respects a textbook case of a … charismatic leader, Castro in power came to be seen as an ascetic, devoted to the revolutionary cause. He flaunted no wealth and appeared morally pure, while seeming, in the words of one observer, "head of everything."
> His charisma, in turn, rested on an electric and messianic link with the masses. He made ordinary people feel a sense of dignity and im-portance.

Economically, what has Cuba achieved? From an early point Castro nationalized most of the economy and implemented a series of social reforms that led to guaranteed employment, free education and health care, the elimination of hunger, and decent housing at a very low cost (Eckstein, 1980). A system of agrarian reform was launched in which land was redistributed in a much more egalitarian manner. Eckstein (1986:520) notes that "among Latin American countries Cuba has the smallest percentage of private holdings and the small-est amount of privately held land in large estates. Also, no other Latin American country has implemented an agrarian reform that has ben-efited as large a percentage of the farm labor force or distributed as large a percentage of the land area as has Cuba." Social distinctions and privilege were attacked in the urban as well as the rural economy, and there was a strong anti-elitist, egalitarian emphasis. As a result of Castro's efforts, Cuba soon came to have the most egalitarian income distribution in all of Latin America (Eckstein, 1986, 1994). For example, in 1953 the poorest quintile (fifth) of the population received only 2.1 percent of the national income, but by 1978 it was receiving 7.8 percent. As the poorest segments of the population benefited, so the best-off segments saw their incomes reduced. The richest quintile had 57.9 percent of the total income in 1953, but this had declined to 33.4 percent by 1978. Similarly, the richest 5 percent of the population saw its share of the total income decline from 26.5 percent in 1953 to 9.5 percent in 1978 (Eckstein, 1986). Cuba also has virtually the lowest infant mortality rate in Latin America, although this is not especially the result of the revolution. Cuba had Latin America's lowest infant mortality rate even in the days of Batista.

However, although Cuba is clearly a more egalitarian society than the rest of Latin America as the result of Castro's economic reforms, its Latin American position in per capita GDP has actually declined. In 1955 Cuba ranked fifth in Latin America. This ranking declined to twelfth in 1970, although it increased somewhat, to ninth, by 1980 (Eckstein, 1986). But by 2004 its rank had slipped all the way to nineteenth, very near the bottom (Central Intelligence Agency, 2004). In this respect Cuba has followed a similar path to that of Soviet and East European state socialism: a more egalitarian, but a poorer, society compared to capitalist societies. Moreover, in assessing the achievements of Cuba, we cannot disregard the mass exodus that has been taking place from Cuba to Florida in the past several decades. Certainly this does not reflect favorably on either the economic or the political situation. Yet, in all fairness, it should be pointed out that Cuba's economic performance has been hindered by U.S. hostility toward it. In fact, the United States tried to overthrow the Castro regime in 1961, when in April of that year President John F. Kennedy sent a small group of forces surreptitiously by boat through the Bay of Pigs to invade the island. When this effort failed—the forces were detected and intercepted—the United States tried to undermine Cuba in other ways, especially by establishing an economic embargo against trade with the United States and by attempting to persuade its allies in Western Europe not to trade with Cuba. Although Cuba is only 90 miles off the tip of Florida, its major trade partner for many years was the Soviet Union, thousands of miles away.

In some respects, then, Cuba has probably been the most successful—or, more accurately, the least unsuccessful—of all state socialist societies. However, as noted at the end of this chapter, because Castro has loomed so large in directing Cuban society, once he dies Cuba is likely to go the way of other state socialist societies and fully reenter the capitalist world-economy.

Nicaragua

Outside of the Eastern European revolutions, the Nicaraguan Revolution is the only example of a social revolution in which the revolutionary movement not only allowed for free elections, but permitted itself to be voted out of power as a result of those elections. Nevertheless, it would be several years before elections were held, and in the meantime a five-person *junta*, known as the Government of National Reconstruction, set itself up as a provisional government. The members of the *junta* were Daniel Ortega, the principal representative of the Sandinista Front for National Liberation (FSLN), two other members of the FSLN, and two persons representing the bourgeoisie. One of this government's first actions was to introduce major economic reforms, which primarily involved seizing private property—both land and industry—and nationalizing it. Among the first properties seized were those that had belonged to Somoza, including not only his landholdings but more than a hundred of his industrial and commercial enterprises (Grynspan, 1991).

However, once the FSLN-dominated *junta* attempted to confiscate other private holdings, and to undertake such actions as nationalizing the banking system, it began to encounter major opposition. The most vigorous opposition came from the bourgeoisie, which had originally allied itself with the FSLN only because of its own hatred of Somoza. The FSLN-bourgeois alliance soon cracked apart, an unsurprising outcome given the sharply opposing economic interests of the two groups. As Dévora Grynspan (1991:102) puts it, "The conflict between the FSLN and the bourgeoisie was inevitable, as it resulted from the inherent contradiction between revolutionary change and socialist goals, on the one hand, and the interests of a capitalist class, on the other, especially the Nicaraguan capitalist class, which had been accustomed to operating in an environment of complete market freedom and low taxation." The two bourgeois members of the *junta*, Alfonso Robelo and Violeta Chamorro, resigned less than a year after it was formed. To make matters worse for the FSLN, when Ronald Reagan became U.S. president in 1981 his administration embarked upon an unrelenting campaign to undermine the Sandinistas, either by evicting them from office, destroying their economy, or both. The Reagan administration introduced an embargo against trade between the United States and Nicaragua, put pressure on Latin American firms to end their own trade with Nicaragua, and tried to block loans to Nicaragua from major financial organizations. The administration also established an alliance with the Nicaraguan *contrarevolucionarios*, or Contras, a military organization that was attempting to topple the Sandinista regime. Incessantly referring to the Contras as "freedom fighters," Reagan implemented policies that led to their being provided with funds and various forms of military aid (Grynspan, 1991; Selbin, 1999).

Elections were finally held in late 1984, and Daniel Ortega was elected president, capturing some 67 percent of the vote. FSLN candidates for the legislature received 63 percent of the vote, which gave them 61 legislative seats. Before the elections took place, the Reagan administration engaged in a vigorous campaign to discredit them, arguing that they would be nothing but a sham. However, the elections were "hailed as free, open, fair, and honest by the six opposition parties that participated and virtually all the international observers not affiliated with the U.S. administration" (Selbin, 1999:50–51).

Strong opposition to the Sandinistas continued, however. Naturally there was still internal opposition from the bourgeoisie, and external opposition from the Reagan administration by no means ceased (if anything, it intensified, for Reagan's second term of office was marked by the infamous Iran-Contra scandal in which the U.S. government illegally funneled money to the Contras through Iran). But there was also opposition from other segments of the population, including peasants and workers, for both political and economic reasons. Although they were considerably less dictatorial than revolutionary elites have normally been, the Sandinistas were not above political repression; they forbade workers from striking, for example, and engaged in some press censorship. And in 1984 the economy entered what was to become a rather long period of stagnation. Nevertheless, the government remained committed to a system of democratic elections, and the next elections were held in early 1990. This time, the Sandinistas received only 41 percent of the vote. Ortega was ousted as president and replaced by Violeta Chamorro of the National Opposition Union (UNO), one of his earliest and most vigorous opponents, who captured 55 percent of the vote. (Chamorro and her family owned the leading newspaper, *La Prensa*, which had been engaged in sustained criticism of Ortega and the Sandinistas.) However, the Sandinistas continued to hold a substantial number of seats in the National Assembly and, thus, were still active in the Nicaraguan halls of power (Grynspan, 1991; Selbin, 1999).

Many observers, and many Nicaraguans, blamed the United States for the defeat of the Sandinistas in the 1990 elections, and there is a great deal of substance to this claim (Selbin, 1999). Much of the opposition to the FSLN resulted from the bad state of the economy, but many Nicaraguans also thought that as long as the FSLN remained in power the United States would continue its economic embargo against Nicaragua and its support of the Contras. As Dévora Grynspan (1991:110) has put it:

> What seemed evident to all Nicaraguans was that a victory by UNO would not only bring an end to the contra war and the U.S. economic embargo but might also bring in fresh U.S. aid to reconstruct the Nicaraguan economy. To the extent that the U.S.-sponsored war and embargo contributed in a significant way to the erosion of support for the revolution, and to the extent that people perceived a vote for the FSLN as a vote for continued U.S. aggression, it can be said that the United States again had a decisive role in determining the course of Nicaraguan politics.

However, the role of the United States should not be overstated. Pressures from the United States certainly played an important role, but there was a great deal of popular sentiment against the FSLN on the basis of purely domestic considerations (Selbin, 1999).

Elections were held again in 1996, and this time the winner was Arnoldo Aléman, who defeated Ortega by 51 percent to 38 percent. Aléman was a forceful opponent of the FSLN, but, because it continued to hold a substantial number of seats in the national parliament, the FSLN remained strong and forced Aléman to tone down his rhetoric and modify some of his more grandiose plans (Selbin, 1999). In 2001, Ortega was defeated in the presidential race for a third time, this time by Enrique Bolanos of the Partido Liberal Constitucionalista, or PLC (56 percent to 42 percent). Nevertheless, the FSLN captured 43 of the seats in the National Assembly, almost as many as the PLC's 47.

The example of Nicaragua shows that the pessimistic view of revolutionary outcomes stated at the beginning of this chapter needn't lead to some sort of fatalism. Revolutions have not produced new authoritarian regimes in every single case (cf. Goodwin, 1994b:749–750). The great accomplishment of the Nicaraguan Revolution was the destruction of the horrendous neopatrimonial dictatorship of Somoza and its replacement by regimes generally committed to democracy and pluralism. Civil society was strengthened in Nicaragua, with "a broad spectrum of political parties, media, trade unions, and other mass organizations [becoming] more vigorous than at any previous time in Nicaraguan history" (Foran and Goodwin, 1993:233).

Iran

Although the shah was deposed in early 1979, the Iranian Revolution was not really finished because a severe power struggle loomed over the form the new government would take. As Foran and Goodwin (1993) suggest, the end of the revolution did not come until more than three years later, when the Islamic fundamentalists gained clear control of the government. The initial revolutionary government was led by Mehdi Bazargan, who held the title of prime minister. The main office holders were middle-class professionals and intellectuals. However, this government had to contend with Khomeini and his fundamentalist followers. In the summer of 1979 major debates broke out over the drafting of a new constitution. Khomeini naturally wanted the constitution to have a strong Islamic grounding, and a provision was introduced in which he was given extensive veto powers over decisions made by the *majlis*, or parliament. Secular progressives were increasingly repressed, as were secular and middle-class women, by the Islamic Revolutionary Guards. After the American embassy in Tehran was seized by radical Muslim students in November, Bazargan resigned (Foran and Goodwin, 1993).

A new government was constituted by Abul Hasan Bani Sadr, an economist as well as politician, who won the first presidential elections in January of 1980. Khomeini's Islamic Republican Party (IRP), stung by its loss of the presidency, redoubled its efforts and in elections held in March won over half of the seats in parliament. For the next year and a half, a major power struggle took place between the IRP and Bani Sadr and his allies. Also involved in the struggle was the radical *Mujahideen*. Although they were religious, they tended to be supportive of Sadr because of their strong dislike of Khomeini's highly fundamentalist version of Islam. In June of 1981, Sadr was forced out of the presidency and driven out of the country by parliament, heavily dominated as it was by the IRP. A major confrontation between the IRP and the *Mujahideen* ensued. The *Mujahideen* killed several top IRP members, including the prime minister and interim president, as well as many members of parliament. The IRP's Revolutionary Guards returned the favor by killing hundreds of *Mujahideen* and arresting and executing many others. However, the actions of the *Mujahideen* essentially led to their demise; they were delegitimated in the eyes of the more moderate left, their organization was broken up, and remaining members were either driven underground or exiled (Foran and Goodwin, 1993; Moshiri, 1991).

Power had shifted dramatically into the hands of the IRP. "By late 1982, the IRP was in clear control of the situation, and could proceed to jail its erstwhile left-wing supporters in the Tudeh and Fada'ian-Majority and to silence its conservative and liberal clerical critics as well" (Foran and Goodwin, 1993:216). A powerful theocracy had been established. Over the course of the coming decade, the IRP consolidated its grip on power and restructured the Iranian state and society along fundamentalist Muslim lines (Foran and Goodwin, 1993).

Why did the IRP emerge from the old revolutionary coalition as the clear winner? Was it because of widespread and highly intense religious feelings among the population? On the surface this might appear to be the case, but surface appearances can be highly misleading (Parsa, 2000). Farrokh Moshiri (1991:131) explains that it was largely a question of control over crucial political resources:

> The theocratic outcome of the Iran revolution is easily explained by the resources at the disposal of the religious elite, namely, the mosques and religious students. The estimated number of mosques was 75,000 in 1982; the estimated number of religious students in 1980 was 1,500 for Qom alone.... To those networks one should add the local committees and the bazaar networks; the network of personnel within the shah's secret service and army who joined the revolutionary government; the revolutionary guards, which had been formed as a counterbalancing organization to the U.S.-trained army; and Sazeman e Basij (Mobilization Organization), Foundations for War Refugees, and the various agencies involved with the reconstruction of the country and land reform such as Jahad e Sazandeghi (Crusade for Reconstruction), and the

Dayereh-ye Amr be Ma'ruf va Nahi az Monker (Center for Combating Sin), which functioned as a morals squad.

Foran and Goodwin (1993) add that the IRP was better organized and better prepared to engage in violent confrontations, that it controlled important economic resources, and that the major oppositional groups were plagued by internal divisions.

What really came to be established in Iran was not any ordinary theocracy but a religious republic that was "anti-rational, anti-Western, [and] xenophobic" (Chirot, 1995:265) and that, in essence, substituted a religious dictatorship for the shah's military dictatorship. The new Islamic Republic had no respect whatsoever for human rights or civil liberties, and religious conformity was demanded of all persons. In this sense it was not even remotely democratic. However, it gained the allegiance of the masses to a very large extent, something obviously totally missing in the shah's regime (Moshiri, 1991).

The Revolutions Against Communism

Eastern Europe

In looking at the revolutionary outcomes in Eastern Europe, we find that there are two major considerations: First, to what extent have these former Communist societies established genuine and relatively stable democratic political regimes, and, second, how have they fared economically?

All of the postrevolutionary societies of Eastern Europe have established formal democracies, but democracy is not an all-or-nothing thing; it varies by degree. The figures given in Table 7.1 provide quantitative indicators of the level of democratization achieved in the Eastern European postsocialist regimes. The democracy score is a composite of the degree of popular participation in politics (as measured by the proportion of the population voting) and the degree of political party competition. Using these figures, we see that the two Eastern European societies that have achieved the highest levels of democratization are the Czech Republic and Slovakia, whereas the least democratic Eastern European society is Romania.

Table 7.1 Democracy and Political Rights in Postsocialist Societies

Country	Democracy Score 1993	Democracy Score 2000	Political Rights Score 2003	Superdemocracy Score 2000/03
Belarus	6.5	7.2	2	21.2
Bulgaria	35.4	24.1	7	73.1
Czech Republic	40.3	39.3	7	88.3
Estonia	17.7	24.1	7	73.1
Georgia	19.8	14.8	4	42.8
Hungary	27.4	25.4	7	74.4
Latvia	19.5	27.7	7	76.7
Lithuania	23.5	28.2	7	77.2
Moldova	8.0	22.0	5	57.0
Poland	19.6	22.3	7	71.3
Romania	27.5	20.7	6	62.7
Russia	27.0	20.7	3	41.7
Slovakia	38.4	36.8	7	85.8
Ukraine	21.7	32.7	4	60.7

Note: Democracy scores are calculated as the rate of voter participation multiplied by the extent of political party competition, which is then divided by 100. A political rights score of 7 indicates the greatest recognition of political rights, a score of 1 the least recognition (these scores have been reversed from the original coding). Superdemocracy scores are calculated by multiplying the political rights score by 7, and then adding the result to the democracy score for 2003. This calculation is designed to give political rights approximately equal weighting with political representation and participation.

Sources: Freedom House Survey Team (2003); Gastil (1989); Vanhanen (2003).

But democracy is more than party competition and voting; it also involves respect for basic political rights and liberties. This dimension of democracy is shown in Table 7.1 in terms of a 7-point scale, with 7 indicating the highest degree of respect for political rights. Here we see that all of the Eastern European societies have achieved the highest level, except for Romania, which has achieved the next-highest level.

Another way of looking at the level of democratization involves classifying societies into what political scientists call *presidential* or *parliamentary* systems (Ágh, 1998; Banac, 1992; Stokes, 1993). A presidential system is one in which a great deal of power is concentrated in the position of president relative to the power of the legislature, whereas a parliamentary system is just the opposite: Presidential powers are circumscribed by legislators much more than in a presidential system. Using these concepts, we can say that only Romania has a presidential system (Ágh, 1998).

However, only in the Czech Republic and Slovakia has the level of democratization approached its level in the long-established Western democracies, and Czechoslovakia was the one society that had begun to establish democratic institutions prior to World War II and its eventual incorporation into the Soviet Empire. Political elites in all of the Eastern European postsocialist societies have resisted to one extent or another high levels of participation by the masses. The Hungarian political scientist Attila Ágh (1998:52) has commented to the effect that "the new system has established democratic political institutions, but it so far has created only a half-made, 'partyist' democracy, that is, a democracy mostly for the party elites. The basic democratic values of competition and participation have not yet been fully developed for the entire population." Ágh adds that the "real participatory democracy of the West European type is thus still missing" (1998:52). Political elites have also been slow to adopt the Western style of strong political tolerance for opponents, often viewing them as enemies needing to be crushed and pushed out of politics altogether (Ágh, 1998).

For the most part, democratic institutions have been strongest in the East Central European countries—the Czech Republic, Slovakia, Hungary, and Poland—and weakest in the Balkan states of Bulgaria and Romania, the latter in particular. Despite the involvement of the masses in the Romanian revolution, in many ways the revolution was actually a *coup d'état* led by Ion Iliescu and a segment of the old Communist *nomenklatura*, who apparently had been plotting the *coup* for some time. Ágh (1998) has described this regime as a "thinly veiled façade democracy" that monopolized power from the beginning and did not engage in negotiations with any other parties. He considers it a highly oppressive regime that essentially stole the revolution. Others, though, suggest that this characterization is too strong (Verdery and Kligman, 1992). Clearly, however, Romanian democracy is a far cry from Western democracy.

What are the prospects for the further consolidation of democracy and its enlargement in this part of the world? I think they are relatively good, especially in East Central Europe. The fact that these societies are becoming increasingly market-oriented, capitalist societies bodes well for democracy, since democracy and capitalism have been closely associated historically (Sanderson, 2004).

What, then, of economic developments? Privatization has occurred throughout Eastern Europe, but most extensively in the Czech Republic, Slovakia, Hungary, and Poland. There seems to be a commitment to producing an essentially capitalist economy in due time. During the early years of economic transition, nearly all of the postsocialist societies experienced negative economic growth and serious economic problems. However, by 1994 positive economic growth had resumed in virtually all of these societies (Ágh, 1998; Holmes, 1997), and this growth has continued into the early 2000s.

Table 7.2 Selected Development Indicators for Postsocialist Societies, Germany, the United States, Japan, the European Union, and the World as a Whole

Country	LE	GDP	GDP-PPP	LFA	TV	TEL	COM
Bulgaria	71.0	1,190	7,600	26	63.1	36.8	5.2
Czech Republic	75.4	6,750	15,700	5	89.3	36.2	17.7
Estonia	71.7	4,650	12,300	7	85.1	35.1	21.0
Hungary	71.9	6,650	13,900	6	89.2	36.1	10.8
Latvia	70.9	3,500	10,200	15	68.4	30.1	17.2
Lithuania	72.6	3,730	11,400	16	72.6	27.0	11.0
Poland	73.9	4,910	11,100	19	82.8	45.1	10.6
Romania	70.6	2,050	7,000	42	52.7	19.4	8.3
Russia	67.0	2,410	8,900	12	76.3	24.2	8.9
Slovakia	73.7	4,390	13,300	6	86.1	26.8	18.0
Ukraine	69.7	850	5,400	20	75.7	21.6	1.9
Germany	78.2	24,200	27,600	3	97.1	65.1	43.1
United States	77.1	35,990	37,800	2	99.5	64.6	66.0
Japan	81.5	31,320	28,200	5	99.1	55.8	38.2
European Union	78.6	22,870	—	4.5	96.6	55.4	31.9
World	65.5	5,200	8,200	40	—	12.9	9.9

Legend: LE = life expectancy at birth (2000–2005 average); GDP = Gross Domestic Product per capita (2001); GDP-PPP = Gross Domestic Product adjusted for purchasing power parity (2003); LFA = percentage of the labor force in agriculture (years vary between 1998 and 2002); TV = number of color televisions per 100 households (2001); TEL = number of telephone lines per 100 population (2001); COM = number of computers per 100 population (2001).

Sources: The Economist (2004); Central Intelligence Agency (2004).

Table 7.2 provides a variety of economic indicators for the postsocialist societies and compares these societies to three highly developed societies, the European Union, and the world as a whole. Levels of per capita GDP are still quite low, although not nearly as low if GDP is assessed in purchasing power parity (PPP) terms. Yet even then the postsocialist societies lag far behind the most developed societies. Can they catch up? Perhaps one or two of them can, but the real question is whether they can continue the considerable economic development that has occurred in the last ten years. That, I think, is highly probable now that the forces responsible for decades of economic stagnation are being increasingly pushed into the background. There seems to be good reason for a cautious optimism.

In any event, the outcomes of the 1989 revolutions, both political and economic, are, with one or two exceptions, the only instances in world history of revolutions actually leading to societies that are both better off economically and more democratic. These are major achievements.

Russia

The Eastern European revolutions had much greater societal support than in Russia. Although the former were primarily revolutions from above, in Russia the revolution was *purely* a revolution from above. This difference has made it much easier for the Eastern European postsocialist societies to make the transition to democracy and a market economy. The new Russian government of Boris Yeltsin carried over most of the old bureaucratic elite and, thus, did not have sufficient autonomy and state capacity to do the things that needed to be done. Gordon Hahn (2002:497–498) has pointed to the special problems encountered by new governments in pure revolutions from above, and he situates the 1991 Russian revolution in this context:

> Unlike revolutions from below, the new regime is not deeply rooted with societal support. Crucially important for a revolution's autonomy, "the bureaucratic state apparatus, or a segment of it," must not be recruited from the "dominant" class(es) and must not form "close personal and economic ties with those classes after their elevation to high office." A non-autonomous state is likely to lack the ideological and institutional cohesion or overall capacity to rule and implement policy

effectively. The state's capacity—its command of financial, material, and human resources—is, in turn, contingent on its ideological and institutional cohesion. In lieu of these state requisites, especially autonomy, revolutionary bureaucrats will be forced to win at least "tacit cooperation from the most influential local interests" in order to institutionalize their power, since they have not mobilized the masses and eschew the use of force in favor of bureaucratic, administrative, legalistic methods of implementing the revolution. The ensuing compromises undermine the revolutionary project, whether it is one of authoritarian modernization or integration into a globalizing, democratizing world.

In sum, the road to democracy and free markets by way of revolution from above has proven to be problematic. Such revolutions tend to produce unstable, illiberal democracies and corrupt state capitalist or corporatist economies.... [T]he illiberal results of revolution from above are evident in Russia. The major reason is the post–Soviet Russian regime's incorporation of many of the former regime's governing institutions and personnel.... Because Russia's revolution from above was led by party-state elites from the Soviet *nomenklatura* class, it lacks sufficient state autonomy from key economic and political interests left over from the *ancien regime* for it to establish an effective democracy or free market.

Indeed, nearly 75 percent of the personnel of the Soviet state in the period 1996–1999 were holdovers from the old *nomenklatura*.

Table 7.1 shows that Russia has the lowest level of democratization of all the postsocialist societies with the exception of Belarus. Russia has a very strong presidential system that is now represented in the form of Vladimir Putin, the former head of the Soviet KGB. Putin has extremely strong authoritarian tendencies and seems only too happy to consolidate his power into a full-blown dictatorship. In September of 2004, for example, he put an end to the direct popular election of Russia's governors and decided to have the Russian parliament elected from slates put together by national leaders over whom he exercises enormous control (Kagan, 2004).

The Russian economy has undergone much less privatization than the economies of Eastern Europe. Many private enterprises and the majority of commercial banks are still dependent on state subsidies; 90 percent of the agricultural land is still owned by the state. Probably less than half of total GDP is contributed by private enterprises (Hahn, 2002). The decade of the 1990s was a disaster for Russia, with the Russian economy deteriorating dramatically after 1991. GDP declined markedly, as did total economic investment and the rate of economic accumulation. Total agricultural and industrial production declined by about 50 percent between 1991 and 1998, and capital investment in 1996 was at less than one-quarter of its level in 1990. Capital flight was a major problem, amounting to more than $150 billion between 1992 and 1999. Science and technology were allowed to decay; transportation and telecommunications infrastructures badly needed repair and lacked necessary equipment; and gas and oil production, which form a critical part of the Russian economy, went into a state of disorganization and decline (Castells, 1996; Ericson, 1995; Kagarlitsky, 2002; Stiglitz, 2003).

Russia is now run by a group of "oligarchs," some forty extremely rich persons who have enormous economic and political power (Hahn, 2002; Kagarlitsky, 2002). The oligarchs, accordingly to Boris Kagarlitsky, are plundering the country and make most of their investments outside it. Hahn (2002) claims that these oligarchs—whom he calls "parasitical kleptocrats"—control some 85 percent of the country's finance capital. According to Kagarlitsky (2002), the oligarchs are not a true capitalist class and are completely incapable of promoting the economic development of Russia. Although they have enormous amounts of capital, they benefit more from investing it abroad than from domestic investment. The oligarchs are deeply enmeshed in the Russian state. Corruption, which was a major problem in the old Soviet Union, continues and may be worse than ever. In Kagarlitsky's view, contemporary Russia more closely resembles a feudal-bureaucratic society than a capitalist one, in that parasitic politicians who work through bribes have much more importance than genuine businessmen.

Yet despite this extremely bleak picture, there are some signs that Russia might have begun to turn the corner. Capital investment declined for eight consecutive years, but in 1999 it increased by some 5 percent and in 2000 by close to 20 percent. In 2001 demand for computer hardware increased by 17 percent, and for computer services by almost 30 percent. And capital flight has begun to slow considerably. It was $1.9 billion in July of 2000, but that had declined to about $800 million in July of 2001. These objective indicators are matched by subjective ones: Russians seem to be feeling more optimistic. On an optimism-pessimism scale in which 100 represents the midpoint, Russians scored 86 in 1999, 101 in 2000, and 137 through September of 2001 (Wines, 2001).

Where things are headed in Russia is very difficult to say, but a reasonable conclusion is that Russia still has a very long way to go, both economically and in terms of democratic government. Russia has a very long tradition of "things never going quite right." In medieval and early modern times its peasants were the poorest in Europe. Peter the Great tried to open a "window to the West," but the country never really got Westernized. In 1861 serfdom was legally ended, but the material conditions of life for peasants hardly changed at all. The famous 1917 revolution made some improvements, but there were many steps backward. Russia is now at another critical juncture. Can it "get it right" this time? We will have to wait and see.

Surviving Communist Regimes and the Future of Socialism

There are only five Communist regimes left in the world today. These are found in China, Vietnam, Laos, North Korea, and Cuba. Do they have a future? The answer, I think, is a resounding "no." China and Vietnam have already completely abandoned socialism as an economic system even though Communist political parties retain their monopoly on political power. But it is likely that this monopoly will last only a short time longer, probably no more than twenty years. Both are likely to experience revolutions from above of the type we have seen in Eastern Europe, especially once capitalist forces develop further. Laos began to introduce market reforms in 1986, along with decentralized control. Although these reforms led to substantial economic growth, Laos is still one of the world's poorest societies (outside of sub-Saharan Africa), and the Leninist regime there cannot possibly have a serious future (Central Intelligence Agency, 2004). North Korea, the most bizarre socialist society ever created, has no real future either, since it is led by a megalomaniacal leader totally out of touch with the rest of Asia, not to mention the world as a whole. North Korea will experience either a revolution from above or a democratic transition once Kim Jong Il dies. It is simply a matter of time. Once that happens, the two Koreas are likely to reunify into a powerful capitalist state that will combine South Korea's economic might with North Korea's military might. As for Cuba, Fidel Castro, the only leader Cuba has had since its 1959 revolution, is now in his late 70s, and with his death there will undoubtedly ensue a struggle for power that will end with the creation of a much more open political system.

Once these Communist regimes are gone, socialism is probably finished for good. Ken Jowitt (1991) sees socialism as having been morally disgraced and indisputably shown to be highly inferior to capitalism on economic grounds. In concurrence with the analysis above, he suggests that the few Communist regimes that remain do so only because the "tough old leaders" of the original revolutionary generation have yet to die (Chirot, 1991). Lipset and Bence (1994:203) see things in essentially the same way:

> Although Marx was right about the failure of efforts to create socialism in pre-industrial societies, he was wrong in anticipating the socialist revolution in advanced industrial ones. The United States apart, they all have significant socialist or social democratic parties, but without exception all of these have now given up socialist objectives; they all endorse the market economy as the best means to produce increased productivity and a higher living standard for the underprivileged. Socialism and Marxism may be considered failures not because of developments in the formerly Communist world, but because of their inability to point the way for the advanced countries.

Epilogue

The Future of Revolutions

WHILE SOCIALISM MAY HAVE NO FUTURE, it doesn't necessarily follow that revolutions do not have one. Nevertheless, a number of scholars are now beginning to ask the question, Is the age of revolutions over? For many of them, the answer is "yes." Goodwin (2001, 2003) sees revolutions as unlikely in the years ahead primarily because of the wave of democratization that has swept over much of the less-developed world in the past two decades (Sanderson, 2004). Why should democratization reduce the probability of revolution? For one thing, it ameliorates (even if it does not eliminate) social conflict, and it institutionalizes it by redirecting it into socially legitimate channels. If people are unhappy with their rulers, they recognize that they have an opportunity to get rid of them in the next election. Democratic modes of government also provide people with the opportunity to engage in popular protests that often allow them to win concessions from economic and political elites. Goodwin's conclusion is that "the ballot box has been the coffin of revolutionaries" (2003:67). Indeed, the evidence gives strong support to this view. As Goodwin notes, no revolution has ever overthrown a democratic regime. Revolutions are most likely to occur against brutal neopatrimonial dictatorships or exclusionary colonial regimes, and these regimes are becoming a relative rarity in the world of the twenty-first century.

Robert Snyder (1999), Ghia Nodia (2000), and Fred Halliday (1999) agree that the spread of democratization is making revolutions less likely, and for reasons very similar to those invoked by

Goodwin. But Halliday suggests three additional reasons for the diminished probability of revolutions in the future: States have generally grown stronger and thus more impervious to revolutionary overthrow; there are no longer any powerful states, such as the Soviet Union, that wish to promote revolutions in the Third World; and the ideological climate has become much less favorable to revolutions (cf. Snyder, 1999:21–24). As Halliday says, "The period of world history that runs from 1789 to 1989, in which the idea of a revolutionary change, at once possible and desirable, attracted large numbers of people, has effectively ended" (1999:332).

Two scholars who disagree with this line of thinking are John Foran (1997c) and Eric Selbin (1997). They see revolutions as being just as likely, if not more likely, in the coming years. And why? Because there is still a great deal of poverty, suffering, and injustice that will continue to create "cultures of opposition." Certainly poverty and suffering continue on a world scale, and there are many groups with strong feelings of injustice. But as Goodwin (2001:304) points out, it takes much more than these things to produce revolutions:

> Yet while these factors may generate widespread popular grievances, history tells us that these grievances are not sufficient to cause revolutions or even to generate significant revolutionary movements or popular rebellions. After all, revolutionary movements develop not simply because people are angry, but because the state under which they live provides no other mechanisms for social change and violently represses those who peacefully seek incremental reforms. And revolutionary movements, even those with strong popular support, rarely succeed in seizing power unless the authoritarian states that they confront are very weak or suddenly weakened.

As we noted in the first chapter, social revolutions are distinctly modern phenomena, occurring only within the past two centuries. They did not occur in premodern times, and their probability of occurrence in our current "postmodern" world seems significantly diminished. A major epoch of world history may have come to an end.

Appendix

Ten Leading Students of Revolutions

THIS APPENDIX SHOWCASES the lives of ten major students of revolution. Some of the students have written autobiographical sketches; in other instances the book's author wrote biographies based on information obtained from websites, faculty résumés, or books. The sketches focus mostly on the intellectual lives of these leading students, but most also contain social background information and material on their personal lives. Jack Goldstone's autobiographical sketch, for example, is as much personal as intellectual and contains an animated discussion of the lives of his parents and his own life over a long period of time. It is hoped that these sketches convey something of the human element in the study of revolutions. Intellectuals are human too, and they have very human needs, desires, goals, and purposes that guide their intellectual work.

John Foran: From Sartre to Marx, Iran to Chiapas—An Intellectual Autobiography

I was born in 1955 in Holyoke, Massachusetts, and grew up in New England. Between 1973 and 1977 I attended Amherst College, and lived in France for two years before coming to the West Coast in 1978 to begin graduate school at the University of California at Santa Barbara. In college I was interested in literature and philosophy, especially French and German. In my senior year, I undertook a thesis on

Sartre, and my advisor, Norman Birnbaum, required me to read Marx (for the first time) before getting to Sartre. This was an eye-opening experience for me, and I remember well my naïve question to my advisor in our next meeting: "This is really interesting; is there some way to apply it to the world?" The encounter with Marx shifted my interest to Sartre's own Marxism, and my thesis work then introduced me to the tradition of Western Marxism, in which I have worked ever since. In France, in my junior year and again a year after graduation, I saw the resonances of May 1968, and attended lectures and seminars by Alain Touraine, Nicos Poulantzas, and Henri Weber (a Trotskyist participant in 1968, the most interesting of them all).

I went to graduate school at Berkeley, having never had an undergraduate course in sociology, but with this budding passion for social theory. In my first year, I learned that I had to think of some way to apply theories empirically, and had the good fortune to take courses in Latin American and Middle Eastern history (there was no way to learn about the Third World in sociology then, which has now changed somewhat for the better). In particular, my eyes were further opened by my encounter with dependency theory as a key to history, and one which in the hands of Fernando Henrique Cardoso and Enzo Faletto, in their classic *Dependency and Development in Latin America* (1978), bore striking similarities to Sartre's dialectical way of blending historical agency and social structure.

I thus undertook a study of the Allende years in Chile for my M.A. The further I got into this tragic story, however, the more my initial inspiration that here was a project capable of changing the world turned to sorrow at its failure. I became unable to read further into the subject. This was in the summer of 1979, and the Iranian Revolution had just occurred. I shifted my research focus to those events, seeing in them something to be hopeful about, and came into contact with the radical political culture of Iranian students abroad, another enormous lesson in the politics of social transformation.

This project held my attention despite the fading of revolutionary hopes. My research took on a resolutely historical approach to the revolution, however, perhaps in response to that fading. The ten years or so I spent on the long history of social movements in Iran resulted in *Fragile Resistance: Social Transformation in Iran from 1500 to the Revolution* (Westview, 1993), and led me into the intricacies of studying social movements in all their complexity, in the process making me a generalist in areas such as theories of the state, political economy, culture and politics, and historical sociology.

After arriving at UC–Santa Barbara to begin teaching in 1989, I became more of a comparativist, or perhaps returned to my initial interest in Latin American studies. In 1990 I embarked on a lengthy journey of learning about the history of revolutions in the Third World, which I finally completed in the spring of 2004 as a book for Cambridge University Press, under the title *Taking Power: On the Origins of Third World Revolutions* (Foran, 2005).

I haven't really answered the question of how I relate to these movements. The question that I have focused on is the one of origins: Under what circumstances has it been possible for coalitions of aggrieved people to come together in a project of social transformation? This is the classic question of the causes of social revolutions, which has occupied the majority of scholars of revolution, and to which I contribute my part. This has meant trying to do justice to the classic antinomies of structure and agency, political economy and culture, internal and external factors. A related question for me has been: Who makes revolutions, and why? Again, this has meant trying to think hard about agency, subjectivity, and culture, as well as race/ gender/class, in a context that constrains or enables them to have effects. These are very large questions, and the empirical evidence bearing on them is vast. They also have pushed me into certain methods, most notably Boolean or qualitative comparative analysis, to handle a study in which the number of cases is too few to quantify (thank God, because I have no ear for it), yet too many to compare directly and simply. The other question that I must someday get around to is: Why do most revolutions fail once in power, and how could it be otherwise? Thus the motivation for the work is clearly from the perspective of an interest in seeing such experiments succeed.

I still dream that societies and individuals can transform themselves. I've seen it happen in my classrooms, and I've studied it on a grand scale. As I state in my syllabi, "I consider teaching a revolutionary act.... Learning and teaching are complex, endlessly fascinating collaborations. I learn enormous amounts from the students in my classes, whom I consider colleagues and companions on an intellectual, potentially life-changing journey." I have developed a social justice–oriented teaching method known as the case method, and invite teachers to consult the website about this at www.soc.ucsb.edu/projects/casemethod/.

Certainly, in both my teaching and research, I find the subject of revolutions one of great hope and inspiration, mixed with tragic outcomes and disappointments. The role of a non-dogmatic existential Marxist is to try to draw the lessons of the past to reflect on and act in the present and lay the groundwork for the future, something I and colleagues in the field undertook in the volume *The Future of Revolutions: Rethinking Radical Change in the Age of Globalization* (2003). My hope is that this work will contribute to the history it describes in some way or another, however indirectly.

I am active in the Green Party, locally and on the state level. I see the need for a party in the United States that will deeply challenge the status quo, and a need for the Greens to make the necessary changes in who they are in order to be that party. I intend to both work in, and draw out the lessons of, the global justice movement, and hopefully retain that link between activism, scholarship, and life that sustains me. If the next generation can do better, there will be some pay-off from what the past and present ones have done along these lines, both in interpreting the world and in changing it.

And where does Chiapas come into it? As the Zapatistas say, "Another world is possible." It's necessary. And it's up to all of us.

Jack A. Goldstone: The Political Demography of Revolutions— An Intellectual Autobiography

My parents were German Jews who were expelled from that country in the 1930s. My mother was only eight years old at the time and traveled to Shanghai with her parents. My father was twenty-four and already working in the family business. He was not quite so lucky. He got a call at work one day from his mother: "The Gestapo just came and took your father and brother, and they're looking for you." He took what cash he could from the cash register, boarded a train, hid in the bathroom at the border crossing, and made it to Czechoslovakia. After further wrong-way travels and stints in border prisons in Poland and a detention camp in Britain, he was finally shipped out to a P.O.W. camp in Australia (where all German passport-holders in Britain, even Jews, were sent during the Battle of Britain). After a few years of whittling trinkets for guards in the desert sun, he was allowed to leave for a neutral country. He too ended up in Shanghai for the last few years of World War II, and he met my mother there. They migrated once more, to San Francisco, where they were married. I was born there in 1953.

I had a conventional life for the son of parents in small business without any formal education. I worked in the family business on weekends from the time I was ten, and read everything I could at other times. I attended the San Francisco public schools, but when I graduated from high school in 1971 I knew little about history and even less about politics. I was especially apt in mathematics and science, won several math/engineering awards, and was granted early admission and a Hertz Fellowship to study physics at the California Institute of Technology. My main interest was in particle physics. Yet when I took a course in economics from Charles Plott (later one of the leaders in the field of experimental economics), I found that analyzing social behavior was just as fascinating as analyzing physical processes. I soon enrolled in several social science courses, including political science with John Ferejohn (then just starting as an assistant professor, later an eminent Fellow at the Hoover Institution at Stanford University), and studied energy policy with John Holdren (also a young assistant professor then, now Heinz Professor of Public Policy at Harvard).

I was very excited, but also very naïve. One day, I passed an exhibit case in the Caltech Humanities Library with Professor Ferejohn and he exclaimed, "Look at that, a first edition of Hobbes!" "Who's Hobbes?" I replied. Ferejohn answered me sternly: "You don't know who Thomas Hobbes was? And you call yourself an educated man?" I had to admit I didn't, and thus was not. If I was ever going to become a social scientist, I had a great deal of learning to do. Although my time at Caltech was short (I was there only a year and half), that period stamped my future intellectual development, both by changing my direction and by setting standards for research that I have ever since aimed to reach.

In 1973 I took a leave from Caltech to visit other schools where I might transfer to pursue a social science education, riding Greyhound buses across the country (I couldn't afford to fly or to have a car at that point; in fact I didn't acquire my first car until age twenty-six, a very odd thing for a Californian). But before I left Caltech I bought a second-hand set of the "Great Books." I read as I rode the bus, trying to remedy my deficiencies as an *un*educated man. I read Hobbes, Greek literature, Shakespeare, Kant, Hume, Montaigne, Marcus Aurelius; I had a lot of catching up to do. I owe some of my best undergraduate education to Greyhound.

I eventually transferred to Harvard and majored in social studies. For the first time, I had to learn to write essays; that was a major struggle. Yet I was fortunate to be able to learn from such scholars as Thomas Schelling, Paul Bator, Howard Raiffa, and Richard Zeckhauser (for whom I worked as a research assistant on an energy policy project) in economics, and Theda Skocpol, Paul Starr, Michael Walzer, and Karl Deutsch in sociology and political science. Deutsch supervised my undergraduate honors thesis, in which I studied how Henry Jackson's U.S. Senate Committee on Energy and Natural Resources used information to inform its policymaking. I spent a delightful summer on Capitol Hill, courtesy of a grant from Harvard's Institute of Public Policy, learning about the life of Senate staff.

Yet I came away disillusioned. Information, I found, was used mainly to backstop decisions already made for political reasons. Politicians paid most attention to the views of folks they most trusted, who were not necessarily the best experts in the field. Their daily agenda was set more by current headlines in the *Washington Post* and *New York Times* than by long-term planning for policy. After completing my thesis, I changed course once again, deciding I would study the history of governance and learn why government so often made poor policy. I stayed at Harvard another five years for graduate study in political sociology.

Again, I was fortunate to be in the right place with the right people at the right time. Skocpol was working on the draft of what would become her classic *States and Social Revolutions*. S. N. Eisenstadt was a visiting professor, also working on revolutions. I decided that the study of revolutions would truly lead me to understand when and how governments went astray. I thought that governments—with all their access to finances, military force, and expert advice—should not normally be easy to overthrow, and that revolutions must indicate some kind of failure or dilemma of government. This view was reinforced by Skocpol's structural theory, and became the basis of my work.

However, the real breakthrough in my understanding came by chance. I had planned to be a teaching assistant one semester for Daniel Bell (another formidable scholar and major influence on me) in his course on macrosociology. But Bell came down with back problems, cancelled the class, and I was left to search for any teaching job I could find, simply to support myself. An opportunity came from George Masnick, of the Harvard School of Public Health, who was teaching a course on American public policy and the post–World War

II baby boom. Frankly, I knew little or nothing of demography; but by then I had much experience in studies of U.S. public policy. Masnick offered to teach me all I needed to know of basic demography, if I would help the students in the class research the issues in public policy.

As the class progressed, it was fascinating to see the issues posed by the baby boom for state and national governments. State and local governments had to build more schools, more houses, more roads, more utilities, and provide more health services. Universities were overflowing with self-confident and rebellious students. The labor market had to absorb huge waves of new workers. Doing all these things while fighting the war in Vietnam fueled inflation and led to major political battles at the federal level over taxation and spending. And the gap between generations led to new proclamations of morality and idealism that challenged the status quo.

At the same time that I was teaching this course, I was starting my own independent research into revolutions, trying to identify recurrent patterns. I had already realized, thanks to work by Skocpol and Eisenstadt, that revolutions often began with conflicts over state spending and taxation and elite battles over conservative versus radical ways to cope with fiscal problems, often involved rebellious students, and were preceded by rising unemployment among workers or struggles over land by peasants. It was this conjunction of factors, affecting local, regional, and national authorities simultaneously and across several dimensions of social organization, that led to the severe social breakdowns that characterized revolutions. Eisenstadt was careful always to remind me that revolutions were borne by heterodox ideologies that had suddenly become more salient.

I was trying to understand what forces could possibly cause all these things to come together—fiscal problems, elite battles, student unrest, worker and peasant distress, and heterodox ideologies—when it dawned on me: If the U.S. government, with its modern and fast-growing industrial economy, was severely challenged by the impact of the postwar baby boom, what would have been the impact of population booms on preindustrial agrarian states, with their far more vulnerable economies and less capable states? I spent several days in the Widener library stacks, looking up the population history of every major state that had experienced a revolution in the last three hundred years. The results were extraordinary and quite clear: All such revolutions had been preceded by two or three generations of strong, often exceptional, population growth. By contrast, periods of political conservatism and stability were, almost without exception, characterized by population stagnation or even slow decline.

I now had a theory, and accumulated evidence, but getting support for it was another matter entirely. When I first proposed my plans to do a dissertation on population pressure in preindustrial societies as a cause of revolution, my advisors firmly rejected it as a return to old-fashioned "pressure-cooker" theories of revolution. Revolutions were not caused by population, but by politics, they assured me; it was the state and not the situation of the masses, much less their sheer numbers, that caused state crises. My theory, they said, treated people like bacteria in a jar, breeding themselves into crisis. It was a throwback to 1930s-style "rise of the masses" anxieties. I will never forget Skocpol's reaction to my dissertation proposal: She told me firmly that given the paucity and poor quality of historical demographic data, it was unlikely that anyone could do such a dissertation. Moreover, she added, even if the data could be used, the difficulty of documenting any causal connection between long-term population movements and political crises was so great that no graduate student like myself could hope to accomplish it. Finally, she argued that even if I could make such a link, no one would care—research had moved on to issues of elite and state conflicts, and popular grievances were merely a more-or-less constant background against which elite and state battles over war and taxation took place. My dissertation proposal was rejected.

Although Skocpol was surely just looking out for a graduate student who was biting off more than he could possibly chew, I was deeply distressed, and nearly gave up. Still, I thought, my population approach *did* address elite and state and fiscal conflicts. It simply placed them in a larger context, and explained why student rebellions, popular grievances, and interest in heterodox ideologies conjoined with them in major revolutionary crises. I looked for a way to make the case, and decided to try again. This time, I found help from George Homans and Nathan Keyfitz. Homans persuaded me to simply focus on the English Revolution of 1640. At the time, interpretations of the event were dominated by theories of a "rising gentry." Yet Homans, a master historian in his own right, was struck by elements of what Christopher Hill had labeled "a world turned upside down," in which issues of law and status were widely challenged, and contention among elite factions and the Crown was more acute than any conflict between classes. He was also struck by the fact that the revolution was fought in the counties as much as between Parliament and the King, as my theory would suggest. Homans guided my readings and helped me focus my work. Keyfitz, a brilliant mathematical demographer who also had deep experience in theory, was intrigued by my notion that population growth could have political consequences, a notion that fit with some of his own experience in studying developing countries. He gave me his wholehearted support. Even Skocpol eventually relented, and after my field statement on theories of revolution (later published as "Theories of Revolution: The Third Generation" in *World Politics* in 1980) persuaded her that I had a good grasp of the issues regarding states and elites, she approved my research.

I was able to publish some earlier work on social movements (a critique of William Gamson's famous study of social protest) and obtain a job at Northwestern University upon getting my Ph.D., but continued to face rejection in my work on population and revolution. My first journal submission on the English Revolution was rejected by *Theory and Society,* my first comparative study on the topic was rejected by *Comparative Studies in Society and History,* and my book manuscript based on my dissertation was rejected by Cambridge University Press. Historians took umbrage at my social science approach to their topic, while sociologists felt I dwelt too much on historical details. Eventually, I was able to get my work published, but it took some years of persistent struggles. Along the way, I was turned down for jobs by Princeton, the University of North Carolina at Chapel Hill, the University of Washington, and the University of Chicago. (Northwestern University, while extremely supportive of my research, entered a fiscal crisis as I arrived and froze salaries; I was advised to try to get outside offers but had little luck.)

Still, I once again had good fortune with people. A young economic historian at Northwestern, Joel Mokyr, and his colleague Jonathan Hughes, brought me into their economic history seminar. There I had a chance to really learn about population history, the history of money and inflation, and state finances. I met future Nobel laureates Doug North and Robert Fogel, both frequent visitors to Chicago-area economic history meetings. And I gained their support to seek access to the Population History Group at Cambridge University, which was just then reconstructing the population history of England in unprecedented detail.

I obtained leave to spend a spring in Cambridge with the Population Group. It was perhaps the greatest intellectual and personal experience of my life. The group's leaders—Peter Laslett, E. A. Wrigley, and Roger Schofield—along with many other brilliant and original scholars, had made the Population Group a home for historical demographers from around the world. Their library alone was a treasure trove. Best of all, even when they disagreed with some of the conclusions I drew, they freely shared their data and their discussions, opening their homes and sharing their ideas.

In the next few years, I had the opportunity to spend time at several other research centers: the Research School of Social Sciences in the Australian National University, where I met the brilliant agricultural historian Robert Allen; the UCLA Center for Chinese Studies, home to Philip Huang, Benjamin Elman, Richard Baum, and many other distinguished scholars; the Berkeley Demography Department, where I benefited from the knowledge of Sheila Johanssen, Eugene Hammel, Kenneth Wachter, and Ron Lee. I even returned to Caltech for a short stint as visiting professor of Political Science.

By 1991, my manuscript, *Revolution and Rebellion in the Early Modern World*, had been published by the University of California Press, and I had moved to the University of California at Davis as director of a new graduate research and training center on comparative history. In 1993, my book was honored with the ASA Distinguished Contribution to Scholarship award. It appeared that I was finally on the way to a flourishing career.

But this was not to be. Instead, dark days lay ahead. The University of California entered its own financial crisis, and my research center was cut back to form mainly a visiting speakers bureau. For the next ten years, I had little or no opportunity to teach graduate courses in political sociology or comparative history. Also in that decade, my wife and I were thrown out of our beds and across the room by the Northridge Earthquake of 1994, which destroyed my wife's home in Los Angeles, where we were staying at the time. This was followed by a series of illnesses and injuries to family members that kept us in and out of hospitals for much of the next seven years.

I became a pretty good undergraduate lecturer, and did what research I could, extending my work into additional areas such as social movements, prison riots (with the wonderful collaboration of Bert Useem), and comparative methods. I also began work on my next major enterprise, an account of the origins of the Industrial Revolution and the rise of the West.

For the study of social movements, I was offered a truly wonderful opportunity by Chuck Tilly, Sid Tarrow, and Doug McAdam, who invited me to join a research group on Contentious Politics that they had begun at Stanford University. Once again, I was fortunate to have brilliant and generous colleagues who stimulated me and encouraged my work. I was also lucky to meet some of the most gifted graduate students in sociology and political science, who were offered fellowships to work with the group. One of my proudest achievements is the edited volume of their work published in 2003 as *States, Parties, and Social Movements* by Cambridge University Press.

In 2004, I was offered an outstanding honor: a chair in public policy at George Mason University, where I would succeed one of the most distinguished political sociologists of the last century, Seymour Martin Lipset. Interest in revolutions had run high again in Washington, with events in Afghanistan, Iraq, and Haiti crowding onto the policy agenda. It seemed like a natural home, and I was grateful to have the opportunity to return to graduate teaching and research in my chosen field.

Looking back on the past twenty years, I realize that it was almost entirely the continued influence of brilliant friends and colleagues, and the encouragement of truly superior scholars, that accounts for anything that is good in my work. About all I did was persevere. If progress in understanding the roots of revolution and conflict helps reduce, in some degree, the incidence of needless violence, and makes peaceful transformations to freer societies more likely, I will be truly delighted. But I know if any of these things happen it will be because the quarter-century between 1980 and 2005 was a truly extraordinary time of intellectual ferment and original scholarship in comparative-historical sociology, and I was very lucky to be around as it happened.

Jeff Goodwin: From Revolutions to Terrorism, 1979–2001—An Intellectual Autobiography

My interest in revolutions crystallized in the summer of 1979, in a basement apartment off Oxford Street in Cambridge, Massachusetts. I could not have guessed then that this interest would powerfully shape my intellectual concerns for the next two decades. I had finished my junior year at Harvard and was trying to come up with a topic for my senior honors essay, a requirement in the interdisciplinary Social Studies program in which I was majoring (or "concentrating," in Harvard lingo). A major revolution had occurred quite unexpectedly earlier that year in Iran, and the Sandinistas would take power in Nicaragua in mid-July. It appeared that revolutionaries in El Salvador might also sweep away the military government in that country. And there was a revolution of sorts on the small Caribbean island of Grenada. The year 1979 was unmistakably a year of revolution. And my own sympathies for the underdog piqued my interest in these revolutions—and in the very idea of revolution.

While these dramatic events were occurring, I was also reading about past revolutions. Two books, in particular, had a profound influence upon me at this time, although they were very different in nature. John Womack's magisterial study of the peasant movement led by Emiliano Zapata, *Zapata and the Mexican Revolution* (1968), was one of the most gripping works of history that I had ever read. *Zapata* is a masterpiece of social history, and I consider it one of the greatest historical works of the twentieth century. (About this time I also saw for the first time Elia Kazan's *Zapata!*, with a brilliant screenplay by John Steinbeck and of course starring the young Marlon Brando as the man himself.) Womack was and is a professor of history at Harvard, and I would take his wonderful, two-semester Latin American history course during my senior year. In fact, I decided to write my senior essay on the Mexican Revolution, and Womack agreed to be my advisor.

The other book that had a profound impact on me at this time was Skocpol's *States and Social Revolutions*. Skocpol was a young sociology professor at Harvard and her book had just been published. I had previously hoped to enroll in Professor Skocpol's course on revolutions, but a scheduling conflict prevented me from doing so. (In fact, I am a rather unusual protégé, having never taken a regular course from Theda at either the undergraduate or graduate level.) I devoured this book, amazed, delighted, and awed that events of such world-historical importance could be explained so clearly, powerfully, and parsimoniously. If Womack's book is a classic of social history, Skocpol's is a masterpiece of comparative and historical sociology. The thought would soon occur to me: Could I explain the Mexican Revolution that Womack wrote about or even the still-unfolding events in Central America with the theoretical tools provided by Skocpol?

My senior essay attempted to provide an analytic explanation for the onset of the Mexican Revolution. I argued, if memory serves, that the collapse of the dictatorship of Porfirio Diaz was brought about not only, or even mainly, by rebellions "from below" but also by the growing alienation of middle-class and elite strata, as well as of the United States government, from the Diaz regime. (International war, a factor emphasized by Skocpol, played no role in this particular state crisis, although geopolitics certainly mattered.) The collapse of the Diaz dictatorship made possible, in turn, the various mobilizations and conflicts that we now remember as the Revolution. Professor Skocpol and Jack Goldstone, a graduate student who was nearing the end of his studies at Harvard, were the two "readers" (i.e., graders) of my essay. I think they liked it well enough, although I recall some doubt as to just how original my arguments were. I was certainly strongly influenced by Walter Goldfrank's cutting-edge analysis of the Mexican Revolution.

I remained intrigued by the possibility of carrying out a comparative analysis of revolutionary movements in Central America, and I applied to the sociology graduate program at Harvard, eager to study with Skocpol. Alas, she went on leave the very year I entered graduate school, and she relocated the following year to the University of Chicago, having been denied tenure at Harvard. As fate would have it, she returned to Harvard as a tenured professor soon after I began working on my dissertation. In the meantime, I studied comparative and historical methods with J. Samuel Valenzuela (now at Notre Dame), and I befriended and learned a lot from a number of junior faculty and graduate students in both the Sociology and Social Studies programs.

My doctoral dissertation examined revolutionary movements in Southeast Asia following World War II, as well as in Central America during the 1970s and 1980s. Revolutionary movements in both these regions had very uneven success, and my dissertation sought to explain why. Strongly influenced by Skocpol, my explanation focused on the nature of the states that would-be revolutionaries confronted. The structure and practices of some states made it comparatively easy for revolutionaries to mobilize people and even take power, but other political contexts were much less conducive to revolutionary mobilization, let alone seizures of power. This claim informed all my subsequent writings on revolutions, and I continue to think it's a darned good idea, even if it fails to explain everything one might wish to know about revolutions.

The year after I completed my doctoral dissertation, Communist regimes were swept away in Eastern Europe. This caught me by surprise, as it did virtually all of the experts on the Soviet bloc. In a number of cases, popular rebellions helped bring down Communist regimes. So were these revolutions? What caused these momentous events? And what accounted for the quite different ways in which Communist regimes were destroyed? I was a new professor at Northwestern University (in the Political Science department) in the fall of 1989, and I began to educate myself about Eastern Europe (Valerie Bunce, now at Cornell, was a huge help). Once again, real-world events had a strong influence on my scholarship.

I soon moved to the sociology department at New York University. As a result, I was able to learn a lot from Charles Tilly, especially while he was based at the New School for Social Research. I continued to read about Eastern Europe, and I threw myself into a number of other projects, mainly having to do with social movements. Eventually, my comparative study of revolutions was published by Cambridge University Press as *No Other Way Out: States and Revolutionary Movements, 1945–1991* (2001). I took the title for my book from Trotsky, who once quipped that people don't make revolutions eagerly, but only when there is no viable alternative. The book included the analyses (much revised) of Southeast Asia and Central America that I developed in my dissertation. It also included a chapter on the events of 1989 in Eastern Europe. And it included a chapter on protracted rebellions—insurgencies that neither seized power nor were simply defeated, but ended in negotiated settlements, or slowly fizzled out, after prolonged conflicts.

I should emphasize that it has been enormously edifying and satisfying to find myself a part of the small but dynamic network of scholars who have produced a genuinely important stream of research about the causes and consequences of revolutions. Scholars such as Skocpol, Goldstone, Tilly, Ellen Trimberger, John Foran, Jeff Paige, Misagh Parsa, Eric Selbin, Farideh Farhi, and others have pushed our understanding of revolutions far beyond where it stood a quarter-century ago. This is surely one of the signal, if often overlooked, achievements of social science during this period.

Only months after my book on revolutions was published, the real world intruded again, pushing my scholarly research in a new direction. The terrorist attacks on the World Trade Center occurred only a short distance from my home in Greenwich Village. These attacks were unsettling both personally and intellectually. Why would the perpetrators of these attacks choose to target civilians? What did they hope to gain thereby? I have subsequently thrown myself into the study of the political strategy known as "terrorism." Of course, terrorism is not entirely unrelated to revolution. It is a strategy that some, but not all, revolutionary movements have employed in order to realize their objectives. (And make no mistake, al-Qaeda is a revolutionary movement.) But why some revolutionaries have chosen to employ this strategy, while others have rejected it, has not been well explained. Most scholars of revolutions are interested in why they happen in certain places, but not others, and at certain times, but not others. The diverse strategies of revolutionaries, of which terrorism is one, have not received as much sustained attention. (Of course, terrorism is a strategy that many types of networks and organizations, including states, with very different political orientations, have adopted.)

My book on revolutions appeared twenty years after I first became interested in the topic. During that time, alas, popular interest in revolutions, at least among North Americans, seemed to wane considerably. The Clinton and Bush years will not be remembered as a time of political radicalism, although strong radical subcultures certainly persisted. I hope my comparative study of terrorism won't take so long to appear! Whether terrorism will continue to be an issue of broad public concern when it does appear remains to be seen. Alas, the owl of Minerva spreads its wings only at dusk.

Ted Robert Gurr: An Intellectual Biography

Ted Robert Gurr, a political scientist, was born in Spokane, Washington, in 1936, the grandson of pioneer settlers in the Pacific Northwest.[1] He majored in psychology at Reed College where his reading of the social-psychological literature on frustration-aggression theory, and coursework in statistics, provided a point of departure for his

---

[1] Information in this biography was obtained from Gurr's website, http://www.cidcm.umd.edu/people.gurr.htm, and directly from Professor Gurr himself. A more detailed biographical account is Ted Robert Gurr, "Conflict and Political Order: An Intellectual Biography," in Hans Daalder (ed.), *European Politics: The Story of a Profession*, London: Pinter, 1997.

later research on the origins of revolutionary political action. After graduating from Reed in 1957, he began working on an M.A. degree in public affairs at Princeton but soon left, turned off by a stultifying and hierarchical program that contrasted too sharply with Reed's lively and creative intellectual environment.

From 1958 to the early 1960s Gurr worked as a research and editorial assistant, then collaborator, with Alfred de Grazia, a political scientist. He soon resumed doctoral study in New York University's African studies program and, in 1964, conceived the idea for a dissertation that looked at the social-psychological origins of the wave of postindependence rebellions that erupted in tropical Africa. His dissertation, which he defended in 1965, became the basis for the classic book *Why Men Rebel,* which won the Woodrow Wilson Prize as best book in political science of 1970.

In 1965 Harry Eckstein invited Gurr to join a small research team working on internal wars at Princeton's Center for International Studies, a position that gave him the opportunity to begin empirical work testing some of the propositions in his dissertation. Publications followed, along with a junior faculty appointment and an opportunity, in the summer of 1968, to take a position with the National Commission on the Causes and Prevention of Violence. The Commission was established by President Lyndon Johnson at the peak of violent urban protest by urban African-Americans and in the immediate aftermath of the assassinations of Martin Luther King and Robert Kennedy. Gurr was teamed with a young historian, Hugh Davis Graham, who was listed as the first author, to prepare the widely publicized two-volume report to the Commission, *Violence in America: Historical and Comparative Perspectives.* Revised editions were issued in 1979 and 1989 but attracted little of the attention—or sales—of the 1969 report.

The publication of two well-reviewed books led to a faculty appointment and chair at Northwestern University in the 1970s and to funding opportunities for a program of systematic work on civil conflict. It also prompted a four-year detour into the comparative history of crime and conflict in Western societies, which documented similar long-term trends in personal and property crime—a nineteenth- and early-twentieth-century decline followed by substantial increases after 1960. This helped stimulate a wave of crime-trend studies in sociology and criminology that continues to the present, but Gurr soon returned to his primary interest in violent political conflict. After the death of his wife Erika in 1980, he spent a Fulbright year in Australia, remarried, and left Northwestern for the University of Colorado.

A number of shifts are evident in Gurr's subsequent work: more substantial use of case and historical studies, more attention to the domestic and international structures that shape conflict, a greater emphasis on group-level conflict processes, and a focus on policies for managing and redirecting deadly conflict. All are exemplified in the Minorities at Risk (MAR) project, which he initiated at the University of Colorado in the mid-1980s. The project was initially prompted by the convergence of James Scarritt's concern about the human rights status of minorities and Barbara Harff's work on the victimization of ethnic groups in genocides and "politicides." The project soon developed a momentum of its own. Housed at the University of Maryland's Center of International Development and Conflict Management (CIDCM) since 1989, the project is devoted to tracking and analyzing the conflicts of approximately 300 ethnic and national peoples throughout the world. A practical goal of the research is to assess the effects of conflict management strategies, especially those designed in response to separatist demands.

Evidence from the MAR project has been summarized in a number of publications, including *Minorities at Risk* (1993), *Ethnic Conflict in World Politics* (1994, rev. ed. 2004, co-authored with Barbara Harff), and *Peoples Versus States: Minorities at Risk in the New Century* (2000). Beginning in 2000 Gurr and Monty Marshall have prepared a series of biennial reports from CIDCM entitled *Peace and Conflict* that provide up-to-date global surveys of armed conflicts, self-determination movements, and democratization. (On MAR and related projects see www.cidcm.umd.edu/inscr/ and www.minoritiesatrisk.com.)

In late 1994 Gurr was invited to help establish the State Failure Task Force, a White House–sponsored empirical study of the precursors of internal wars and regime breakdowns since 1955 that has been continued by the Bush administration (and is now known as the Political Instability Task Force). Key to the Task Force's work is the principle that "the international consequences of state failures are profound. A vital policy question is whether failures can be diagnosed far enough in advance to facilitate effective international efforts at prevention or peaceful transformation." The Task Force analyses of these issues are widely circulated among U.S. intelligence and foreign policy specialists. Parallel to this policy research Gurr has done extensive collaborative work with Barbara Harff on risk assessment and early warning of ethnopolitical conflicts (Gurr) and humanitarian crises (Harff).

In 1995 Gurr was awarded the title of Distinguished University Professor at Maryland, where he has taught courses on theories and comparative analyses of ethnic and revolutionary conflict at both the graduate and undergraduate levels. International recognition of Gurr's work includes the Olaf Palme Visiting Professorship at the University of Uppsala, Sweden (in 1996–97) and a stint at the Interdisciplinary Program on Root Causes of Human Rights Violations of the University of Leiden, The Netherlands. He has received numerous grants and awards, including a 1988–89 appointment as Peace Fellow of the U.S. Institute of Peace and a recent grant from the Carnegie Corporation that supports the ongoing work of the Minorities at Risk project on self-determination movements. In October of 2002 he received an honorary doctorate from the University of Sofia, Bulgaria.

Retired from the University of Maryland since 2003, Gurr and his wife Barbara Harff, a professor at the U.S. Naval Academy, divide their time between homes on Chesapeake Bay in Annapolis, Maryland, and in Summerlin, Nevada. His daughter Lisa Anne is a cultural anthropologist, and his daughter Andrea is a university administrator. His stepson, Timothy Gribben, is a mineral processing engineer.

Krishan Kumar: An Autobiographical Sketch

I lived for most of my life in England, attending school in London. I studied history as an undergraduate at Cambridge University and sociology as a postgraduate at the London School of Economics. My Ph.D. dissertation began as a study of Darwinism, evolutionism, and sociology, an interest that I have retained. But I found I had bitten off more than I could chew for the purposes of a dissertation, so I ended up doing a study of the idea of postindustrial society, as promoted by such thinkers as Daniel Bell and Alain Touraine. This dissertation was published as *Prophecy and Progress: The Sociology of Industrial and Post-Industrial Society* (1978). By that time I had moved to the new University of Kent at Canterbury as a lecturer in sociology (having in the early 1970s also had a stint as a BBC Talks producer, an experience that has given me a lasting interest in public-service broadcasting).

But before I continued work on *Prophecy and Progress* I had already during my graduate years developed an interest in revolution and published my first book, an edited volume, *Revolution: The Theory and Practice of a European Idea* (1971). In the ninety-page introduction to that book—a collection of historical and theoretical documents—I advanced an idea of revolution drawing on concepts from the history of art and science. I also attempted to give a general theory of the causes of revolution, drawing particularly on the ideas of Plato, Tocqueville, Burckhardt, and others who might be said to have had a "state-centered" view of revolution, and who put the stress on elite rather than class conflicts as the principal dissolving forces of *ancien régimes*. Perhaps I might say, rather immodestly, that I think this brief initial sketch anticipates in many ways Skocpol's much more elaborate and more theoretically sophisticated "structuralist" account of revolution in *States and Social Revolutions*.

My work in the 1980s continued the themes of my *Prophecy and Progress*, being mainly about the history, theory, and practice of industrial societies. I wrote about work and unemployment, about economic growth and its problems, and about the future of industrial societies. In 1983 I co-edited with Adrian Ellis a volume of essays stimulated by the work of the British economist Fred Hirsch. It was called *Dilemmas of Liberal Democracies: Studies in Fred Hirsch's Social Limits to Growth*. I also got involved in work on the "informal economy," and on the new, "post-Fordist" developments in work and work organization taking place in central Italy. Much of this work was connected with my involvement in a journal, *New Universities Quarterly*, and with a non-profit think tank, the Acton Society, of which I was trustee. We organized numerous conferences in Britain and Italy, and published the papers and the discussions in the *New Universities Quarterly* and several Acton Society volumes. Many of my own essays and articles of this period were republished in my *The Rise of Modern Society: Aspects of the Social and Political Development of the West* (1988).

While working on *Prophecy and Progress* I had also got interested in utopias. This took me off on a longer journey than I had expected, leading to the publication of *Utopia and Anti-Utopia in Modern Times* (1987) and *Utopianism* (1991). I found the material fascinating, both as literature and as a form of social and political theory. I also discovered that an interest in utopias put one in touch with scholars in a wide range of disciplines—literature, history, political theory, sociology, even theology (my books on utopias have been shelved by bookshops in all these categories). This led to numerous international conferences on utopias, the most stimulating and agreeable being the ones organized by the literature department of the University of Bologna. In the early 1990s Stephen Bann and I organized a conference at Kent to celebrate the work of the French scholar Louis Marin; the papers appeared in a jointly edited volume, *Utopias and the Millennium* (1993). I also published editions, with introductions and critical notes, of William Morris's *News from Nowhere* (1995) and H. G. Wells's *A Modern Utopia* (1993).

My work on post-Fordist developments in the "Third Italy" also renewed my interest in theories of industrial society, leading eventually to the publication of *From Post-Industrial to Post-Modern Society: New Theories of the Contemporary World* (1995, new edition forthcoming). I had also, following a year as a visiting scholar at Harvard, started working with Jeff Weintraub on a number of projects, one of which led to our jointly edited volume, *Public and Private in Thought and Practice: Reflections on a Grand Dichotomy* (1997).

But during this time, revolution had by no means been forgotten. In the mid-1980s I had been commissioned to write a book on revolution by Fontana Press. By 1989 I had written three chapters, including one on the origins of the French Revolution. The 1989 revolutions in Central and Eastern Europe stopped me in my tracks. Here, precisely on the bicentenary of the French Revolution, were a new and quite unexpected series of revolutions. It seemed impossible to carry on the writing of my book—especially as one of my main aims was to trace the tradition of revolution and revolutionary ideas, what I called "revolutionism," since the eighteenth century—without investigating the 1989 revolutions and their aftermath. Over the next six years I spent a good deal of time in Central and Eastern Europe, helped by having a base at the Central European University in Prague, where I was a visiting professor in the sociology department. I wrote a number of essays on the character of the 1989 revolutions, from the perspective both of their relation to Central European societies and of their place in the general Western revolutionary tradition, to which—cautiously—they claimed heir. Most of these writings were later collected in my book *1989: Revolutionary Ideas and Ideals* (2001).

In 1996 I left the University of Kent for the University of Virginia, where I am currently William R. Kenan, Jr., Professor of Sociology.

My most recent work has been on nationalism and national identity. In 2003 Cambridge published my *The Making of English National Identity*. Building on that work I now wish to do a comparative study of "Empire and Identities," focusing especially on England, France, and Russia as imperial nations. A good part of that work I hope to do in 2004–05 as a Member of the School of Social Science at the Princeton Institute of Advanced Study. I am also co-editing (with Gerard Delanty) for Sage Publishers a *Handbook of Nations and Nationalism*.

So, to conclude where I began, with revolution. The unfinished book, interrupted by the 1989 revolutions, remains to be completed, and will be, though it will probably look very different from the way I originally envisioned it. What remains a guiding thread for me is that revolution is a phenomenon in history and with a history. Abstract theoretical schemas, of the kind that often appear in textbooks, seem to me useless unless firmly anchored in history. As a modern phenomenon revolution arose at a specific time and in a specific place, eighteenth-century Europe and its North American offshoot. What happened in the American and French revolutions affected practically every subsequent revolution, not just in Europe but in the rest of the world as it came under European rule and influence. The study of revolution has to be principally concerned with the effects of that process of invention and diffusion. This means that while revolutions will show a "family resemblance" to each other, they will also differ according to time and place.

There will be some similarity in concept, causation, course, and consequences, but we should not look for or expect identity. The Russian Revolution clearly borrowed from the French Revolution, but it did not replicate it, any more than the Chinese Revolution that culminated in 1948 replicated the Russian Revolution to which it was indebted in complex ways. When Trotsky accused the revolutionaries of 1848 of being "shabbily wise" with the experience of 1789, he was making an important point about how one revolution relates to another. Revolutionaries as well as counter-revolutionaries learn from past experiences; that is bound to affect how they and their enemies think and act. The 1989 revolutions are the most recent example of this, as one can readily see from the writings of such thinkers as Vaclác Havel and Adam Michnik.

I have sketched out a brief prospectus for myself, similar to the above, in a forthcoming article on revolution for the *New Scribner's Dictionary of the History of Ideas*. Now all I need is the time to finish that book I started twenty years ago!

Barrington Moore, Jr.: A Biographical Sketch

Born in Washington, D.C., in 1913, Barrington Moore, Jr., studied Greek and Latin at Williams College and then went on to work for a doctorate at Yale.[2] He served as a political analyst during World War II in the U.S. Department of Justice as well as the U.S. Office of Strategic Studies. Moore taught briefly at the University of Chicago after the war and then moved to Harvard in 1948. He was part of the Department of Social Relations, but his way of doing sociology, as well as his theoretical and political views, made him an ill fit in the department. He thus became based in the Russian Research Center. In his early years he wrote books on the Soviet system: *Soviet Politics* in 1950 and *Terror and Progress USSR* in 1954. After several other books and articles, he published his masterpiece in 1966, *Social Origins of Dictatorship and Democracy: Lord and Peasant in the Making of the Modern World*. This book received almost immediate recognition and fame, made his reputation, and increased the audience for all of the remaining books he would write. By 1975 *Social Origins* had been reprinted nine times. It received the Woodrow Wilson Foundation Award in 1968 and the MacIver Award in 1969. At the time it was written, *Social Origins* was one of the very few works in sociology to use a comparative-historical approach and to be extensively informed by historical materials. In a sense, Moore's book helped initiate a new direction in sociological analysis, for by the mid-1970s a comparative-historical revolution was under way.

In *Social Origins* Moore's aim was to understand the nature of the various paths that had been taken in the past two hundred years to the modern world. He used a loosely Marxian approach that considered the form of economy and the nature of the major social class divisions as primary. Three paths to modernity were identified. The first path, which occurred in England, France, and the United States, was capitalist and democratic. As in the other two paths, both landlords and peasants were an important part of this process. They either contributed to the process of capitalist development and democratization (which, Moore argues, was the case in England) or, if they were opposed to it, were swept aside through revolution or some other form of collective violence (the French Revolution, the American Civil

---

[2]Much of this biographical sketch is based on Dennis Smith, *Barrington Moore, Jr.: A Critical Appraisal*, M. E. Sharpe, 1983.

War). The second path was also capitalist, but it led to fascism rather than to democracy, at least for a time. Germany and Japan took this path. Since the bourgeois or capitalist impulse was much weaker in these countries, their revolutions were revolutions from above rather than from below. The third path was the Communist path, followed most strongly by Russia and China. These were largely agrarian societies with limited capitalism and commercialism. Here the urban classes were not strong enough to help modernize their societies, and the peasants were huge in number. It was the peasantry in these societies that constituted the main force in the Russian Revolution of 1917 and the Chinese Revolution of 1949, and it was the Communist Party that tried to modernize these societies.

Of Moore's later books, the most important were *Reflections on the Causes of Human Misery and on Certain Proposals to Eliminate Them* (1972) and *Injustice: The Social Bases of Obedience and Revolt* (1978). In *Reflections* he identified four main sources of human misery: poverty, hunger, and disease; war; persecution for one's beliefs; and social injustice and oppression. Moore's book had strong moral overtones, for he wished to suggest certain lines of possible action by which these forms of misery could be alleviated. One of his central concerns was the question, What is a good social and political order? Rulers and their authority are inevitable, but what are just forms of rule? Moore set forth three criteria by which political regimes can be judged: the extent to which rulers pursue goals that will tend to reduce the amount of misery, the extent of rulers' competence to rule, and a reciprocal relationship between rulers and subordinates in which the subordinates obey and give legitimacy to the rulers in exchange for the provision of services by rulers that contribute to overall societal welfare.

Moore went on to consider various types of political systems and their strengths and weaknesses. Despite the obvious advantages of parliamentary democracy, in practice it tends to be committee-ridden and thus to get bogged down in trivial issues that prevent it from finding good resolutions of major moral disagreements. Socialist regimes have suffered from even worse problems, the most central of which has been the abuse of the population by rulers despite rulers' claims to be acting in behalf of the general social welfare. Anarchist proposals for removing all centralized authority are totally unrealistic because of the enormous likelihood of disorder and even violent conflict. Eliminating centralized authority would, moreover, probably be only temporary, since most likely a new centralized authority would sooner or later emerge in response to disorder and conflict.

These conclusions are rather dismal, but the only way to get beyond them is through greater and freer intellectual inquiry. A good society is one that permits a maximum amount of objective pursuit of truth and beauty, and this pursuit should be undertaken "irrespective of the consequences" (Moore, 1972:93). Such inquiry may lead to the discovery of "inconvenient facts," but it must be undertaken nonetheless. We cannot know in advance whether the knowledge we create or discover will support or contradict certain moral positions already held. And "philosophies incongruent with the pursuit of a reduction in misery should be permitted since the basis of rationality is strengthened through argument" (D. Smith, 1983:72), and "all opinions, however obnoxious or however passionately held, [should] be heard and subjected to the test of rational criticism" (1983:74).

But the good society requires more than the completely free and unfettered pursuit of truth and beauty. It should also be free from foreign threats, its members should have emotional security and possess high levels of technical and intellectual competence, and it should have an approximate social and economic equality. The main obstacles to the achievement of these ends are the economic and political inequalities within societies and the realities of international political competition and conflict. Moore is a realist, however. He recognizes that

> many of the "causes" of human misery are endemic in social relationships and cannot be "eliminated." ... [T]he causes of human misery include the following factors: conflicts arising from moral disagreements about the principles which should be expressed within political orders; competition between individuals, groups and societies in the course of modernisation (which has the effect of continually revising upwards the prevailing definitions of scarcity and deprivation); the irreducible uncertainty which prevails in international relations; and the constant temptation facing individuals to avoid the commands and sanctions of moral rules for their own advantage and to the detriment of others. Moore's analysis suggests that only the first of these causes may to some extent be removed. (D. Smith, 1983:74–75)

In *Injustice* Moore focused mostly on the struggles of the German working class throughout the nineteenth century and into the early twentieth century. He looked at the involvement of German workers in the Revolution of 1848, trends in the working class from the mid-nineteenth century until the beginning of World War I, and the attempt at revolutionary reform in 1918–1920. Later in the book he examined such major themes as the reasons for the outcomes of the Russian and German revolutions of the early twentieth century and the conditions that produced the Nazi regime. In the book's final chapters he looked at authority, principles of distribution, the difficulties in defining what exploitation is and how to conceptualize it, and the sense of moral outrage.

Since *Injustice,* Moore has written three more books: *Authority and Inequality Under Capitalism and Socialism* (1987), *Moral Aspects of Economic Growth and Other Essays* (1998), and *Moral Purity and Persecution in History* (2000). *Authority and Inequality* was based on the Tanner Lectures on Human Values, which Moore presented at Oxford University in May of 1985. It focused on the United States, the Soviet Union, and China. *Moral Aspects* looked at changes in political and economic beliefs and behavior throughout the past several hundred years. And in his highly provocative *Moral Purity,* Moore explored the notable tendency of people to persecute others regarded as having political, economic, or religious ideas that are "impure" and "polluting." Moore looked at such religions as Judaism and Christianity, at the violent repression of Protestants by Catholics in the French Wars of Religion after the Reformation, and at the terrors of the French Revolution. He also examined the search for moral purity in Mao's China and the extraordinary persecutions that occurred there. Monotheistic religion was identified as one of the major causes of extreme intolerance.

As these latest books demonstrate, Moore has continued to be intellectually active into his late eighties. Like the eminent sociologist George Homans, Moore was one of those rare sociologists born into the upper class. But unlike Homans, who was a relatively conservative Republican who reflected his class background, Moore took his politics in a direction different from his upbringing. Homans thought that society was largely acceptable as it was and believed that sociology could contribute nothing of any real value to improving it (and should not attempt to do so), but Moore, as has been made clear already, had a deep sense of the injustices that occur in societies, especially as the result of class inequality. He went against the grain of his class background in a way that Homans did not. Although Moore accepted authority and hierarchy as inevitable, he wanted to reduce hierarchy as much as possible. Theoretically, he leaned in a Marxian direction.

As the leading historical sociologist at Harvard when Skocpol was a student there, Moore influenced her significantly. However, this influence had more to do with the methodological style of his work than with its content or theoretical substance, for she has been quite critical of his major assertions (Skocpol, 1994:25–54). As a state-centered theorist, Skocpol thought that Moore gave too much attention to economics and class struggles and not enough attention to the independent role of the state in producing revolution. In her words, "Moore remains within the Marxist theoretical tradition, for he retains the fundamental Marxist propensity to explain political struggles and structures as functions of class structures and struggles" (1994:37).

Barrington Moore, Jr., was a very private man, a loner who never attracted personal disciples. He preferred to work on his yacht and to rely only on his wife as a sounding board for ideas and as a critic of his manuscripts. The Section on Comparative and Historical Sociology of the American Sociological Association honored him by creating a prize in his name, which is given annually to the best paper in comparative and historical sociology published within the previous two years.

Theda Skocpol: A Biographical Sketch

Theda Skocpol was born in 1947 and grew up in Wyandotte, Michigan.[3] She attended Michigan State University as an undergraduate on a National Merit Scholarship. Completing her B.A. in sociology in 1969, she had the extraordinary distinction of earning the highest grade-point average in a class of 4,000 students. Skocpol then went to Harvard University for her M.A. in 1972 and her Ph.D. in 1975. She then taught in the sociology department at Harvard from 1975 until 1981. Denied tenure by Harvard, she accepted an offer of a tenured professorship at the University of Chicago in both the sociology and political science departments, a position she held until 1986. At about this time she became the center of a national academic controversy over Harvard's refusal to grant tenure to a scholar of the eminence Skocpol had attained. Embarrassed by the unwanted unfavorable publicity, Harvard responded by inviting her to return to Harvard with tenure. She accepted the offer and between 1986 and 1994 was located in the sociology department. Since that time she has held a joint position in the departments of sociology and government,

---

[3]Adapted from the "Biographical Note" located at http://www.wjh.harvard.edu/soc/faculty/skocpol.

and in 1998 was named the Victor S. Thomas Professor of Government and Sociology. Since 2000 she has served as the director of Harvard's Center for American Political Studies.

Skocpol's first book, based on her dissertation, was her legendary *States and Social Revolutions*. It won the 1979 C. Wright Mills Award and the 1980 American Sociological Association Award for a Distinguished Contribution to Scholarship and has been translated into six languages. It has been called the best book ever written on revolutions and one of the most influential books in both political science and sociology. Skocpol's other major work on revolutions is *Social Revolutions in the Modern World* (1994), which reprints some of her most important essays on revolutions along with new contributions. A leader in comparative and historical sociology, Skocpol has also edited two major works in this area, *Vision and Method in Historical Sociology* in 1984 and (with Peter Evans and Dietrich Rueschemeyer) *Bringing the State Back In* in 1985.

For the past two decades Skocpol's research has focused mainly on American politics in historical and comparative perspective. Many of her wide-ranging analyses have been collected in her *Social Policy in the United States: Future Possibilities in Historical Perspective* (1995). In 1992 she wrote a magisterial book, *Protecting Soldiers and Mothers: The Political Origins of Social Policy in the United States*. It won five major awards, including the 1993 Woodrow Wilson Foundation Award of the American Political Science Association, given annually for the "best book published in the United States during the prior year on government, politics, or international affairs"; and the 1993 Ralph Waldo Emerson Award of Phi Beta Kappa, given to honor "a comprehensive study that contributes significantly to historical, philosophical, or religious interpretations of the human condition." She has also published many articles in scholarly journals and books of collected readings, as well as numerous articles in such magazines for the educated public as *The American Prospect, The Atlantic Monthly, MotherJones, Slate, The New Republic, The Brookings Review,* and *The Chronicle of Higher Education*.

Skocpol's most recent books include *Boomerang: Clinton's Health Reform and the Turn Against Government* (1997); *Civic Engagement in American Democracy* (1999, co-edited with Morris P. Fiorina); *The Missing Middle: Working Families and the Future of American Social Policy* (2000); and *Diminished Democracy: From Membership to Management in American Civic Life* (2003).

At Harvard Skocpol has taught such courses as American Society and Public Policy; History, Institutions, and Political Analysis; Civic Engagement in American Democracy; Civic Engagement: Theories, Research, and Strategies; and Methods of Historical Macroanalysis.

Skocpol served as president of the Social Science History Association in 1996 and the American Political Science Association in 2002–03. She has been elected to the American Academy of Arts and Sciences and the National Academy of Social Insurance, and has held fellowships from the John Simon Guggenheim Foundation, the Institute for Advanced Study in Princeton, New Jersey, the Russell Sage Foundation, and the Robert Wood Johnson Foundation. She is active in civic as well as academic life and has been included in policy discussions with President Clinton at the White House and Camp David. She has appeared on television and radio and is frequently quoted by journalists. Skocpol has been married since 1967 to Bill Skocpol, who teaches physics at Boston University. Although he also attended Michigan State University on a National Merit Scholarship at the same time, they actually met at Rust College in Mississippi while working on a civil rights education project. They are the parents of Michael Allan Skocpol, who was born in 1988. The Skocpols live in Cambridge, Massachusetts, throughout the academic year and in Mount Desert, Maine, during the summer.

Charles Tilly: An Intellectual Biography

Born in 1929 in Lombard, Illinois, Charles Tilly graduated from York Community High School in Elmhurst, Illinois. He attended Harvard University, receiving an A.B. *magna cum laude* in 1950 and a Ph.D. in sociology in 1958. Between his undergraduate and graduate degrees, he served in the U.S. Navy's amphibious forces, studied at Balliol College, Oxford, and the Facultés Catholiques de l'Ouest, Angers, and began full-time teaching. While a student, Tilly worked at various times as newsboy, grocery clerk, office boy, factory hand, construction laborer, janitor, night watchman, camp counselor, and psychiatric hospital researcher.

Tilly's first teaching position was at the University of Delaware, where he was located from 1956 until 1962. While on a postdoc at Princeton in 1962–63, he looked for another job. He found one at Harvard, teaching there from 1963 until 1966. He then taught at the University of Toronto (1965–1969), the University of Michigan (1969–1984), and the New School for Social Research (1984–1996). He is currently Joseph L. Buttenwieser Professor of Social Science at Columbia University. At Columbia he has regular membership in the departments of sociology and political science, serves as a fellow of the Institute for Social and Economic Research and Policy, and also as a fellow of the Center for Historical Social Science. Tilly has held visiting appointments at the Center of International Studies at Princeton University (1962–63), Sir George Williams University in Montréal (1967), the Center for Advanced Study in the Behavioral Sciences in Palo Alto, California (1968–69 and 1997–98), the Institute for Advanced Study in Princeton, New Jersey (1970–71, 1972), the École des Hautes Études en Sciences Sociales in Paris (1974–1978, 1980, 1982, 1986, 1990), l'Université de Paris I/Sorbonne (1983), the Russell Sage Foundation (1987–88), the University of Stockholm (1996), and Stanford University (1997–98).

Most of Tilly's work has focused on large-scale social change and its relationship to contentious politics, especially in Europe since 1500. His most important books are *The Rebellious Century, 1830–1930* (with Louise Tilly and Richard Tilly) (1975), *From Mobilization to Revolution* (1978), *Big Structures, Large Processes, Huge Comparisons* (1985), *The Contentious French* (1986), *Coercion, Capital, and European States, 990–1990* (1990), *European Revolutions, 1492–1992* (1993), *Popular Contention in Great Britain, 1758–1834* (1995), and *Durable Inequality* (1998). His most recent books are *Stories, Identities, and Political Change* (2002), *The Politics of Collective Violence* (2003), *Contention and Democracy in Europe, 1650–2000* (2004a), and *Social Movements, 1768–2004* (2004b). Tilly's books have been translated into Spanish, French, Italian, Portuguese, Swedish, Greek, Croatian, Turkish, Chinese, and Korean. In all likelihood Tilly will publish many more books in the coming years. This is an easy prediction, because writing is perhaps the most natural thing Tilly does. He writes rapidly and with great elegance. It is difficult, if not impossible, to think of another sociologist whose prose is as beautiful as his.

Tilly is a member of the U.S. National Academy of Sciences, a fellow of the American Academy of Arts and Sciences, and a fellow of the American Association for the Advancement of Science. He belongs to the American Philosophical Society, the Sociological Research Association, and the Society for Comparative Research, and is a *chevalier* of l'Ordre des Palmes Académiques. He has received the Common Wealth Award in sociology (1982) and the Eastern Sociological Society's Merit Award for Distinguished Scholarship (1996), as well as honorary doctorates in social sciences from Erasmus University in Rotterdam (1983), the Institut d'Études Politiques of the University of Paris (1993), the University of Toronto (1995), the University of Strasbourg (1996), the University of Geneva (1999), and the University of Crete (2002).

In 1987, Tilly's book *The Contentious French* shared the C. Wright Mills Award of the Society for the Study of Social Problems, and in 1989 the same book won the Award for Distinguished Scholarship of the American Sociological Association. In 1995 his book *European Revolutions* received the Premio Europeo Amalfi. In 1996, the American Sociological Association's Section on Collective Behavior and Social Movements gave his *Popular Contention in Great Britain* its Distinguished Scholarly Publication Award. In 1999, the Eastern Sociological Society selected his *Durable Inequality* for its first annual Book Award. The American Sociological Association gave the same book its Award for Distinguished Scholarship in 2000. In 2001, Columbia University's sociology graduate students named him Professor of the Year.

Tilly's current research and writing include:

- studies of contention and social change in Great Britain, France, and Europe as a whole since 1650;
- syntheses of research on inequality, work, and labor markets;
- critical reviews of causal explanation and historical analysis in the social sciences;
- syntheses on contentious politics, democracy, nationalism, collective violence, and related topics;
- co-authorship of a textbook on world history;
- co-editorship and co-authorship of a handbook on contextual political analysis; and
- books on trust networks in politics and reason-giving in social life.

He is helping run the Russian Academy of Sciences–U.S. National Academy of Sciences joint project on conflict in multiethnic polities. He is also now emerging successfully from chemotherapy for lymphoma and actually wrote an entire book during treatment as part of his recovery plan.

Among the negative distinctions that he values the most are

- never having held office in a professional association;
- never having chaired a university department or served as a dean;
- never having been an associate professor;
- being rejected every single time he has been screened as a prospective juror.

He had also hoped never to publish a book with a subtitle, but subtitles somehow slipped into two of his co-authored books.

Timothy P. Wickham-Crowley: An Autobiographical Sketch

I grew up in Elizabeth, New Jersey, in a mostly working-class and Catholic neighborhood. After beginning my school years in our parish school, I finished my last eight years in the public school system, finally attending a citywide, all-boys' public high school, Thomas Jefferson. In retrospect, my experiences there must have strongly shaped my later career choices to study sociology and Latin America, because of the exceptional socioeconomic, religious, and ethnic diversity of the student body—with notably large contingents of southern and eastern European Catholics, Jews, African-Americans, and Puerto Rican and Cuban Americans. The last groups provided my motivation to begin studying Spanish after four years of Latin.

I was the first member of my family line to finish four years of college. I attended Princeton University, getting my A.B. in 1973. My time at Princeton was indeed well spent, because I soon abandoned ill-conceived childhood ambitions to become a lawyer. I first moved toward Latin American studies after taking two sterling history courses offered by Stanley Stein, but by my junior year I had focused on sociology as my major and my future career. As the son of a truck driver in that bastion of privilege I was sensitized to class differences, to be sure, and thus came to reject recurring attempts by certain social theorists to treat disprivileged groups in society (e.g., the working class) as if they were, for all intents and purposes, too "collectively brain-damaged" to understand their own lives and their own interests (and I thank Frank Parkin for coining that lethal metaphor). Such a contrarian stance is surely found in my recurring positive references to the key ideas developed by James Scott (especially in his *Weapons of the Weak,* 1990), Peter Berger (from his *Pyramids of Sacrifice,* 1975), and Barrington Moore, Jr. (from his *Injustice,* 1978). My own reflections and the influence of these and other thinkers led me forcefully to reject any viewpoints that endorse or advocate as key concepts, in reference to the lower classes, the ideas of "false consciousness," "ideological hegemony," or the presumed necessity of "consciousness-raising," and I reject them most notably in an essay about ideology and revolution from my 1991 book of essays, *Exploring Revolution.*

I obtained my Ph.D. degree in sociology from Cornell in 1982. When I entered the Ph.D. program at Cornell, I quickly discovered the complementary strengths available to me in their Latin American Studies program, and used the flexibility of Cornell's committee system to merge the two interests. While at Cornell, I also met my wife, and from that union came our hyphenated surnames (and lucky we are to be graced with a mellifluous example of that genre). I don't really mind being at the end of alphabet now, having spent three decades at the front of it.

During this time at Cornell my major research interests crystallized, which, again, expressed the perspectives of my two interests. From Latin American Studies I gained a value-based yet still scholarly interest in profound forms of social transformation that did and still do affect the lives of tens of millions around the world: economic underdevelopment and social revolutions. (On the latter subject I have published widely; on the former I teach and am doing current research.) That is, I was interested in spending my career pursuing *Reflections on the Causes of Human Misery,* as Barrington Moore entitled a book epitomizing his characteristically intellectual yet morally committed meditations on such "big" issues. From Latin Americanists, as well as from Moore and other theorists, I certainly was reinforced in my concerns with social justice. Yet Moore's intellectual approach also nurtured the type of sociology I wished to pursue. Like Moore and in accord with Weber's value-freedom thesis, my sociological vocation has called me to "see society plain" rather than to project my own hopes and fears upon reality, even granting the imperfections of my actual published attempts to approach such grails. Also from sociology I absorbed the field's conceit that the only really interesting sociology is that which explains why the social world works the way it does. My interest in sociological theory (a course I regularly teach) thus has always been informed by the mission statement given us by the late George Homans: The office of theory is to explain. Therefore

I have been singularly unimpressed by those increasingly prevalent versions of "theory" which are nothing but ineffectual and unending efforts in philosophical debate or worrying over conceptual issues: battles in the ether rather than attempts to roll up our sleeves and get on with the business of understanding social life.

The best-known writing that has expressed the merger of my sociological drive to understand and explain with my ethical interests was my blushingly well-received work, *Guerrillas and Revolution in Latin America* (it was nominated for the Bryce Wood Award given by the Latin American Studies Association, as well as for the Distinguished Publication Award given annually by the American Sociological Association). About half of that work comes from my Cornell dissertation, the rest from a two-decade extension of the period and movements analyzed and from a rethinking of my core political ideas and methods inspired by the writings of Theda Skocpol, Charles Tilly, and Charles Ragin. More recently, those twin concerns are clearly partly embedded in two recent books I co-edited with Susan Eckstein on justice issues in Latin America, *What Justice? Whose Justice?* (Eckstein and Wickham-Crowley, 2003a), and *Struggles for Social Rights in Latin America* (Eckstein and Wickham-Crowley, 2003b).

As I think about what I most want to see in sociology and in Latin American studies, my aims are actually quite prosaic, in both possible senses of that term. Thus I again side with Homans in my interest in getting rid of "the guff" in sociology. Along these lines, I have consistently tried to strengthen my writing so that I will not be the typical sociologist whose prose readers fear to encounter. Whatever my own merits in that regard, I have also tried politely but insistently to focus on style as an important element in evaluation of our peers' work. I harbor the dream that, if enough of us complain regularly about our bad writing while praising the good, we will finally improve. If we get really lucky the whole field will drift in the direction of one of our epitomes of powerful, clear, and evocative prose, Charles Tilly (perhaps not by accident himself a former student of Homans).

My second concern revolves around the fact that I first call myself a teacher. Since my interests in two very large fields are not narrowly circumscribed by the two topics of revolutions and development, but rather reflect a deeper and passionate vocation for the life of the mind, I have sought to pass on that passion and convey the virtues of sociological analysis to my students.

My commitment to teaching is also reflected in the fact that at Georgetown University, where I have been located since 1986, I have taught a wide range of courses: political sociology, social theory, sociology of religion, sociology of revolution, Latin American studies, social inequality, social movements, comparative sociology, and the sociology of science. In 1991 I became an honorary faculty member of Alpha Sigma Nu, the national Jesuit honor society. Although it may seem immodest to say so, I have twice been nominated by Georgetown's seniors in the School of Foreign Service for a university-wide teaching award, and my department has nominated me three times for the Dean's Award for Excellence in Teaching given by the College of Arts and Sciences.

Teaching young people continues to provide me with my greatest career satisfaction, that almost electrical, yet profoundly human "charge" from intellectual engagement in the classroom that has no professional equal. I seek in that encounter precisely what Max Weber (in "Science as a Vocation") hoped for and sought in the teacher's presentation of ideas, that "an untutored but receptive mind can understand them and—for us what alone is decisive—can come to think about them independently."

Eric R. Wolf: A Biographical Sketch

Eric Wolf was born on February 1, 1923, in Vienna, Austria.[4] He held a lifelong interest in other cultures; as a young man, Wolf attended school in England, where he discovered a love for science. After moving to the United States, Wolf attended Queens College (now part of the City University of New York). After marrying in 1943 and serving in World War II, he resumed his studies once the war had ended. He earned a bachelor's degree in sociology and anthropology the year after the war ended, and then a Ph.D. in anthropology a few years later. Wolf subsequently divorced his first wife (in 1972) and married Sydel Sylverman, another anthropologist.

Wolf suggested that the categories of race, ethnicity, and culture were products of the specific social practices characteristic of Western capitalist societies, and he also believed that other categories might be forthcoming in other kinds of social forms. He saw discourse on

---

[4]Adapted from the discussion by Jacque Braun at http://www.mnsu.edu/emuseum/information/biography/uvwxyz/wolf_eric.html.

race predominant in the nineteenth century and discourse on culture increasing in the twentieth century. Ethnicity, he noted, was a popularly emerging topic in the 1980s and 1990s, especially as world events caused renewed attention to be given to it. He saw definitions of ethnicity shifting to "formulas of cultural distinctiveness" as though the two were almost synonymous.

Wolf was considered a major anthropologist of his time and wrote extensively. He published articles in such journals as the *American Anthropologist, Comparative Studies in Society and History,* and *Revista Mexicana de Antropologia.* The most important theme that ran through his works was the various situations of peasants. This is evident in his most important books: *Peasant Wars of the Twentieth Century* (1969), *Peasants* (1966), and the widely celebrated *Europe and the People Without History* (1982). In *Peasant Wars* he applied a Marxian perspective to understand revolutions and revolutionary movements of various types. In *Peasants,* a little book of barely more than 100 pages, he delved into numerous aspects of peasant society in both traditional and ancient societies and in the modern world, looking at ecology, economics, politics, culture, and ideology.

Wolf was particularly concerned with the integration of peasants into the modern capitalist and industrial world, and thus in *Europe and the People Without History* he broke new ground by applying Immanuel Wallerstein's world-system perspective to the study of the impact on peasant life of the emerging and expanding capitalist world-economy. He argued that to understand peasant life after around C.E. 1400 one had to look at its connection to this world-economy. It could not be understood apart from it. This book explored the nature of modes of production and peasant life prior to 1400, and then discussed the early development of capitalism and its impact on native cultures and societies. Wolf examined Spanish and Portuguese colonization of the New World, the search for silver, the *hacienda* system of plantation agriculture, the slave trade, and slavery in Brazil and elsewhere. A whole chapter was devoted to the fur trade and its impact on such North American Indian populations as the Abenaki, the Huron, and the Iroquois in the northeast, and the Kwakiutl and various other groups in the northwest. Other chapters dealt with the impact of European colonialism in Asia.

Eric Wolf died on March 6, 1999, after a distinguished career as a leading anthropologist.

Suggested Readings

On conceptualizing revolutions, see Cohan (1975), Skocpol (1979), Goldstone (1991), and Tilly (1978, 1986, 1993). On modes of production in history, see Marx (1965) and G. A. Cohen (1978). On feudalism, see Bloch (1961), Critchley (1978), and Anderson (1974a). On the development of capitalism, Paul Sweezy's *The Theory of Capitalist Development* (1942) is a superb introduction to a Marxian analysis of the evolution of the capitalist system. Although old, it is a classic and well worth reading. Works on the 500-year history of capitalism by Braudel (1981, 1982, 1984) and Wallerstein (1974a, 1974b, 1979, 1980, 1989) are also classics and essential reading. See also Chase-Dunn (1989), Beaud (1983), Kriedte (1983), and Smith (1991). On the less-developed world see Frank (1978, 1979), Warren (1980), So (1990), McMichael (2004), and Bradshaw and Wallace (1996). Good sources on colonialism are Magdoff (1978), Murray (1980), and Ferro (1997).

Lenski's *Power and Privilege: A Theory of Social Stratification* (1966) is a classic analysis of stratification in a wide range of human societies. See also Bendix and Lipset (1966) and McCord and McCord (1977). Important works that deal primarily with classes in modern capitalist societies are Laumann, Siegel, and Hodge (1970), Giddens (1980), Giddens and Held (1982), Westergaard and Resler (1975), and Wright (1979, 1985). On states, see Evans, Rueschemeyer, and Skocpol (1985), Kennedy (1987), Tilly (1990), Anderson (1974b), Carnoy (1984), Poggi (1978, 1990), and Clark (1995). On the development of democracy see Rueschemeyer, Stephens, and Stephens (1992), Markoff (1996), Schaeffer (1997), Vanhanen (1997, 2003), and Sanderson (2004). Sanderson (1999a, 1999b) and Sanderson and Alderson (2005) discuss all of these phenomena in considerable detail over a very long period of time. See also Chirot (1977, 1986).

James DeFronzo's *Revolutions and Revolutionary Movements* (1996) contains useful narrative discussions of the Russian and Chinese revolutions. There is a huge literature on the French Revolution, which is an academic industry in France. Very good brief works in English are Popkin (2002) and Doyle (1999). Doyle provides an excellent assessment of the historical development of the debate over whether the French Revolution was a bourgeois revolution. There is a smaller, though still large, literature on the Russian Revolution. Two excellent sources are Fitzpatrick (1994) and Pipes (1995). An early classic on the Russian Revolution was written by the eminent historian Edward Hallett Carr, *The Bolshevik Revolution, 1917–1923* (1950). It takes up three full volumes. The first volume examines the revolution itself, whereas the other two deal with its economic and political consequences. An exceptionally well-written and captivating (and also succinct) work on the Chinese Revolution is Lucien Bianco's *Origins of the Chinese Revolution, 1915–1949* (1971; original French version 1967). Schrecker (2004) is a more detailed work that is not as captivating but still very good.

Good narratives of the Cuban, Nicaraguan, and Iranian revolutions can be found in DeFronzo (1996). Although chapter-length rather than book-length, like his discussions of the Russian and Chinese revolutions mentioned above, they are far more detailed than the brief sketches presented in the present book. Misagh Parsa's *States, Ideologies, and Social Revolutions* (2000) discusses the Iranian, Nicaraguan, and Philippine revolutions. Marifeli Pérez-Stable's *The Cuban Revolution* (1999) is a very good source on Cuba. Also on Cuba, see Ruiz (1968) and Aguila (1994). Additional sources on Nicaragua are Walker (1982, 1986), Grynspan (1991), and Chavarría (1986); on Iran, see Abrahamian (1982, 1989), Green (1982), Milani (1988), Moshiri (1991), Moaddel (1993), and Foran (1993); and on the Philippines, see Chapman (1987) and Kessler (1989, 1991).

A. S. Cohan (1975) is a good older discussion of various theories of revolution. More recent discussions can be found in Goldstone (1980, 1982). Two very good recent general treatments of theories of revolutions and the problems encountered in explaining them are the collections of essays by Keddie, *Debating Revolutions* (1995), and Foran, *Theorizing Revolutions* (1997b). Davies (1962) and Gurr's *Why Men Rebel* (1970) are the best known of the social-psychological theories of revolution. Tucker (1978) contains a wide range of selections from Marx's writings, some of which include his theoretical views on revolutions. Wolf's *Peasant Wars of the Twentieth Century* (1969) and Paige's *Agrarian Revolution* (1975) are two of the best examples of modern Marxian theorizing on revolutions. Skocpol and Trimberger (1978) provide an excellent critique of Marxian theories. Tilly's *From Mobilization to Revolution* (1978) established resource mobilization theory, which quickly led to state-centered theories of revolutions and state breakdowns. Skocpol's *States and Social Revolutions* (1979) analyzed the Great Revolutions and produced the first major state-centered theory of these revolutions. Goldstone's *Revolution and Rebellion in the Early Modern World* (1991) followed in the state-centered tradition but looked at social and political revolutions in both Europe and Asia. It was the first work to attempt a general theory that could explain revolutionary patterns on both continents. Tilly's *European Revolutions, 1492–1992* (1993) discusses, largely descriptively, revolutions, rebellions, civil wars, and other forms of collective violence throughout Europe during the past 500 years. See also Tilly (1964, 1986, 1995) and Tilly, Tilly, and Tilly (1975).

Wickham-Crowley's *Guerrillas and Revolution in Latin America* (1992) is perhaps the most important book on Third World revolutions ever written. Jeff Goodwin's *No Other Way Out* (2001) applies a state-centered perspective very similar to Wickham-Crowley's to a wider range of Third World revolutions and offers a systematic appraisal of the strengths and weaknesses of this perspective. Foran (1997b) contains important essays. Skocpol's *Social Revolutions in the Modern World* (1994) reprints some of her most important articles and essays and offers replies to her critics. See also Goldstone (1980, 1982), Goodwin and Skocpol (1989), Collins (1993), and Goodwin (1994a, 1994b). In a very insightful article, Wickham-Crowley (1997) discusses theories of revolution in terms of the answers they give to four fundamental questions: What are the sources of grievances in a population? What makes peasants or other groups revolutionary? Which societies experience successful revolutions and which do not? What explains the similarities and differences in state policies following the revolutionary seizure of power?

János Kornai's *The Socialist System: The Political Economy of Communism* (1992) is an extremely insightful and useful work on how state socialist economies function and on why they stagnated. *Socialist States in the World-System* (1982), edited by Christopher Chase-Dunn, contains important essays by Marxists debating the nature of state socialism and how it relates to the capitalist world-system. Djilas's *The New*

Class (1957) is a classic work on the failure of state socialist societies to become egalitarian and democratic. Lane (1992) examines *perestroika* and *glasnost* and looks briefly at the collapse of the Soviet Union in 1991. Nove (1989) provides a discussion of *glasnost* before the collapse. Three important collections of essays on the Soviet collapse are Blackburn (1991), Lapidus (1995), and Dallin and Lapidus (1995).

Good accounts of the Communist collapse throughout Eastern Europe are Stokes (1993), Ágh (1998), and the essays in Brown (1991) and Banac (1992). Zeman (1991) provides a useful historical backdrop to the Communist collapse, as well as a brief overview of the collapse itself. See also Jowitt (1992). Krishan Kumar's masterly *1989: Revolutionary Ideas and Ideals* (2001) is a collection of the author's important essays on the Eastern European revolutions brimming with major insights. Gil Eyal's *The Origins of Postcommunist Elites* (2003) focuses on why Czechoslovakia split into two sovereign states in 1993. Gordon Hahn (2002) provides a detailed treatment of the reasons for the Soviet collapse from the beginnings of Gorbachev's reform efforts to his replacement by Yeltsin. On why social scientists should have predicted the collapse of Communism, see Goldstone (1995) and Lipset and Bence (1994). Lipset and Bence provide a fascinating discussion of actual predictions of the collapse.

Good discussions of the outcomes of the French Revolution are Popkin (2002) and Doyle (1999); of the Russian Revolution, Fitzpatrick (1994) and Pipes (1995); and of the Chinese Revolution, Bianco (1971) and Schrecker (2004). Skocpol (1979, 1986) and Goldstone (1991) provide somber analyses of what the Great Revolutions produced, and of what revolutions usually produce. See also Goldstone (1986:Part 6). The French historian Stéphane Courtois, along with five other European historians, provides a comprehensive and much-needed assessment of the horrendous human consequences of Communism in *The Black Book of Communism* (1999).

On the outcomes of the Cuban Revolution, see two articles by Susan Eckstein (1980, 1986), a sociological specialist in Cuban society and politics, as well as her book *Back from the Future: Cuba Under Castro* (1994; 2nd ed. 2003). As a socialist, Eckstein perhaps exaggerates the actual accomplishments of the Castro regime and underplays its negative dimensions. Also on Cuba, see Pérez-Stable (1999). On Nicaraguan outcomes, see Grynspan (1991) and Foran and Goodwin (1993). Selbin (1999) discusses revolutionary outcomes in Cuba and

Nicaragua and, to some extent, Latin America more generally. Eckstein (1982) discusses revolutionary outcomes in several Latin American countries. On Iran, see Foran and Goodwin (1993) and Moshiri (1991). On a variety of revolutionary outcomes, see the last section of the edited volume by Goldstone (1986).

Good accounts of post-Communism can be found in Holmes (1997) and Ágh (1998). A good journalistic account of postsocialist Russia is found in Remnick (1997). In his *Russia Under Yeltsin and Putin,* Boris Kagarlitsky (2002) provides a very grim and pessimistic assessment of Russia since 1991. Kagarlitsky argues that in order for real modernization to occur in Russia, another economic revolution is needed—one that will overthrow the entrenched political and economic oligarchy that continues to enrich itself at the expense of the Russian people as a whole.

The Future of Revolutions (2003), edited by John Foran, is a collection of essays that addresses the question of whether revolutions are likely to occur in a future marked by massive economic and political change, especially globalization. The book contains the unique feature of three sets of thematic discussions among the authors at the University of California at Santa Barbara. See also Goodwin (2001:293–306), Halliday (1999:331–338), Snyder (1999), and Nodia (2000).

References

Abonyi, Arpad. 1982. "Eastern Europe's reintegration." In Christipher Chase-Dunn (ed.), *Socialist States in the World-System*. Beverly Hills, CA: Sage.

Abrahamian, Ervand. 1982. *Iran Between Two Revolutions*. Princeton, NJ: Princeton University Press.

———. 1989. *The Iranian Mojahedin*. New Haven, CT: Yale University Press.

Aganbegyan, Abel. 1988. "New directions in Soviet economics." *New Left Review* 169:87–93.

———. 1989. *Inside Perestroika: The Future of the Soviet Economy*. Trans. Helen Szamuely. New York: Harper & Row.

Ágh, Attila. 1998. *The Politics of Central Europe*. Thousand Oaks, CA: Sage.

Aguila, Juan M. 1994. *Cuba: Dilemmas of a Revolution*. Boulder, CO: Westview Press.

Amalrik, Andrei. 1970. *Will the Soviet Union Survive Until 1984?* New York: Harper & Row.

Anderson, Perry. 1974a. *Passages from Antiquity to Feudalism*. London: New Left Books.

———. 1974b. *Lineages of the Absolutist State*. London: New Left Books.

Arjomand, Said Amir. 1992. "A demographic theory of revolution; or, sociology as sorcery." *Contemporary Sociology* 21:3–8.

Aya, Rod. 1979. "Theories of revolution reconsidered: Contrasting models of collective violence." *Theory and Society* 8:39–99.

Banac, Ivo. 1992. *Eastern Europe in Revolution*. Ithaca, NY: Cornell University Press.

Beaud, Michel. 1983. *A History of Capitalism, 1500–1980*. New York: Monthly Review Press.

Bendix, Reinhard, and Seymour Martin Lipset. 1966. *Class, Status, and Power: Social Stratification in Comparative Perspective*. New York: Free Press.

Berger, Peter L. 1975. *Pyramids of Sacrifice*. New York: Basic Books.

Bianco, Lucien. 1971. *Origins of the French Revolution, 1915–1949*. Trans. Muriel Bell. Stanford, CA: Stanford University Press. (Original French version 1967.)

Blackburn, Robin (ed.). 1991. *After the Fall: The Failure of Communism and the Future of Socialism*. London: Verso.

Bloch, Marc. 1961. *Feudal Society.* 2 vols. Trans. L. A. Manyon. Chicago: University of Chicago Press.

Boyce, James K. 1993. *The Philippines: The Political Economy of Growth and Impoverishment in the Marcos Era.* Honolulu: University of Hawaii Press.

Bradshaw, York W., and Michael Wallace. 1996. *Global Inequalities.* Thousand Oaks, CA: Pine Forge Press.

Braudel, Fernand. 1981. *The Structures of Everyday Life.* (Vol. 1 of *Civilization and Capitalism, 15th–18th Century.*) New York: Harper & Row.

———. 1982. *The Wheels of Commerce.* (Vol. 2 of *Civilization and Capitalism, 15th–18th Century.*) New York: Harper & Row.

———. 1984. *The Perspective of the World.* (Vol. 3 of *Civilization and Capitalism, 15th–18th Century.*) New York: Harper & Row.

Brown, J. F. 1991. *Surge to Freedom: The End of Communist Rule in Eastern Europe.* Durham, NC: Duke University Press.

Bruszt, Laszlo, and David Stark. 1992. "Remaking the political field in Hungary: From the politics of confrontation to the politics of competition." In Ivo Banac (ed.), *Eastern Europe in Revolution.* Ithaca, NY: Cornell University Press.

Brzezinski, Zbigniew (ed.). 1969. *Dilemmas of Change in Soviet Politics.* New York: Columbia University Press.

———. 1989. *The Grand Failure: The Birth and Death of Communism in the Twentieth Century.* New York: Scribner.

Cardoso, Fernando Henrique, and Enzo Faletto. 1979. *Dependency and Development in Latin America.* Berkeley: University of California Press.

Carnoy, Martin. 1984. *The State and Political Theory.* Princeton, NJ: Princeton University Press.

Carr, Edward Hallett. 1950. *The Bolshevik Revolution, 1917–1923.* 3 vols. New York: Norton.

Castells, Manuel. 1996. *The Information Age: Economy, Society, and Culture* (Vol. 1: *The Rise of the Network Society.*) Oxford: Blackwell.

Central Intelligence Agency. 2004. *World Factbook 2004.* Available online at www.cia.gov/cia/publications/factbook.

Chapman, W. 1987. *Inside the Philippine Revolution.* New York: Norton.

Chase-Dunn, Christopher. 1989. *Global Formation: Structures of the World-Economy.* Oxford: Blackwell.

Chase-Dunn, Christopher (ed.). 1982. *Socialist States in the World-System.* Beverly Hills, CA: Sage.

Chavarría, Ricardo E. 1986. "The revolutionary insurrection." In Jack A. Goldstone (ed.), *Revolutions: Theoretical, Comparative, and Historical Studies.* San Diego: Harcourt Brace Jovanovich.

Chirot, Daniel. 1977. *Social Change in the Twentieth Century.* New York: Harcourt Brace Jovanovich.

———. 1986. *Social Change in the Modern Era.* San Diego: Harcourt Brace Jovanovich.

——. 1991. "Introduction." In Daniel Chirot (ed.), *The Crisis of Leninism and the Decline of the Left.* Seattle: University of Washington Press.

——. 1995. "After socialism, what? The global implications of the revolutions of 1989 in Eastern Europe." In Nikki R. Keddie (ed.), *Debating Revolutions.* New York: New York University Press.

Clark, Samuel. 1995. *State and Status: The Rise of the State and Aristocratic Power in Western Europe.* Montreal: McGill-Queen's University Press.

Cobban, Alfred. 1964. *The Social Interpretation of the French Revolution.* Cambridge, UK: Cambridge University Press.

Cohan, A. S. 1975. *Theories of Revolution.* London: Thomas Nelson & Sons.

Cohen, G. A. 1978. *Karl Marx's Theory of History: A Defence.* Oxford: Oxford University Press.

Collins, Randall. 1986. *Weberian Sociological Theory.* New York: Cambridge University Press.

——. 1993. "Maturation of the state-centered theory of revolution and ideology." *Sociological Theory* 11:117–128.

Collins, Randall, and David Waller. 1992. "What theories predicted the state breakdowns and revolutions of the Soviet bloc?" In Louis Kriesberg (ed.), *Research in Social Movements, Conflicts and Change.* Vol. 14. Greenwich, CT: JAI Press.

Courtois, Stéphane, Nicholas Werth, Jean-Louis Panné, Andrzej Paczkowski, Karel Bartošek, and Jean-Louis Margolin. 1999. *The Black Book of Communism: Crimes, Terror, Repression.* Trans. Jonathan Murphy and Mark Kramer. Cambridge, MA: Harvard University Press.

Critchley, John. 1978. *Feudalism.* London: Allen & Unwin.

Dallin, Alexander, and Gail W. Lapidus (eds.). 1995. *The Soviet System: From Crisis to Collapse.* Rev. ed. Boulder, CO: Westview Press.

Davies, James C. 1962. "Toward a theory of revolution." *American Sociological Review* 27:5–18.

de Dios, Emmanuel S., and Paul D. Hutchcroft. 2003. "Political economy." In Arsenio M. Balisacan and Hal Hill (eds.), *The Philippine Economy: Development, Policies, and Challenges.* New York: Oxford University Press.

DeFronzo, James. 1996. *Revolutions and Revolutionary Movements.* 2nd ed. Boulder, CO: Westview Press.

Djilas, Milovan. 1957. *The New Class.* New York: Praeger.

Doyle, William. 1999. *Origins of the French Revolution.* 3rd ed. Oxford: Oxford University Press.

Dunn, John. 1972. *Modern Revolutions: An Introduction to the Analysis of a Political Phenomenon.* Cambridge, UK: Cambridge University Press.

Eckstein, Susan E. 1980. "Capitalist constraints on Cuban socialist development." *Comparative Politics* 12(3):253–274.

——. 1982. "The impact of revolution on social welfare in Latin America." *Theory and Society* 11:43–94.

————. 1986. "The impact of the Cuban Revolution: A comparative perspective." *Comparative Studies in Society and History* 28:502–534.

————.1994. *Back from the Future: Cuba Under Castro.* Princeton, NJ: Princeton University Press (2nd ed. 2003, Routledge).

Eckstein, Susan E., and Timothy P. Wickham-Crowley (eds.). 2003a. *What Justice? Whose Justice? Fighting for Fairness in Latin America.* Berkeley: University of California Press.

————. 2003b. *Struggles for Social Rights in Latin America.* New York: Routledge.

The Economist. 2004. *Pocket World in Figures 2005.* London: Profile Books.

Eisenstadt, S. N. 1992. "The breakdown of Communist regimes and the vicissitudes of modernity." *Daedalus* 12(2):21–42.

Ericson, Richard E. 1995. "The Russian economy since independence." In Gail W. Lapidus (ed.), *The New Russia: Troubled Transformation.* Boulder, CO: Westview Press.

Evans, Peter B., Dietrich Rueschemeyer, and Theda Skocpol (eds.). 1985. *Bringing the State Back In.* New York: Cambridge University Press.

Eyal, Gil. 2003. *The Origins of Postcommunist Elites: From Prague Spring to the Breakup of Czechoslovakia.* Minneapolis: University of Minnesota Press.

Ferro, Marc. 1997. *Colonization: A Global History.* Trans. K. D. Prithipaul. St-Hyacinthe, Quebec: World Heritage Press.

Fitzpatrick, Sheila. 1994. *The Russian Revolution.* Oxford: Oxford University Press.

Foran, John. 1993. *Fragile Resistance: Social Transformation in Iran from 1500 to the Revolution.* Boulder, CO: Westview Press.

————. 1997a. "Discourses and social forces: The role of culture and cultural studies in understanding revolutions." In John Foran (ed.), *Theorizing Revolutions.* New York: Routledge.

————. 1997c. "The future of revolutions at the *fin-de-siècle.*" *Third World Quarterly* 18:791–820.

————. 2005. *Taking Power: On the Origins of Third World Revolutions.* New York: Cambridge University Press.

Foran, John (ed.). 1997b. *Theorizing Revolutions.* New York: Routledge.

————. 2003. *The Future of Revolutions: Rethinking Radical Change in the Age of Globalization.* London: Zed Books.

Foran, John, and Jeff Goodwin. 1993. "Revolutionary outcomes in Iran and Nicaragua: Coalition fragmentation, war, and the limits of social transformation." *Theory and Society* 22:209–247.

Frank, Andre Gunder. 1978. *World Accumulation, 1492–1789.* New York: Monthly Review Press.

————. 1979. *Dependent Accumulation and Underdevelopment.* New York: Monthly Review Press.

Freedom House Survey Team. 2003. *Freedom in the World: The Annual Review of Political Rights and Civil Liberties, 2003.* New York: Freedom House.

Gastil, Raymond. 1989. *Freedom in the World: Political Rights and Civil Liberties, 1988–89.* New York: Freedom House.

Giddens, Anthony. 1980. *The Class Structure of the Advanced Societies.* 2nd ed. London: Hutchinson.

Giddens, Anthony, and David Held (eds.). 1982. *Classes, Power, and Conflict: Classical and Contemporary Debates.* Berkeley: University of California Press.

Goldstone, Jack A. 1980. "Theories of revolution: The third generation." *World Politics* 32:425–453.

———. 1982. "The comparative and historical study of revolutions." *Annual Review of Sociology* 8:187–207.

———. 1991. *Revolution and Rebellion in the Early Modern World.* Berkeley: University of California Press.

———. 1995. "Predicting revolutions: Why we could (and should) have foreseen the revolutions of 1989–1991 in the U.S.S.R. and Eastern Europe." In Nekki R. Keddie (ed.), *Debating Revolutions.* New York: New York University Press.

Goldstone, Jack A. (ed.). 1986. *Revolutions: Theoretical, Comparative, and Historical Perspectives.* San Diego: Harcourt Brace Jovanovich.

———. 2003. *States, Parties, and Social Movements.* New York: Cambridge University Press.

Goodwin, Jeff. 1994a. "Old regimes and revolutions in the Second and Third Worlds: A comparative perspective." *Social Science History* 18:575–604.

———. 1994b. "Toward a new sociology of revolutions." *Theory and Society* 23:731–766.

———. 2001. *No Other Way Out: States and Revolutionary Movements, 1945–1991.* New York: Cambridge University Press.

———. 2003. "The renewal of socialism and the decline of revolution." In John Foran (ed.), *The Future of Revolutions: Rethinking Radical Change in the Age of Globalization.* London: Zed Books.

Goodwin, Jeff, and Theda Skocpol. 1989. "Explaining revolutions in the contemporary Third World." *Politics and Society* 17:489–509.

Graham, Hugh Davis, and Ted Robert Gurr (eds.). 1969. *Violence in America: Historical and Comparative Perspectives.* New York: Praeger (2nd ed. 1979, 3rd ed. 1989, Sage).

Green, Jerold D. 1982. *Revolution in Iran.* New York: Praeger.

Gross, Jan T. 1992. "Poland: From civil society to political nation." In Ivo Banac (ed.), *Eastern Europe in Revolution.* Ithaca, NY: Cornell University Press.

Grynspan, Dévora. 1991. "Nicaragua: A new model for popular revolution in Latin America." In Jack A. Goldstone, Ted Robert Gurr, and Farrokh Moshiri (eds.), *Revolutions of the Late Twentieth Century.* Boulder, CO: Westview Press.

Gurr, Ted Robert. 1970. *Why Men Rebel.* Princeton, NJ: Princeton University Press.

———. 1993. *Minorities at Risk: A Global View of Ethnopolitical Conflicts.* Washington, DC: U.S. Institute of Peace Press.

———. 1997. "Conflict and political order: An intellectual biography." In Hans Daalder (ed.), *European Politics: The Story of a Profession.* London: Pinter.

———. 2000. *Peoples Versus States: Minorities at Risk in the New Century.* Washington, DC: U.S. Institute of Peace Press.

Gurr, Ted Robert, and Barbara Harff (eds.). 1994. *Ethnic Conflict in World Politics.* Boulder, CO: Westview Press. (Rev. ed. 2004.)

Hahn, Gordon M. 2002. *Russia's Revolution from Above, 1985–2000: Reform, Transition, and Revolution in the Fall of the Soviet Communist Regime.* New Brunswick, NJ: Transaction.

Hall, John A. 1992. "Malthus and modernity." *Contemporary Sociology* 21:1–3.

Halliday, Fred. 1995. "A singular collapse: The Soviet Union, market pressure, and inter-state competition." In Nikki R. Keddie (ed.), *Debating Revolutions.* New York: New York University Press.

———. 1999. *Revolution and World Politics: The Rise and Fall of the Sixth Great Power.* Durham, NC: Duke University Press.

Hibbert, Christopher. 1980. *The Days of the French Revolution.* New York: William Morrow (Quill).

Holmes, Leslie. 1997. *Post-Communism: An Introduction.* Durham, NC: Duke University Press.

Huntington, Samuel P. 1968. *Political Order in Changing Societies.* New Haven, CT: Yale University Press.

Jowitt, Kenneth. 1978. *The Leninist Response to National Dependency.* Berkeley: Institute of International Studies.

———. 1991. "The Leninist extinction." In Daniel Chirot (ed.), *The Crisis of Leninism and the Decline of the Left.* Seattle: University of Washington Press.

———. 1992. *New World Disorder: The Leninist Extinction.* Berkeley: University of California Press.

Judt, Tony R. 1992. "Metamorphosis: The democratic revolution in Czechoslovakia." In Ivo Banac (ed.), *Eastern Europe in Revolution.* Ithaca, NY: Cornell University Press.

Kagan, Robert. 2004. "Stand up to Putin." *Pittsburgh Post-Gazette,* Sept. 19, p. B-3.

Kagarlitsky, Boris. 2002. *Russia Under Yeltsin and Putin.* London: Pluto Press.

Kaneda, Tatsuo. 1988. "Gorbachev's economic reforms." In P. Juviler and H. Kimura (eds.), *Gorbachev's Reforms.* New York: Aldine de Gruyter.

Keddie, Nikki R. 1981. *Roots of Revolution.* New Haven, CT: Yale University Press.

Keddie, Nikki R.(ed.) 1995. *Debating Revolutions.* New York: New York University Press.

Kennedy, Paul. 1987. *The Rise and Fall of the Great Powers.* New York: Random House (Vintage).

Kessler, Richard J. 1989. *Rebellion and Repression in the Philippines*. New Haven, CT: Yale University Press.

——. 1991. "The Philippines: The making of a 'people power.'" In Jack A. Goldstone, Ted Robert Gurr, and Farrokh Moshiri (eds.), *Revolutions of the Late Twentieth Century*. Boulder, CO: Westview Press.

Kornai, János. 1992. *The Socialist System: The Political Economy of Communism*. Princeton, NJ: Princeton University Press.

Kriedte, Peter. 1983. *Peasants, Landlords and Merchant Capitalists: Europe and the World Economy, 1500–1800*. Cambridge, UK: Cambridge University Press.

Kumar, Krishan. 1971. *Revolution: The Theory and Practice of a European Idea*. London: Weidenfeld and Nicholson.

——. 1978. *Prophecy and Progress: The Sociology of Industrial and Post-Industrial Society*. New York: Viking Press.

——. 1987. *Utopia and Anti-Utopia in Modern Times*. Oxford: Blackwell.

——. 1988. *The Rise of Modern Society: Aspects of the Social and Political Development of the West*. Oxford: Blackwell.

——. 1991. *Utopianism*. London: Taylor & Francis.

——. 1992. "The revolutions of 1989: Socialism, capitalism, and democracy." *Theory and Society* 21:309–356.

——. 1995. *Fom Post-Industrial to Post-Modern Society: New Theories of the Contemporary World*. Oxford: Blackwell.

——. 2001. *1989: Revolutionary Ideas and Ideals*. Minneapolis: University of Minnesota Press.

——. 2003. *The Making of English National Identity*. New York: Cambridge University Press.

Kumar, Krishan, and Stephen Bann (eds.). 1993. *Utopias and the Millennium*. London: Reaktion Books.

Kumar, Krishan, and Adrian Ellis (eds.). 1983. *Dilemmas of Liberal Democracies: Studies in Fred Hirsch's Social Limits to Growth*. London: Routledge.

Kumar, Krishan, and Jeff Weintraub (eds.). 1997. *Public and Private in Thought and Practice: Reflections on a Grand Dichotomy*. Chicago: University of Chicago Press.

Kurzman, Charles. 2004. *The Unthinkable Revolution in Iran*. Cambridge, MA: Harvard University Press.

Kushnirsky, F. I. 1988. "Soviet economic reform: An analysis and a model." In S. Linz and W. Moskoff (eds.), *Reorganization and Reform in the Soviet Economy*. Armonk, NY: Sharpe.

Lane, David. 1992. *Soviet Society Under Perestroika*. Rev. ed. London: Routledge.

Lapidus, Gail W. 1988. "Gorbachev's agenda: Domestic reforms and foreign policy reassessments." In P. Juviler and H. Kimura (eds.), *Gorbachev's Reforms*. Hawthorne, NY: Aldine de Gruyter.

—— (ed.). 1995. *The New Russia: Troubled Transformation*. Boulder, CO: Westview Press.

Larkin, John A. 1993. *Sugar and the Origins of Modern Philippine Society*. Berkeley: University of California Press.

Laumann, Edward O., Paul M. Siegel, and Robert W. Hodge (eds.). 1970. *The Logic of Social Hierarchies*. Chicago: Markham.

Lefebvre, Georges. 1939. *Quatre-Vingt-Neuf*. Paris: Institut pour l'Histoire de la Révolution Française, Université de Paris. (English translation, *The Coming of the French Revolution*. Trans. R. R. Palmer. Princeton, NJ: Princeton University Press, 1947.)

Leggett, Robert E. 1988. "Gorbachev's reform program: 'Radical' or more of the same?" In S. Linz and W. Moskoff (eds.), *Reorganization and Reform in the Soviet Economy*. Armonk, NY: M. E. Sharpe.

Lenski, Gerhard E. 1966. *Power and Privilege: A Theory of Social Stratification*. New York: McGraw-Hill.

Levin, Bernard. 1993. "One who got it right." *National Interest* 31:64–65. (Originally published 1977.)

Lipset, Seymour Martin, and Gyorgy Bence. 1994. "Anticipations of the failure of Communism." *Theory and Society* 23:169–210.

Magdoff, Harry. 1978. *Imperialism: From the Colonial Age to the Present*. New York: Monthy Review Press.

Markoff, John. 1996. *Waves of Democracy*. Thousand Oaks, CA: Pine Forge Press.

Marx, Karl. 1965. *Pre-Capitalist Economic Formations*. Trans. Jack Cohen. Ed. E. J. Hobsbawm. New York: International Publishers. (Originally written 1857–1858.)

McCord, William, and Arline McCord. 1977. *Power and Equity: An Introduction to Social Stratification*. New York: Praeger.

McMichael, Philip. 2004. *Development and Social Change: A Global Perspective*. 3rd ed. Thousand Oaks, CA: Pine Forge Press.

Milani, Mohsen M. 1988. *The Making of Iran's Islamic Revolution*. Boulder, CO: Westview Press.

Moaddel, Mansour. 1993. *Class, Politics, and Ideology in the Iranian Revolution*. New York: Columbia University Press.

Moore, Barrington, Jr. 1950. *Soviet Politics*. Cambridge, MA: Harvard University Press.

———. 1954. *Terror and Progress USSR*. Cambridge, MA: Harvard University Press.

———. 1966. *Social Origins of Dictatorship and Democracy: Lord and Peasant in the Making of the Modern World*. Boston: Beacon Press.

———. 1972. *Reflections on the Causes of Human Misery and on Certain Proposals to Eliminate Them*. London: Allen Lane.

———. 1978. *Injustice: The Social Bases of Obedience and Revolt*. Armonk, NY: M. E. Sharpe.

———. 1987. *Authority and Inequality Under Capitalism and Socialism*. Oxford: Oxford University Press.

————. 1998. *Moral Aspects of Economic Growth and Other Essays*. Ithaca, NY: Cornell University Press.

————. 2000. *Moral Purity and Persecution in History*. Princeton, NJ: Princeton University Press.

Moore, Wilbert. 1963. *Social Change*. Englewood Cliffs, NJ: Prentice-Hall.

Morris, William. 1995. *News from Nowhere*. Ed., with an introduction, notes, and bibliography, Krishan Kumar. Cambridge, UK: Cambridge University Press. (Originally published 1890.)

Moshiri, Farrokh. 1991. "Iran: Islamic revolution against Westernization." In Jack A. Goldstone, Ted Robert Gurr, and Farrokh Moshiri (eds.), *Revolutions of the Late Twentieth Century*. Boulder, CO: Westview Press.

Moynihan, Daniel Patrick. 1979. "Will Russia blow up?" *Newsweek,* November 19, pp. 144, 147.

Murray, Martin J. 1980. *The Development of Capitalism in Colonial Indochina (1870–1940)*. Berkeley: University of California Press.

Naimark, Norman M. 1992. "'Ich will hier raus': Emigration and the collapse of the German Democratic Republic." In Ivo Banac (ed.), *Eastern Europe in Revolution*. Ithaca, NY: Cornell University Press.

Nodia, Ghia. 2000. "The end of revolution?" *Journal of Democracy* 11:164–171.

Nove, Alec. 1989. *Glasnost in Action: Cultural Renaissance in Russia*. Boston: Unwin Hyman.

Paige, Jeffery M. 1975. *Agrarian Revolution: Social Movements and Export Agriculture in the Underdeveloped World*. New York: Free Press.

Parsa, Misagh. 2000. *States, Ideologies, and Social Revolutions: A Comparative Analysis of Iran, Nicaragua, and the Philippines*. New York: Cambridge University Press.

Pérez-Stable, Marifeli. 1999. *The Cuban Revolution: Origins, Course, and Legacy*. 2nd ed. New York: Oxford University Press.

Pipes, Richard. 1984. *Survival Is Not Enough: Soviet Realities and America's Future*. New York: Simon & Schuster.

————. 1995. *A Concise History of the Russian Revolution*. New York: Random House (Vintage).

Poggi, Gianfranco. 1978. *The Development of the Modern State*. Stanford, CA: Stanford University Press.

————. 1990. *The State: Its Nature, Development, and Prospects*. Stanford, CA: Stanford University Press.

Popkin, Jeremy D. 2002. *A Short History of the French Revolution*. 3rd ed. Upper Saddle River, NJ: Prentice-Hall.

Prins, Gwyn. 1990. "Editorial note" to Jan Urban, "Czechoslovakia: The power and politics of humiliation." In Gwyn Prins (ed.), *Spring in Winter: The 1989 revolutions*. Manchester, UK: Manchester University Press.

Remnick, David. 1997. *Resurrection: The Struggle for a New Russia*. New York: Random House.

Rueschemeyer, Dietrich, Evelyne Huber Stephens, and John D. Stephens. 1992. *Capitalist Development and Democracy.* Chicago: University of Chicago Press.

Ruiz, Ramon Eduardo. 1968. *Cuba: The Making of a Revolution.* New York: Norton.

Sanderson, Stephen K. 1999a. *Macrosociology: An Introduction to Human Societies.* 4th ed. New York: Addison Wesley Longman.

———. 1999b. *Social Transformations: A General Theory of Historical Development.* Updated ed. Lanham, MD: Rowman & Littlefield.

———. 2001. *The Evolution of Human Sociality: A Darwinian Conflict Perspective.* Lanham, MD: Rowman & Littlefield.

———. 2004. "World democratization, 1850–2000: A cross-national test of modernization and power resource theories." Paper presented at the annual meeting of the American Sociological Association, San Francisco.

Sanderson, Stephen K., and Arthur S. Alderson. 2005. *World Societies: The Evolution of Human Social Life.* Boston: Allyn & Bacon Longman.

Schaeffer, Robert K. 1997. *Power to the People: Democratization Around the World.* Boulder, CO: Westview Press.

Schrecker, John E. 2004. *The Chinese Revolution in Historical Perspective.* 2nd ed. Westport, CT: Praeger.

Scott, James. 1990. *Weapons of the Weak.* New Haven, CT: Yale University Press.

Selbin, Eric. 1997. "Revolution in the real world: Bringing agency back in." In John Foran (ed.), *Theorizing Revolutions.* New York: Routledge.

———. 1999. *Modern Latin American Revolutions.* 2nd ed. Boulder, CO: Westview Press.

Sewell, William H., Jr. 1985. "Ideologies and social revolutions: Reflections on the French case." *Journal of Modern History* 57(1):57–85.

Skocpol, Theda. 1979. *States and Social Revolutions: A Comparative Analysis of France, Russia, and China.* New York: Cambridge University Press.

———. 1982. "Rentier state and Shi'a Islam in the Iranian Revolution." *Theory and Society* 11:265–283.

———. 1984. *Vision and Method in Historical Sociology.* New York: Cambridge University Press.

———. 1986. "Old regime legacies and Communist revolutions in Russia and China." In Jack A. Goldstone (ed.), *Revolutions: Theoretical, Comparative, and Historical Studies.* San Diego: Harcourt Brace Jovanovich.

———. 1992. *Protecting Soldiers and Mothers: The Political Origins of Social Policy in the United States.* Cambridge, MA: Harvard University Press.

———. 1994. *Social Revolutions in the Modern World.* New York: Cambridge University Press.

———. 1995. *Social Policy in the United States: Future Possibilities in Historical Perspective.* Princeton, NJ: Princeton University Press.

———. 1997. *Boomerang: Clinton's Health Reform and the Turn Against Government.* New York: Norton.

————. 2000. *The Missing Middle: Working Families and the Future of American Social Policy.* New York: Norton.

————. 2003. *Diminished Democracy: From Membership to Management in American Civic Life.* Norman: University of Oklahoma Press.

Skocpol, Theda, and Morris Fiorina (eds.). 1999. *Civic Engagement in American Democracy.* Washington, DC: Brookings Institution Press.

Skocpol, Theda, and Ellen Kay Trimberger. 1978. "Revolutions and the world historical development of capitalism." *Berkeley Journal of Sociology* 22:100–113.

Smith, Alan K. 1991. *Creating a World Economy: Merchant Capital, Colonialism, and World Trade, 1400–1825.* Boulder, CO: Westview Press.

Smith, Dennis. 1983. *Barrington Moore, Jr.: A Critical Appraisal.* Armonk, NY: M. E. Sharpe.

Snyder, David, and Charles Tilly. 1972. "Hardship and collective violence in France, 1830 to 1960." *American Sociological Review* 37:520–532.

Snyder, Robert S. 1999. "The end of revolution?" *Review of Politics* 61:5–28.

So, Alvin Y. 1990. *Social Change and Development: Modernization, Dependency, and World-System Theories.* Newbury Park, CA: Sage.

Stiglitz, Joseph E. 2003. *Globalization and Its Discontents.* New York: Norton.

Stokes, Gale. 1993. *The Walls Came Tumbling Down: The Collapse of Communism in Eastern Europe.* New York: Oxford University Press.

Sweezy, Paul M. 1942. *The Theory of Capitalist Development.* New York: Monthly Review Press.

Tilly, Charles. 1964. *The Vendée.* Cambridge, MA: Harvard University Press.

————. 1978. *From Mobilization to Revolution.* New York: McGraw-Hill.

————. 1985. *Big Structures, Large Processes, Huge Comparisons.* New York: Russell Sage Foundation.

————. 1986. *The Contentious French.* Cambridge, MA: Harvard University Press (Belknap Press).

————. 1990. *Coercion, Capital, and European States, A.D. 990–1990.* Oxford: Basil Blackwell.

————. 1993. *European Revolutions, 1492–1992.* Oxford: Blackwell.

————. 1995. *Popular Contention in Great Britain, 1758–1834.* Cambridge, MA: Harvard University Press.

————. 1998. *Durable Inequality.* Berkeley: University of California Press.

————. 2002. *Stories, Identities, and Political Change.* Lanham, MD: Rowman & Littlefield.

————. 2003. *The Politics of Collective Violence.* New York: Cambridge University Press.

————. 2004a. *Contention and Democracy in Europe, 1650–2000.* New York: Cambridge University Press.

————. 2004b. *Social Movements, 1768–2004.* Boulder, CO: Paradigm Publishers.

Tilly, Charles, Louise Tilly, and Richard Tilly. 1975. *The Rebellious Century, 1830–1930.* Cambridge, MA: Harvard University Press.

Todorova, Maria N. 1992. "Improbable maverick or typical conformist? Seven thoughts on the new Bulgaria." In Ivo Banac (ed.), *Eastern Europe in Revolution*. Ithaca, NY: Cornell University Press.

Tucker, Robert C. (ed.) 1978. *The Marx-Engels Reader.* 2nd ed. New York: Norton.

Vanhanen, Tatu. 1997. *Prospects of Democracy: A Study of 172 Countries*. London: Routledge.

———. 2003. *Democratization: A Comparative Analysis of 170 Countries*. London: Routledge.

Verdery, Katherine, and Gail Kligman. 1992. "Romania after Ceauşescu: Post-Communist Communism?" In Ivo Banac (ed.), *Eastern Europe in Revolution*. Ithaca, NY: Cornell University Press.

Walker, Thomas W. 1982. *Nicaragua in Revolution*. New York: Praeger.

———. 1986. "The economic and political background." In Jack A. Goldstone (ed.), *Revolutions: Theoretical, Comparative, and Historical Studies*. San Diego: Harcourt Brace Jovanovich.

Wallerstein, Immanuel. 1974a. "The rise and future demise of the world capitalist system: Concepts for comparative analysis." *Comparative Studies in Society and History* 16:387–415.

———. 1974b. *The Modern World-System: Capitalist Agriculture and the Origins of the European World-Economy in the Sixteenth Century*. New York: Academic Press.

———. 1979. *The Capitalist World-Economy*. New York: Cambridge University Press.

———. 1980. *The Modern World-System II: Mercantilism and the Consolidation of the European World-Economy, 1600–1750*. New York: Academic Press.

———. 1989. *The Modern World-System III: The Second Era of Great Expansion of the Capitalist World-Economy, 1730–1840s*. San Diego: Academic Press.

Warren, Bill. 1980. *Imperialism: Pioneer of Capitalism*. London: Verso.

Weber, Max. 1968. *Economy and Society*. 2 vols. Berkeley: University of California Press. (Originally published 1923.)

Wells, H. G. 1993. *A Modern Utopia*. Ed., with an introduction, notes, and critical responses, Krishan Kumar. Everyman edition. London: Dent and Sons. (Originally published 1905.)

Westergaard, John, and Henrietta Resler. 1975. *Class in a Capitalist Society: A Study of Contemporary Britain*. New York: Basic Books.

Wickham-Crowley, Timothy P. 1991. *Exploring Revolution: Essays on Latin American Insurgency and Revolutionary Theory*. Armonk, NY: M. E. Sharpe.

———. 1992. *Guerrillas and Revolution in Latin America*. Princeton, NJ: Princeton University Press.

———. 1997. "Structural theories of revolution." In John Foran (ed.), *Theorizing Revolutions*. New York: Routledge.

Wines, Michael. 2001. "At last, signs of economic revival in Russia." *New York Times*, November 17.

Wolf, Eric R. 1966. *Peasants.* Englewood Cliffs, NJ: Prentice-Hall.

———. 1969. *Peasant Wars of the Twentieth Century.* New York: Harper & Row.

———. 1982. *Europe and the People Without History.* Berkeley: University of California Press.

Womack, John. 1968. *Zapata and the Mexican Revolution.* New York: Knopf.

Wright, Erik Olin. 1979. *Class Structure and Income Determination.* New York: Academic Press.

———. 1985. *Classes.* London: Verso.

Zeman, Z.A.B. 1991. *The Making and Breaking of Communist Europe.* Oxford: Blackwell.

Zemtsov, Ilya, and John Farrar. 1989. *Gorbachev: The Man and the System.* New Brunswick, NJ: Transaction Books.

Index

About the Author

Stephen K. Sanderson is Professor of Sociology at Indiana University of Pennsylvania. He is the author of seven previous books and numerous articles in scholarly journals and edited collections. His most recent book is *World Societies: The Evolution of Human Social Life* (Allyn & Bacon, 2005), coauthored with Arthur S. Alderson.

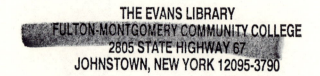